*f*P

HURRICANE SEASON

A COACH, HIS TEAM, AND THEIR TRIUMPH
IN THE TIME OF KATRINA

NEAL THOMPSON

FREE PRESS
New York   London   Toronto   Sydney

FREE PRESS
A Division of Simon & Schuster, Inc.
1230 Avenue of the Americas
New York, NY 10020

First Free Press hardcover edition July 2007

FREE PRESS and colophon are trademarks of Simon & Schuster, Inc.

For information about special discounts for bulk purchases, please contact Simon & Schuster
Special Sales at 1-800-456-6798 or business@simonandschuster.com

Manufactured in the United States of America

1   3   5   7   9   10   8   6   4   2

Library of Congress Cataloging-in-Publication Data

Thompson, Neal.
Hurricane season : a coach, his team, and their triumph in the time of Katrina / Neal
Thompson.
p.   cm.
Includes bibliographical references.
1. John Curtis Christian School (River Ridge, La.)—Football.   2. Football—Social
aspects—Louisiana—River Ridge.   3. Hurricane Katrina, 2005—Social aspects.
I. Title.
GV958.J64T56 2007
796.332'630976338—dc22   2007006563

ISBN-13: 978-1-4165-4070-0
ISBN-10:   1-4165-4070-9

For Mary,
for my sons, Leo and Sean, . . .
and for Mr. Curtis

I firmly believe a man's finest hour, his greatest fulfillment to all he holds dear, is that moment when he has worked his heart out in a good cause, and lies exhausted on the field of battle—victorious.

—Vince Lombardi
(Painted on the concrete block wall
of the John Curtis Patriots' locker room.)

Some say this world of trouble is the only world we'll ever see. But I'm waiting for that morning when the new world is revealed.

—from "When the Saints Go Marching In"

Contents

Prologue

John Curtis defensive lineman Jerahmie Collins and his two brothers are sleeping in the upstairs bedroom of their home in La Place, twenty-five miles west of New Orleans, when Katrina arrives. She announces herself with screeching winds that violently shake the house and rattle the windows, awakening the whole family. Jerahmie had tried to convince his parents to evacuate, but like many thousands across the city and its suburbs, the Collinses decided to take their chances and to stay put.

They now desperately wish they had fled.

As Katrina's squalls begin to pummel the house, the electricity is knocked out. The Collins boys, their two sisters, an uncle, and his two kids decide to crowd together in Jerahmie's parents' room. Toward dawn, as the winds grow more violent and the house begins to sway, Jerahmie and his older brother, Michael, a linebacker at John Curtis, urge everyone to head downstairs with their blankets and pillows and to sleep in the living room, where it'll be safer. They grope their way down the steps and spread out to find spots to curl up, then pretend to fall back asleep as the relentless winds howl and rage.

Jerahmie tries to doze in a corner of the living room floor, but he's bothered by a nagging feeling that he's forgotten something. He decides to run back upstairs to find his portable CD player. Music always helps him sleep.

Using his cellphone screen as a flashlight, he climbs up the steps to his room. While looking for his CD player, he hears a rustling noise that makes him jump. Shining his cellphone around the room, he sees a moving lump under the covers on his brother's bed, and pulling back the bedsheets he sees that the lump is his younger brother Jermaine, an eighth grader at Curtis. He must have crawled back into his own bed as the others were making their way downstairs, and in the commotion no one noticed that he wasn't with them. Jerahmie wakes his brother and takes him downstairs, where the two of them finally drift off to sleep late in the morning, despite the furious racket outside.

A short while later, the entire family is awakened by a violent crashing sound upstairs. They run to investigate and Jerahmie, all 285 pounds of him, gets there first. A huge section of the roof has collapsed, jagged shards of it landing right on Jermaine's bed. Jerahmie's little brother just missed being killed.

All across Greater New Orleans, Katrina is only just beginning to inflict her brutality.

1

Patriots' Game

In the corner of the blue carpeted, concrete-walled room, a giant floor fan whines, pushing around sweat-odored air. The locker room stinks, but at least it's air-conditioned. Sort of. It's better than being outside in the late-day, late-August New Orleans sun. So, the Patriots of John Curtis Christian School, more than a hundred of them, hang out in this dank room with missing ceiling tiles and funky smells. It barely contains them all.

The floor is littered with broken shoulder pads, socks, spools of athletic tape, Adidas sneakers, and the bright red or blue rubber Croc moccasins the players wear in the showers. A quote hand-painted on a scrap of plywood that's duct-taped to the wall reads, WINNERS CONCENTRATE ON WINNING, LOSERS CONCENTRATE ON GETTING BY.

They're trading gossip, razzing each other about girls, or arguing about what to expect from tonight's opponent, all fired up for a new season and the start of a new school year on Monday. A multiracial, multicultural gumbo of kids from all over the city and the suburbs, they're sons of the wealthy and the just scraping by, they're scrawny ninth-grade third stringers and oversized, muscle-bound starting seniors, and they're all united in determination to bring the mighty John Curtis Patriots to yet another state championship this year. A few boys sit alone on stools, headphones blocking out the roar.

3

Others are curled up in a corner trying to nap, while a few enact pregame rituals, getting their heads ready to play.

Offensive guard Andrew Nierman, a bruising six-foot-one, 300-pounder, ties the shoes of his good friend, 325-pound defensive tackle Jonathan "Tank" English. Tank earned his nickname in fourth grade, when he and Andrew dressed as army guys for Halloween. A snarky janitor told Jonathan, nearing two hundred pounds even then, that he looked like an army tank. In grammar school, he developed a bad habit of never tying his laces tight enough, so Andrew always tightens them for him before games.

Tank and Andrew are both the ambitous, determined sons of hard-working single moms. Tank's father died of a heart attack two years ago, after a decade of battling heart disease, high blood pressure, and kidney problems. He was only forty-nine. Tank and his mom, Althea, who runs a day-care center, live in mostly African-American section of Kenner, a suburb just west of River Ridge, and Tank has attended Curtis since the third grade. Andrew, who has contended with growing up biracial in a still strongly segregated New Orleans, commutes from thirty miles away, where he and his mother live alone. He has no relationship with this father, who left years ago.

Andrew and Tank, both juniors, anchor the Patriots' front line—Andrew on offense, Tank on defense. They're both savvy, physical players who run faster than 300-pounders should, and the coaches are relying on each of them to play leadership roles this year. Off the field, their demeanor is more preacher—Tank—and teacher—Andrew—than bone-breaking tacklers. Tank is a warm, happy-go-lucky man-boy with a deep laugh and a melodious voice as smooth and sweet as jelly. He leads his teammates in prayer before games and is a great motivator on the field. Andrew is thoughtful, studious, and serious, with dark, intense eyes; a beefy bookworm in shoulder pads. He's one of the smartest kids in the school and dreams of attending a top academic college, maybe even Harvard.

Linebacker Mike Walker and quarterback Kyle Collura practice their pregame handshake, a hand dance of high-fives, low-fives, and a fist-to-fist punch. They plan to do it after every touchdown this year. Mike and Kyle are also juniors, getting their first shot at full-time varsity this year. Mike has a linebacker's stout body but a face that's pure teenager, with braces, faint freckles, wisps of facial hair, and spots of acne that look like they've been digitally transposed there from a seventh-grade school photo. He's chatty and a bit of a clown who loves to crack jokes in class. Mike joined Curtis only three years ago, commuting from Metairie, east of River Ridge, so that he could join the Patriots. He's worked hard to impress the coaches and has just learned that he's been made a starter this season.

Kyle is lean and loose-limbed, with droopy, Nicolas Cage–like eyes. He always seems half asleep, with slouched shoulders and a laconic, jazzy way of dropping words out of the side of his mouth, as if he couldn't care less where they land.

Kyle was third-string quarterback last year, but was thrust into the starter's job five months ago when the Patriots' rocket-armed quarterback Johnnie Thiel unexpectedly left the school in a huff. Kyle knows he's no Johnnie Thiel, who was all handsome and slick and funny and stylish, confidently strutting his stuff on the field and off.

Johnnie had attended John Curtis since the third grade, and was the Patriots' great hope for this season. In 2003, he had started a few games as a freshman, even playing in the state championship game, a 12–7 heartbreaking loss that left him crying on the sidelines of the Superdome, where the state's high-school championship games are played. Last year, Johnnie split time with a senior quarterback and helped bring the Patriots again to the championship. Johnnie scored twice in that game, leading the Patriots to a 29–14 victory—and their tenth undefeated season—and was named the game's most outstanding player.

He was in line to take sole possession of quarterback in 2005, but his desire to make dazzling runs and hurl touchdown bombs that made the highlight tapes conflicted with the school's old-fashioned, grind-it-out offense. What he really wanted was to be a star, and to catch the eyes of college recruiters. But Curtis is no place for that kind of star, favoring only hard-working, obedient, team players. So, he transferred to East St. John High School in the town of Reserve, twenty miles west but closer to his home.

That's how Kyle, a virtual nobody on the 2004 championship squad, was tapped as the new starter. To make matters worse, shortly after taking over the job, Kyle fell on a tackler in a spring scrimmage and snapped his own collarbone. It has since healed, though still a bit lumpy, and Kyle returned to practice only a few weeks ago. He still seems protective of his collarbone in practice, and the coaches worry that he may not be ready for tonight's game, mentally or physically.

Kyle's well aware that all the fans in the stands tonight will be wondering, This is our new quarterback? This quiet third-stringer? *This* is who's going to lead us to the championship? He's anxious to prove he can carry his team, nervous, but eager to play.

Equally anxious is the team's speedy, all-purpose playmaker, Joe McKnight, who's in the trainer's room getting his ankles taped. Joe has commuted to Curtis from Kenner since he was eight years old. A moody, sometimes stormy young man, he is mad at the world for sticking him with an absentee father and a mom who struggles to put food on the table. Joe and his mother have a complicated relationship and he's been living in and out of their home, staying with friends and extended family members. Coach J. T. Curtis has offered him a room in his home repeatedly, but Joe always says no; he feels awkward about living with his coach, and about how it would look for an African-American kid to be living with a white family.

Joe is six feet tall, just shy of two hundred pounds, and combines the lightning speed of a Jerry Rice with the explosive power of a Barry Sanders, one of his heroes. Each of his biceps is covered in tattoos, one of which reads JOE above a picture of a tiger.

Joe and Johnnie Thiel were a daunting duo on the field last year, each making weekly headlines on the sports pages of the *Times-Picayune*. The coaches mainly used Joe as a defensive safety and on special teams, occasionally putting him in at running back, which is where Joe really wants to play. Last year, he made a strong case for that job by returning forty-three punts for 872 yards and nine touchdowns, averaging twenty-plus yards per return. On kickoff returns, he averaged thirty-one yards and scored three touchdowns. In the state championship game, when the Patriots were stalled in a 14–14 second-half tie, Joe broke free for a long punt return, which set up a go-ahead quarterback sneak by Johnnie.

Joe and Johnnie were also close friends, and when Joe decided—not for the first time—to move out of his mom's house for a few months last year, he moved in with Johnnie's family. The two boys shared a bedroom, the walls covered with football posters, and always drove to and from school and practice together. They considered themselves as much brothers as friends, and Joe was looking forward to two more years of Thiel-and-McKnight headlines. Johnnie asked Joe to come with him to East St. John, but Joe wasn't up for that, and was deeply hurt by Johnnie's transfer. A few weeks later, he moved out of the Thiels' home and temporarily back with his mom. He's since been in and out of her house, spending most of his nights on the couches of friends or relatives.

He hasn't let any of that affect his playing, though. In fact, Joe worked harder than anyone in practices through the spring and summer. He is the team's best all-around player, ranked among the nation's top high-school prospects. Already he's being wooed by USC, Miami, Notre Dame, and others, whose coaches have gasped at highlight tapes showing Joe accelerating past tacklers on one after another rocket-fast, touchdown-scoring punt or kick return. Joe is a beautiful, graceful runner, but also a bruiser who can make split-second decisions look easy: *Should I hurdle this guy or plow into him?*

Joe has a handsome face with a dark, intent gaze. Unlike most jumpy teens, who look everywhere but in your eyes, Joe makes hard, unflinching eye contact. He's quiet, with a surprisingly sly, mischievous wit, but he rarely smiles, not even at his own jokes, not even when he scores.

As the trainer tapes up his ankles, Joe listens to a recording of a speech Al Pacino gives in *Any Given Sunday*, about how football, like life, is a game of inches, and how fighting and clawing for the extra inch can make the difference "between *winning* and *losing*, between *living* and *dying* . . .

"I'll tell you this, in any fight it is the guy who is willing to die who is going to win that inch," Pacino tells his team. "That is what *living* is. The six inches in front of your face . . . That's football, guys. That's all it is. Now, whattaya gonna do?"

The 2005 season begins tonight, and game time is just two hours away.

The Patriots all have their own goals and expectations this year, their own pressures and anxieties. The start of a season is always a time of nerves, when bluster and cocky talk are masks for insecurities. But everyone knows, no matter how positively they spin it, this year's Patriots are but a shadow of last year's championship team.

Graduation took nine offensive starters, including all but one of the offensive linemen, as well as a couple of running backs and receivers, safeties and linebackers. Then there was Johnnie Thiel's transfer. This team is as young and unproven as any group of Patriots has been in many years, with the first-team offense and defense both comprised mostly of juniors, and even a few sophomores. Many of them are getting their first shot at varsity, and this season will be their chance to prove themselves to the coaches, to secure a spot on the first team, and to show their stuff to college recruiters.

Tonight's game is the annual jamboree scrimmage, a preseason New Orleans ritual. All across southern Louisiana, schools are pairing off for abbreviated matches—two fifteen-minute halves instead of four twelve-minute quarters. After a summer of grueling weightlifting sessions, two-a-day practices, and scrimmages, tonight is the real deal, the first chance of the season for players to test themselves in actual play. Sportswriters are in the press box, and parents and girlfriends are in the stands. The stomach butterflies are aflutter.

John Curtis will travel tonight to Salmen High in Slidell, thirty miles northeast of New Orleans, on a night featuring six teams paired off into three games. The Patriots are last on the schedule, facing the Bulldogs of Fontainebleau High. Rather than sit through the first two games, they'll wait here in the locker room until head coach J. T. Curtis hollers for them to load the buses. J.T. decided long ago never to use an opponent's locker room or endure the taunts of home-team fans while waiting for the start of play. His psychological strategy is to show up barely on time, thirty to forty minutes before kickoff, sometimes less. The team steps off the bus and finishes dressing right there, pulling on shoulder pads with their game jerseys prestretched over them. They walk right onto the field, ready to go, to the hair-pulling annoyance of opposing coaches.

Across thirty-six years of leading the Patriots, J. T. Curtis has become one of the nation's most successful high school football coaches, winning more than four hundred games en route to nineteen state championships. No Louisiana school has won even half as many titles and, in the entire history of high school football in America, only one coach has won more games—seventy-eight-year-old John McKissick, who last year notched his five hundredth win, having coached the Green Wave of South Carolina's Summerville High for a half-century.

The John Curtis Patriots' *only* losing season remains J.T.'s first, in 1969, and they've gone undefeated ten times since. His overall record, 417–47–6, represents a winning percentage just shy of .900, a loss in only one of every ten games.

J.T. is as much a counselor as he is a coach to his players, their mentor, guru, and, for some, father figure. During the day, J.T. holds court in his small office, off the high school's main hallway. Three decades of football memorabilia and family photos cover the walls, along with two clocks that haven't worked for years. Visitors sink deep into a blue, fake-leather couch whose springs have been mashed by gargantuan football players plopping themselves down. When he's not lecturing a student about a discipline problem or discussing a personal situation or spiritual matter, or conferring with a teacher or an assistant coach, he might meet with the manager of the Superdome or a college recruiter or some alumni who just stopped by to reminisce.

If he's not in his office or on the practice field or in the coaches' room, he's stalking the halls, barking at students, playfully punching them in the arm, quick with a gibe or tease: *That's the worst haircut I've ever seen!* When he's not in coaching gear, he's smartly dressed in a pressed white shirt and a tie. He has thick, black hair, blue eyes, and the square jaw and bright-white smile of a TV news anchor. One eye appears to be a different shade of blue from the other, but is actually permanently dilated, the result of taking a line drive to the face while coaching the baseball team. He's sixteen months shy of sixty, but looks a decade younger, despite an aging athlete's paunch. His presence is looming, physical.

J.T. has the gift of making visitors feel they're all that matters to him, that he's got all the time in the world. Among the steady stream of visitors he attends to are a number of college coaches, such as USC's Pete Carroll, Florida State's Bobby Bowden, and Texas's Mack Brown, who sometimes stop by to watch a practice. Former

LSU coach Nick Saban was a regular visitor until he left Louisiana to become head coach of the Miami Dolphins.

J.T. could have taken a job at that level. His success has brought lucrative offers, including assistant coaching jobs at Louisiana State and Tulane universities, and the head coaching job at the University of Southwestern Louisiana. When the Saints were looking for a head coach in the 1990s, an LSU coach suggested they consider J.T. But he's turned down all suitors.

Rather than scrum for a career in the big leagues, J.T. is content to remain what he's been his entire adult life: one of the nation's top high-school coaches. He prefers working with high-school kids, and gets enormous satisfaction from turning raw, untamed talents into players who'll make Pete Carroll's jaw drop. Just as his father created the John Curtis Christian School to give every child who walks through the door a chance to succeed, J.T. feels his job—his mission in life, really—is to give every kid he coaches a chance to fulfill his potential. His primary goals: to help players understand their special relationship with God, and to help them to develop confidence and believe in themselves, to learn the value of hard work and team work, to do their best. The championships have followed.

J.T., who recently became the school's acting headmaster, frequently reminds kids that he wants them to be good football players and to win championships. But, as he once put it, "If you do not leave John Curtis Christian School a better person, prepared to take the next step in your life, then we feel like we have failed."

After the Patriots won two championships in a row, in 1987 and 1988, they lost in the playoffs in 1989. That night, when the buses got back to the school, J.T. kept his team on the field for a late-night practice, telling them they needed to set a goal for themselves: to get back to the championship in 1990. He also examined his own mistakes, and told his assistants it was up to the entire coaching staff to raise their own expectations and set the tone for the players. The team went 15–0 and won their eleventh state championship that year. After the game, in the Superdome locker room, J.T. gave a speech that epitomized his decades-long philosophy on football and on life. "Any time you set a goal in your life, you don't always know if you're gonna make that goal, but what you have to do is give it your best shot every day . . . If you give that commitment from now 'til the day you die, you'll be a successful person, no matter what you do."

What makes J.T.'s record of success all the more remarkable is that John Curtis is hardly a sprawling, megarich school with a 20,000 seat stadium and wealthy alumni donors pouring money into the athletic programs. John Curtis is night and day from Texas-style, football-dominated high schools.

John Curtis Christian School sits on a nondescript street in River Ridge, in Jefferson Parish, a suburb ten minutes west of downtown New Orleans, snug up against the Mississippi. An unassuming, middle-class, mostly white community of ranch houses with postage-stamp yards, River Ridge is a place where kids ride their bikes without fear of traffic and play basketball in the street. The main drag, Jefferson Highway, is lined with po'boy shops, a couple of bars, and the popular Dot's Diner.

At the corner of Jefferson Highway and Manguno Drive squats a modest complex of low-slung white buildings, most with white-painted concrete block walls and aluminum roofs. Unlike the imposing multistory monoliths sitting on vast lawns that personify so many modern American high schools, you could easily drive by John Curtis's upper school, which caters to grades seven through twelve, and not even know a school was there. The elementary school, which contains pre-K through sixth grade, is a few blocks down Jefferson Highway, an equally unpretentious group of one-story buildings that could pass for a budget motel.

Visitors are often amazed to discover that one of the nation's best football teams is housed in buildings of corrugated metal and concrete block, where the architectural style is more warehouse than schoolhouse. At the upper school, a combined junior high and high school, students attend physical education classes in a fieldhouse-style gymnasium with a rusty roof and, until recently, no air conditioning. The cafeteria is in a converted barn. The students' lockers are outside, beneath a makeshift metal overhang. Some improvements have been made in recent years: A new façade and awning have spruced up the front entrance. And the practice field, which years ago was a lumpy mud pit, is now in pristine shape.

Still, visitors are also shocked to learn that the vaunted John Curtis Patriots don't have their own athletic stadium. In place of the massive grandstands and klieg lights typical of many high schools, Curtis has two short metal bleachers that can seat about two hundred, and the small parking lot can only fit a couple of dozen cars. The field itself is squeezed, just barely, between two side streets. Early in his career, J.T. considered buying land adjacent to the school to build a stadium. But, after a 1977 flood, property values in River Ridge soared, due to the desirable higher elevation of the land, and he lost his best chance. That's why all the Patriots' games are, technically, away. Even their occasional home game is at a borrowed stadium miles from the school.

Monday, the start of the 2005–06 school year, will bring 648 students to John Curtis, 400 of them to the upper school. Parents choose to send kids here not for the impressive facilities or the high-tech equipment or the prestige. It's always been more about the community, the Christian values, the quality of teaching, and the careful attention to the nurturing of children.

Unlike other private schools, John Curtis isn't a pressure cooker when it comes to grades. J.T.'s father actually forbade talk of grades at home, preferring to focus on whether his children were well-rounded, happy, and *engaged*. Likewise, J.T. stresses academic fundamentals over perfect grades, believing it's better to focus on the drills and the basics and on the execution rather than the results, believing that, if you can perfect the fundamentals, the scholarships—and the championships—will come.

J.T.'s father, John T. Curtis Sr., known to all as "Mr. Curtis," had always urged students simply to seek the truth.

Mr. Curtis was born in 1919 in the working-class Irish Channel neighborhood of New Orleans. His father died when he was a toddler, and his mother worked in a box factory for a dollar a day while raising four children and a niece. Curtis roamed freely along the Mississippi River and the nearby wharfs, among the stevedores and prostitutes. He loved to box at a nearby gym and worked construction jobs with an uncle.

After that unfettered adolescence, John left New Orleans to stay with an uncle in Memphis, where he bounced from job to job. Liquor, fights, and women were constant distractions. He was always looking for something, never sure what, so he stuck with liquor, fights, and women. Then, while working at a clothing store, two elderly Christian coworkers warned him that his carousing was going to be the death of him. "Go to church," they'd tell him. "Read your Bible." He'd just laugh, and they'd shake their heads and say, "We're praying for you, Johnny."

One night in the small bedroom of his aunt and uncle's house, he crashed. He put his head in his hands and wept. He was twenty-two and had achieved nothing with his life. Maybe the old ladies at the store were right, he thought. He cried most of the night. He was lost, and he tried—for the first time in his life—to pray. He said, "God, I don't know who you are or if you really exist. But I know this. What I'm doing is not enough."

The next morning, he put on his nicest clothes and told his aunt and uncle he was going to church. Thinking he was being sarcastic, they told him not to make such jokes. He walked down the street, got lost, and ended up in front of a Methodist church. He entered, took a seat, and instantly felt as if the preacher was talking straight at him. When the services were over, he told the preacher he wanted to repent and turn his life over to God. Two years later he enrolled at Louisiana College, a Baptist school in central Louisiana, where he met a brilliant and beautiful student named Merle Manguno, an Italian girl from an upscale New Orleans neighborhood. She was drawn to his gruff intensity and dark good looks, and the two students soon married.

During his final two years of college, he began traveling on weekends to preach at a rural sawmill town with a small makeshift church for workers. After graduating from Louisiana College, he continued to pursue his religious studies at the New Orleans Baptist Theological Seminary. In 1946, he and Merle welcomed their first child, John Thomas Curtis Jr., calling him "J.T." from the start. After finishing at the seminary, Curtis moved his family to Paradise, Louisiana, a scrubby little town that was anything but paradise. So began a frenetic life as a missionary preacher, his job to establish Baptist churches in the middle of nowhere. He would arrive in some dusty town, seek out Southern Baptist families or others willing to convert, corral them into a congregation, build them a church, preach for awhile, then move on.

Curtis's salary was meager, and the family was very poor. He had to pick up second jobs to pay the bills. Some nights, he'd come home red as a beet after working all day at a construction site or on a ditch-digging crew. Along the way, four more children were born: another son, Leon, and three daughters, Debbie, Kathy, and Alicia.

In 1956, Curtis moved his family back to his hometown, New Orleans. After a few years teaching at an inner-city high school, he opened his self-named school in 1962.

Drawing on the construction skills he learned during his troubled youth and his cash-poor missionary days, he built many of the school's buildings with his own hands. Aesthetics were never a priority. For years the gymnasium was half finished, with rain pouring through incomplete walls. Inside the tin-roofed classroom buildings he painted inspirational words in large, block letters—LOYALTY, SPIRIT, PRIDE, UNDERSTANDING, EXCELLENCE, GOODNESS. In the center of each hallway he painted GOD, reflecting his philosophy that God should be at the center of all that his students do and all that they are. He also sprinkled the drab hallways with artwork, sculptures, and a bright color scheme of red, white, and blue.

Generations of students entering the front lobby off Manguno Street have stepped around a seven-foot bronze sculpture of a sea nymph swimming with tropical fishes and a sea turtle, all of them in an underwater dance around a twist of coral. The sculpture is a perfect expression of Mr. Curtis's whimsical, somewhat eccentric, love of art and of life.

Curtis was hardly a seasoned educator or an experienced administrator. What he had was an ambitious vision of a co-ed, mixed-race school with a nondenominational Christian ethic. The school's mission was *to give all children a chance*, and it was far less exclusive than most private schools. The admission policy declared that "students of all nationalities, races, creeds, religions, and ethnic origins are welcome," glaringly at odds with the trends of greater New Orleans, where segregation was, and still is, an entrenched way of life. The percentage of New Orleans area students enrolled in mostly white parochial schools still ranks as the highest in the nation, reaching nearly half in some parishes.

Mr. Curtis's plan was to cast a wide net and pull in a geographically, religiously, racially, and culturally diverse mix of kids. Tuition was more affordable than at most private schools, and enrollment grew quickly. As he had hoped, students came from the inner city, from bayou and river towns, from farms and suburbs; they were working class, middle class, and upper class alike. Some lived in overcrowded shotgun houses in New Orleans East, while others lived in their own *pied-à-terre* apartments near the school during the week and commuted home on the weekends. For parents struggling to pay tuition, Mr. Curtis often made special arrangements, allowing them to pay by driving a school bus or working in the cafeteria. The school became something of an eccentric newcomer, offering an attractive alternative to the costlier private schools, which were mostly white, and the underfunded public schools of the city, which were mostly black. The minority population at John Curtis has hovered consistently around twenty percent, and the school remains among the rare examples of voluntary integration in an otherwise de facto segregated system.

One of the first non-Catholic private schools in Jefferson Parish, Curtis offered parents an environment that inculcated moral, ethical, and spiritual values based in Christianity, but *not* based on any particular church or religion. The school eventually attracted a solid academic team of Christ-centered teachers who shared Mr. Curtis's passion for working with students and, as he put it, displayed four important qualities: "love, leadership, understanding, and trust."

In time, the school's low-pressure academic atmosphere would send nine of ten students to college, many of them to top institutions, including Harvard, Brown, Columbia, Georgetown, Boston College, and West Point.

Mr. Curtis's passion for the school had a magnetic effect on his family. One after another, his kids made their way back to River Ridge and the family business. J.T. was first. He had been a promising football player in high school and college, and his father lured him into taking over the football team in 1969. Leon, after serving with the Marines for two years as an accountant in San Diego, joined J.T. on the coaching staff in 1971.

Their three sisters returned not long thereafter, though they didn't exactly come rushing back. Kathy made it clear throughout her teens that she was never going to be a teacher. She was going to be an actress on Broadway. After graduating from college, she married a Navy man and they moved all over the country to different submarine bases. She came home in her mid-twenties, with a four-month-old baby, having decided she could teach better than the professors she'd had in college. She now teaches speech and English and works as a counselor in the guidance office.

Debbie returned to River Ridge to become a teacher right after college, in 1975. After earning a master's degree, she was named the elementary school principal. Alicia, the youngest, was as adamant as Kathy about never becoming a teacher, which made it difficult for her to call her father one day and admit that she'd changed her mind. "Baby, there will always be a place for you at school if that's what you want," he told her. She now teaches civics and government and also works in the guidance office.

Curtis's wife, Merle, worked by his side and his brother-in-law, Larry Manguno, became the high-school principal. By the late-1970s, the entire Curtis clan was involved, making his mission theirs. In time, grandchildren became employees, great-grandchildren became students, and John Curtis Christian evolved into the Curtis family school.

A workaholic and control freak, Mr. Curtis constantly schemed to make his school better, and his vigor was both infectious and annoying. He not only built many of the school buildings himself, but was constantly making changes and additions, never satisfied.

He performed so many menial tasks around the school that he'd get his clothes dirty—streaks of black tar on his white pants, paint smears on his shirt. Visitors often mistook him for a janitor. Once, when a fire damaged one of the buildings, while a few of the Curtises met with insurance agents and called contractors, they heard the *scrape, scrape, scrape* of Mr. Curtis shoveling debris into a wheelbarrow.

The man never slept, staying up late at night watching television, the mental wheels churning. He was the kind of guy who'd wake early one morning and announce that he'd decided to tear down a wall in his house or retile the school bathrooms or plant some trees or renovate the library. At dawn, he'd be on the phone, calling family members, telling them, "Meet me at the school." J.T. always felt that his father would have been perfectly capable of walking into school one day to announce they were changing from a Monday-through-Friday schedule to a Thursday-through-Sunday schedule, and after laying out his reasons, he'd convince the others it was a brilliant plan. Mr. Curtis was also a loud, stubborn, iron-willed, and opinionated man, whose pride sometimes boiled over into egotism, and who would always tell everyone just what to do and just how to do it. Some family members dreaded his schemes, which always required an abundance of time and sweat, but his enthusiasm usually won out.

More than two dozen members of the extended Curtis family now live in the modest neighborhood near the school, in simple ranch homes. Their salaries are moderate, but they wouldn't trade their jobs for anything. They're proud of what their father created, and also proud that his humble little school came to be known for such a powerhouse of a football team.

Despite having just four hundred kids in the high school, the Patriots will start the 2005 season ranked by *USA Today* as the ninth-best high-school football team in America.

When asked to explain the Patriot's success, J.T. says it's less about calling great plays or outsmarting other coaches and more about teaching his players about the values and life lessons that form the foundation of the school's ethic. His philosophy of coaching grew out of the culture his dad created at the school.

J.T. often tells his kids to respect the game and to play "like Christian gentlemen." He's capable of flying off the handle and screaming at dumb mistakes, but he's no bully and, as long as a kid is trying, he's patient. He often shrugs off setbacks, like a fumble or interception, that would give most coaches fits, and he uses those moments to remind players that "things in your life aren't always gonna go well. You're gonna have to learn to get up, dust yourself off, and go again."

He encourages them to move past setbacks by having faith that things will always work out. "God has a plan," he tells them. However, he also demands that players respect the game, and hurls vein-popping outbursts at those who commit personal fouls during games. Those players get yanked and benched, sometimes for the rest of the game.

A few years ago, J.T. got a visit from a former New Orleans Saints coach, Wimp Hewgley, who had sent his two sons to John Curtis. His eldest, Troy, graduated a few years back, went to LSU, then became an Air Force fighter pilot, eventually stationed in Afghanistan. When the kid received a big promotion, his superior officer wrote on the promotion letter that Troy displayed the qualities of an "elite warrior." The kid's dad, full of pride, brought a copy of the letter to J.T. and thanked him for making his son a better man. That afternoon, J.T. brought the dad to practice, read the "elite warrior" comments, and told his players, "This is what I prepare you for. I prepare you to be elite warriors. Not elite warriors on the football field, but elite warriors in life."

J.T. has never managed to develop pastimes or hobbies, except for occasionally cooking big batches of gumbo or red beans and rice. When he's not engaged in football, he gets restless and edgy. In the evenings, he flips through TV channels like a kid in need of Ritalin. Like his father, he's an insomniac. One of the few exercises in his life not directly related to the school has been cohosting a popular local TV show, *Friday Night Football*, a weekly wrapup of prep football.

He is comically oblivious to everyday matters. He never knows how much is in his checking account. He doesn't use e-mail or voice mail, and has a hard time keeping track of keys: He's lost so many keys to the doors of the school that the others don't give him keys anymore. He has to call a relative to get into the school. He sometimes even forgets his own wedding anniversary: It's September 16, fast approaching as the season starts.

He has, however, honed an uncanny ability to pay close attention to the issues affecting kids' lives, to their problems and aspirations. As with Troy Hewgley, his relationships with players and students transcend the football field. He remembers the smallest details about his students and regularly asks after their families, "How's your mom's new job?" and "Is your grandma feeling better?" He's known many of them since they were toddlers and, these days, finds himself coaching the *sons* of former players.

Over the years, the lines between J.T.'s home life, work life, church life, coaching life, and family life have become completely blurred.

The front door of his house is rarely locked, and his wife, Lydia, is always ready with a meal for hungry linebackers and tight ends.

If a player is having trouble at home, he might start visiting J.T. and Lydia after school or on weekends. Sometimes, when a kid's home life has turned especially difficult, J.T. and Lydia have invited him to live with them. One of those tenants was Melvin Hayes, an enormous offensive tackle with a towering Afro haircut that made him look six inches taller than his six-and-a-half-foot frame, who slept on the Curtises' living-room couch for *three years*. Hayes played at Mississippi State after graduation and went on to play for the New York Jets.

J.T.'s mission is about more than winning football games. At John Curtis there are no tryouts and no one gets cut. If a kid shows up for practice, he's on the team. There's no guarantee he'll play much, but if he attends each practice and works hard, who knows? J.T. stresses to players that they're always just one play away from getting called upon.

The no-cut policy leads to unusually large teams: more than a hundred aspiring players most years, at a school with fewer than three hundred males. A team that size requires an unusually large coaching staff, a dozen strong. As Bear Bryant, the godfather of southern football, once said: one of the three golden rules of coaching is "surround yourself with people who can't live without football." Fortunately for J.T., the Curtis family is large, and pathologically crazy about the game.

J.T.'s right-hand man is his brother, Leon, the defensive coordinator and linebacker coach. As J.T.'s smirking alter ego, Leon happily cedes the limelight and interviews to his big brother. A jumble of contradictions, Leon appears gruff and unpolished, but he has a master's degree and is a deeply devout man who, when he can't sleep, flips through channels in search of religious TV shows. Leon usually responds to small talk with grunts or silence. One college recruiter who frequently visited the school said it took two years before Leon said a single word to him.

With players, Leon is full of goofy jokes one day, acerbic sarcasm the next. "If you can't play intelligently, you'll have to switch positions, son," he'll say. The kids can't ever figure him out. He'll tell a joke, then yell at anyone who laughs. He's also endearing, and rarely boring. Leon usually calls his players "son," but when he's unhappy, he just calls them the number on their jersey. Worse is when he doesn't call them anything. Leon's silence is more unnerving than his jibes.

The rest of the assistant coaches—"the boys," their wives call them—are an entertaining, devoted group of born-and-bred New Orleanians. Many have been with the school for decades, a few since birth. All but three are named Curtis, or are related to one.

One of the few non-Curtises is Leon's best friend, Mike Roberson, a 1968 John Curtis graduate and the offensive line coach, whom everyone calls Coach Rob. By day, he wears plaid shirts and khakis and teaches history. As a coach, he's a workhorse who's always quietly doing little jobs, like washing uniforms or loading gear onto buses. Normally jovial and easygoing, on gameday, a Jekyll–Hyde thing overcomes him and he'll get unhinged at the site of a player's mistake, yelling like a caveman and wildly flapping his arms as if he's trying to fly.

Coach Rob has coached since the 1970s, as has the coach of the elementary school team, Corey Buttone, a tall, balding man with a reputation for whacking kids in the helmet with the fat championship rings he wears on two fingers. Francis Lanzetta, a parent and teacher aide at the school, also coaches.

The younger generation of coaches includes J.T.'s sons, Jeff and Johnny; his son-in-law, Tommy Fabacher; Leon's three sons, Preston, Matt, and Steve; J.T. and Leon's nephew, Lance; and Jeff's best friend, Jerry Godfrey, an ex-Patriot.

Even with such a big staff, a team of one hundred or more kids is a challenge. J.T. wants to give every kid a chance to prove himself, though. At other schools, anyone less than 150 pounds would be chased off to the track team or chess club. But J.T. likes the potential to be surprised by a scrawny freshman who becomes a two-hundred-pound senior. "I think the greatest ingredient they have is patience," says Pete Jenkins, a defensive coach for the Philadelphia Eagles who previously coached at LSU, where he had gotten to know J.T. "And his patient approach rubs off on his players."

Gary Greaves, one of J.T.'s most satisfying surprises, was an extreme example of that patience. Greaves weighed ninety-seven pounds as a freshman, and got his butt kicked. J.T. worried he might get hurt, and told his parents so. But Gary's father pleaded with J.T. to keep his son on the team. "If he can't play, he'll run away from home." J.T. relented. As a sophomore, Gary again came out for the team, a bit heavier, but broke his arm in practice and was out for the season. By his senior year, the kid had packed on fifty pounds but was still just five-foot-eight and still among the team's pipsqueaks.

During summer camp, Gary played with such surprising ferocity that J.T. took a chance and made him a varsity starter. Greaves went on to lead the defense with nine interceptions that year. "That's what makes high school football so special," J.T. once said about the no-cut policy. "I can't ever tell what a kid can do until I continue to work with him. I don't care how tall, fat, skinny, or short they are." All he expects is a positive attitude and great effort.

Over the years, a handful of J.T.'s players, like Melvin Hayes, have ended up in the NFL, and he's sent hundreds to top colleges. Most players, though, will see their football careers end the day they graduate from high school, and they know it. That doesn't stop them from subjecting themselves to excruciating workouts.

J.T. may be patient, but he's not afraid to push kids *very* hard.

His time-tested method is to put players through endless drills, relentlessly working on footwork, timing, and strength. Every season begins just weeks after the previous season ends, with meticulous workouts in the weight room, the domain of J.T.'s gravel-voiced son-in-law, Tommy, who could pass for a New York City cop, or a *Sopranos* Mafioso. Tommy attended John Curtis and was a standout defensive back, playing on two of J.T.'s championship teams. He earned a football scholarship to LSU, and afterward married J.T.'s daughter, Joanna, whom he had been dating since the eighth grade. Tommy coaches the defensive backs and is also the team's strength and conditioning coach, spending many hours overseeing the action in the team's modest weight room. Gruff as he is, Tommy treats the weight room as if it's a holy place. Though *holy* is probably the last word players would use to describe his winter workouts.

Come spring, players switch from weight-lifting to running, two to four miles a day, depending on their position. Then, for two awful weeks in late spring they partake in a Patriots' ritual known as *running the levee*, a term that even twenty years later players will spit out as if it's a lemon rind. They absolutely *loathe* the levee.

Viewed from above, New Orleans looks like the last place humans should live. Often called the Crescent City, it is nestled in between the rounded southern shore of large Lake Pontchartrain looming to the north, and the meandering curves of the Mississippi River to the south, with the city forming a vaguely crescent shape. One of the country's busiest ports sits in a bend of the river, a central hub in a 14,500 mile inland waterway system.

The swampy, spongy lowlands of the Mississippi Delta stretch out south and east from the city for miles into the gulf, a hardscrabble region dappled with fishing shacks, citrus groves, and oil rigs. Various smaller lakes dot the nearby landscape. The city is surrounded by water.

Ever since the French founded New Orleans in 1718, the city has struggled to hold back those waters on all sides, and is striated by canals and waterways that drain the waters toward the Delta. Omnipresent levee walls border the various waterways and run along the Mississippi and the shore of Lake Pontchartrain, forming the world's largest levee system. Begun by the French settlers, hundreds of miles of levees now loom above the neighborhoods of the city, many of which sit well below sea level. The city has been likened to a bathtub, a saucer, or half an oyster shell. Making matters worse is that, much like Venice, the city has been sinking.

With so many parts of the city and its suburbs below sea level, the levees are as essential a part of New Orleans as beignets and jazz. Some are concrete, some steel, and some are grass-covered slopes of earth that look more like parks than protective barriers.

Suburban River Ridge and Jefferson Parish, most of which are slightly above sea level, are protected not only by levees but a sophisticated pumping system. The earthen, grass-covered levee running along the southern edge of River Ridge is just two blocks from John Curtis, towering above the residential backyards butting up against its base. On the other side of the levee, giant ships and tankers regularly lumber up river above eye level. A paved walkway snakes along the top of the levee, the highest point for miles around.

Soon after the Patriots' intense winter weightlifting sessions, spring running begins and, each afternoon, the Patriots jog over to that levee and line up in rows. With each tweet of a coach's whistle, they scramble forty yards straight up the steep slope. Then they do it sideways, then backwards, then in a zigzag pattern around orange cones. Then on all fours. Over and over and over. Players heave for air, retch their lunch, and sometimes collapse onto the grass. Some wide receivers make it look easy. Out-of-shape freshmen watch with awe and disgust as three-hundred-pound linemen defy physics and outrace them to the top. Coach Leon frequently asks gasping players, "What color's my shirt?" It's red—seeing white is a sign of heatstroke.

Coaches bark out, "When you get tired, what's the first thing to go?" And the Patriots bark back in raspy voices, "Your mind!" Again and again. It sometimes takes until their senior year for players to realize that running the levee isn't just sadistic. It's designed to work their minds as much as their bodies, to help them survive mentally and physically when they're faced with a do-or-die fourth down in the final moments of a do-or-die game.

And yet, as distasteful as running the levee is, J.T.'s summer camp is even worse.

Most high-school players experience the awful pain of practicing twice in the same day, the summer ritual known as two-a-days. But J.T. takes his summer camp session up a notch. After three days of two-a-days, the next four days of camp feature three-a-days. The players arrive at dawn, perform blocking and passing drills for two hours before breakfast, then lie down for a short rest on sleeping bags they've laid out in the gym. The seventy-minute midday practice is always the worst, with the temperatures hovering near a hundred and the air a humid soup. After lunch, they review films, then get to rest again until four o'clock, when they're called back onto the field for another two hours of sun-baked drills. Finally, after dinner, they head home to collapse, returning the next day at dawn. It's hot, brutal, and dirty; a rite of passage. They'll forget many things about their high-school days, but none will forget the bitter aches and the tastes of grass and bile and blood and sweat from their three-a-days.

After more than six months of painfully honing their bodies, their character, and their fortitude, tonight's jamboree game will be the players' first big test of the season and, for the coaches, a glimpse at whether this year's Patriots are a championship caliber team. J.T. has already told sportswriters he considers this "a rebuilding year."

But, as with many of J.T.'s public comments, the response from other coaches is, *Gimme a break*. In a city and state so obsessed with football, the winning record of teeny little John Curtis school has generated an enormous amount of resentment.

Nothing about New Orleans is moderate, certainly not football, which, thanks to the perpetually mediocre Saints, is more about high schools and LSU than the pros.

New Orleans is a city that spends half its life in summer; a city of racial tension and crime; eccentricities and promiscuity; where music, dance, violence, sex, food, and sport are stirred into a primal, cultural gumbo; a city where every day holds the promise of adventure, and every night the steamy scent of danger.

For a city of just under 500,000, outranked in size by such vague metropolises as Columbus and Jacksonville, Charlotte and Phoenix, with just one Fortune 500 company to brag about, it's incredible how much New Orleans has contributed to American culture. To visitors, New Orleans is the French Quarter and Mardi Gras, restaurants and jazz clubs. Away from the tourist spots, many of the city's neighborhoods are plagued by extreme poverty, violence, and drugs.

The inner city is carved by racial lines, a mix of African-American communities such as Tremé and the Lower Ninth Ward to the east and, toward the heart of town, whiter, more touristy neighborhoods, such as the Garden District and Uptown. East, west, and south of downtown are suburban neighborhoods where women work in the health-care industry and men in the boom-or-bust oil or shipping industries. Further south, down into the Delta, they are cattlemen, lumbermen, and duck hunters. Greater New Orleans melds Old Europe and Old South, black and white, country clubbers and roughnecks.

Words and inflections from Cajun, French, Spanish, Caribbean, African, and even voodoo infect the region's dialogue and dialect, so much so that outsiders sometimes can't understand what locals are saying. Many of them speak a jazzy, Big Easy patois, which sounds a bit Texan, a bit southern, and a bit French, but with a New Yorky edge—like a laid-back Brooklynite faking a southern and a French accent at the same time.

They've got names that outsiders can't pronounce, Cajun-inflected ditties like Arceneaux, Duplessis, Badeaux, Dufrene, LaChute, and Ponce de Leon. Their lexicon is also unique. New Orleans isn't divided into counties, but *parishes*. The grassy strip between two lanes of asphalt isn't the median, but the *neutral ground*, and sidewalks are still sometimes called *banquettes*. Like New Yorkers, New Orleanians drop Gs from their *ing* words or sometimes just lop off the last syllable entirely. *This*, *that*, and *these* become *dis*, *dat*, and *deze*; oil is *earl*, and boil is *berl*. Grammar also gets bent, so if Coach Leon agrees with something, he'll usually say, "Yeah . . . you right."

As a popular local newspaper columnist, Chris Rose, once put it, New Orleanians are "fiercely proud and independent . . . We talk funny and listen to strange music and eat things you'd probably hire an exterminator to get out of your yard . . . We talk too much and laugh too loud and live too large and, frankly, we're suspicious of those who don't."

New Orleanians also love their sports, especially football, and the proud and stubborn way of doing things affects that devotion as well. Kids grow up dreaming of LSU or Tulane becoming national champs. They're so committed to the Saints—often derided as the Ain'ts, due to their years of losing—and to their beloved LSU Tigers that, as Rose put it, "Sometimes we bury our dead in LSU sweatshirts."

Texas, Ohio, and Alabama are more often thought of as hard-core football states, but polls have ranked Louisiana well ahead of them, propelled largely by the competitive juices of sports-obsessed Greater New Orleans. Based on such statistics as fan interest, percentage of boys who play in high school, and number of players reaching the NFL, Louisiana is America's third-most football-crazed state, behind Mississippi and Georgia.

As a local high-school coach once said: "This is Louisiana. When it's crawfish season, you catch crawfish. The rest of the time, you play football."

Some of the John Curtis Patriots grew up playing football in the neutral ground, but the lucky ones had a nearby playground. Not a playground with swings and slides, known locally as *shoot-the-chutes*. In New Orleans, *playgrounds* are neighborhood athletic fields, home to Little League teams known as the playground leagues.

The city has 150 playground teams, with hundreds more in the suburban parishes. That entrenched system has produced its share of star athletes, including the Manning boys, Peyton, now the Indianapolis Colts' quarterback, and brother Eli, the New York Giants' quarterback. Their dad, Archie was also a star, who stubbornly insisted on playing for his hometown Ain'ts, despite their years of mediocrity.

Most of the 2005 Patriots are products of the playground system.

Critics have accused J.T. of recruiting players right off those playgrounds, right out of grammar school, and of doling out secret scholarships and other perks. The harshest critics have flat out accused John Curtis of being nothing more than a front for a football-obsessed band of academically challenged meatheads, and of sacrificing academics for state championships, all of which leaves J.T. gape-mouthed. The reality is that his players have qualified to attend top universities all over the country.

As J.T. sees it, John Curtis offers a great education and, more than that, a close-knit and nurturing community that grounds kids, morally, spiritually, and academically, for life ahead. But, as with every private school in America, their success is number driven, and he and the other Curtises work hard every day to boost enrollment. "Certainly, we do everything that we can to entice people to come into our school," J.T. once told a TV interviewer. "That's the nature of the business. We're a *private* school."

J.T.'s father never bothered with diplomacy in responding to critics, and was so perpetually proud of his school and his Patriots that he once boasted aloud, "We're the Rolls-Royce of athletic factories," which made big news in a 2000 *Times-Picayune* story.

J.T. responded to follow-ups from reporters with characteristic directness: "We give our kids the best, and I don't apologize for that."

J.T. has battled all kinds of accusations throughout his career. Usually, he steers clear of what he considers petty squabbles. He once attended a meeting of the Louisiana High School Athletic Association, or LHSAA, and listened to another high school coach disparage his school: *The kids at John Curtis are on steroids, they never go to class, they live in the weight room.* J.T. stood up and calmly introduced himself to the coach, then said, "Listen, I don't know who you are, and I've never even seen you in my school. You've never walked down my halls or sat in on my classes or even seen my weight room. You don't know anything about me or my school. Do you?" The guy sheepishly admitted that J.T. was right.

The encounter reminded J.T. that his team might be a powerhouse, but they're also an underdog, and he's never going to convince everyone that his success is simply the result of hard work and a deep commitment from his players.

Another battle the school has waged is with the LHSAA itself, which oversees high-school sports programs and determines which teams play which. High schools are broken into five levels, based on enrollment; small schools are Class 1A and big ones are Class 5A. Schools vie for state championships against schools in the same division. John Curtis's small size had put it in the Class 2A level but, in 1985, enrollment was boosted by a New Orleans–area oil boom and they were bumped up to Class 3A. In 1993 they jumped another level to play in Class 4A. Even after enrollment dropped, the Patriots kept playing at the 4A level and J.T. came to prefer playing bigger teams, *playing up*, in high school athletics parlance. But the other teams didn't like getting beaten by little John Curtis Christian School, which reached the 4A state championship game eleven of the next twelve years, and won eight times. Last year, the LHSAA reshuffled its classifications, and they bumped John Curtis all the way back to 2A, restricting the team from playing up. The 2A teams were hardly pleased.

After a group of 2A coaches complained about facing Curtis as their new opponent, the LHSAA shifted Curtis to a different 2A district, whose schools are at least a half hour west of River Ridge, forcing all of the Patriots' sports teams to travel long distances to and from games. Mr. Curtis, who had had a long-running public feud with LHSAA president Tommy Henry, resigned in late 2004 as head-master, in protest of the ruling. J.T. chose not to dwell on the setback, and instead began trying to fill his 2005 schedule with occasional out-of-district games against larger schools.

The first full game of this season, just a week from tonight, is against Cottonwood High, a big 5A team flying in from suburban Salt Lake City, Utah. The week after that, the Patriots are scheduled to play in Alabama against another 5A team.

J.T. does things his way, not worrying about what his competitors gripe about. "People don't know what's inside my heart," he once told the *Times-Picayune*. "So I don't care what some people think of me. As long as I continue to do what I think is right."

He also doesn't worry about what anyone thinks of his playbook. He's maintained a decades-long reliance on an old-fashioned offensive strategy, the simplicity of which doesn't make him any more popular with rival coaches. His offense may be something of a dinosaur, but in J.T.'s hands, it has become something of a T-Rex.

In 1975, he implemented a triple-option offense known as the Houston Veer, and he's used it, some would say stubbornly, for three decades. His offense relies less on a vast number of specific plays and more on allowing the quarterback to read the defense and make split-second decisions based on his reads. *Triple* refers to the quarterback's three options: hand off to the halfback, pitch out to the other half-back, or run it himself. J.T. likes the old-style running game because it's unselfish and unpredictable. On three out of four plays, not even the Patriot coaches know who'll carry the ball. "The defense doesn't know what we're going to do because *we* don't know what we're going to do," J.T. says.

The veer is less exciting than the West Coast–style passing game most high schools use. It also doesn't allow running backs to rack up yardage or break records, which is what parents love to see. "A self-ish player can't run my offense," J.T. once said. "Because a selfish player wants to run the ball." Indeed, J.T. has never had a back rush for more than two thousand yards in a season, because so many different backs get a chance to carry the ball. Instead of big gains, the Patriots chew up yardage in small bites. Three-and-a-half yards per play is a first down. A string of first downs is a touchdown.

His success with this strategy infuriates competitors, and some Curtises view the football-factory complaints as merely sour grapes from teams the Patriots have beaten with their simple style. Every opponent knows exactly what to expect from the Patriots. They could watch a scouting tape from 1976 or 1986 or 1996, it wouldn't matter. They'd all look like the same team. Knowing that Curtis runs more or less the same plays year after year is like having a copy of their playbook. And, still, other teams can't stop the Patriots. It's like getting whooped by your aunt.

"Love him or hate him, you've got to respect him," Bill Stubbs, the head coach at Salmen High, a long time Curtis rival, once said of J.T. and his methodical offense.

J.T. has by now given up on trying to convert his critics. Instead, he lets his record speak for itself, and he's taught his players to do the same. When opponents taunt them during games, part of the psychological warfare of the sport, he tells them just to point at the scoreboard—which usually reflects a Patriot lead—and coolly walk away. "Play with poise," is among his mantras.

Local sportscaster Ed Daniels, with whom J.T. co-hosts *Friday Night Football,* has a theory: "J.T. has committed the ultimate sin in America. . . . He succeeded."

Tonight is time to see whether all the pain of the weight-lifting, levee-running, and three-a-days will pay off. The coaches all know this is a green team; as J.T. put it, this will likely be a rebuilding year. Then again, no one really knows what a player is capable of until he's out there under the lights, in the heat of battle, amidst the roar of the crowd.

The Patriots will soon face the Fontainebleau Bulldogs beneath the klieg lights of the Salmen High stadium, in front of a clamorous crowd of three thousand.

2

Friday Night Jamboree

Each afternoon before a game, J.T. goes home for his vaguely super-stitious pre-game ritual: he eats a bowl of soup with a diet Coke, then lies down for a short nap. Refreshed by that bit of zenlike calm, he drives the half mile back to the school.

Fifteen minutes before tonight's departure time, J.T. arrives at the coaches' room, knowing his assistants will have already loaded the equipment truck, passed out clean jerseys, and gassed up the buses. Jeff, who coaches the quarterbacks, is grading the written test he gives his players before each game. In the veer offense, so many decisions are in the quarterback's hands that Jeff, who played quarterback for his dad and at Tulane, drills his guys endlessly. Johnny, who coaches the special teams and linebackers, eats his usual pregame Quarter Pounder and fries. Tommy shuns the superstitious stuff, claiming it's just voodoo. As always, a few coaches are watching video footage, studying tonight's opponent. Like a group of doctors studying X rays, they fast forward and rewind through a DVD of the Fontainebleau Bulldogs in action, searching for clues, any weakness to exploit tonight. Their main concern is the Bulldogs' speedy quarterback.

After briefly conferring with Leon and Coach Rob, J.T. shouts, "Let's load 'em up," and the entire coaching staff snaps into action, grabbing rain suits, baseball caps, headsets, erasable white boards, and pens. The trainers, team managers and statisticians scurry around packing their gear. Tonight, they're letting J.T.'s six-year-old grandson,

John Thomas Curtis the fourth, ride along, representing the coaching staff of the future.

Down in the noisy, sweaty locker room, Tank English calls the players around for a pregame prayer: "Father, we thank you for the ability to play football tonight. Give us clear minds and clear thoughts . . ."

He's interrupted as Coach Jerry bursts into the locker room shouting, "Load up." The players pour out the door, cleats clacking on the sidewalk. The varsity starters climb into the first of three buses; the second-team guys take the next bus; freshman and third-team players go to the last. Riding point as usual is Coach Rob, driving the team's equipment truck, a Ford cube van called "Mike Neeley's war wagon," named for a former player who was killed in a traffic accident in college. Neeley's father donated the truck, which now features a FALLEN PATRIOTS plaque on the side, listing Patriots who've died over the years, including two recently killed in Iraq.

Jefferson Parish police officers Craig Gardner and Red Lindsay have been escorting Patriot buses to and from games for years. Gardner played for J.T. years ago and, after graduating and becoming a cop, he volunteered to escort his old team. Because every game is away, the Patriots always battle Friday night rush-hour traffic. More than a few times they've arrived late, and it helps to have cops plowing a noisy path for them.

Traffic is thick along Airline Drive and Clearview Parkway, but commuters obediently move aside for the screaming sirens and flashing lights of the Patriots caravan. At red lights, the officers block the intersection and the Curtis buses barrel right through.

Tonight, the officers have decided to avoid Interstate 10 through downtown and to take the slightly longer route to Slidell, across the Lake Pontchartrain Causeway—the longest bridge in the world, at twenty-four miles—to the lake's North Shore. The players sit in absolute silence as they cross Pontchartrain's gray-brown waters. J.T. forbids any talking. They should be getting their heads in the game.

With three games on tap for the jamboree, thousands of fans from six different schools have come out to Salmen High on this sweltering sauna of an August night.

The second of tonight's three games is underway when the Patriots' buses arrive. The players unload and finish suiting up to the blare of marching bands, the rhythmic chants of opposing cheerleaders, and taunts being traded across sides of the field. Fans mingle in the parking lot, hosting tailgate parties around sizzling grills. A line snakes out from the small concession stand, where fried oyster po'boys are sold along with hot dogs and nachos. With six teams playing tonight, the grandstands and sidelines are a rainbow of team colors. Some of the boys have painted their bodies, hair, and faces in their team's colors. The crowd is reveling in the rites and rituals that mark the ecstatic kickoff to another season of high-school football in America.

In the night's first game, the host team, Salmen, has lost to its crosstown rival, Slidell, 22–14. In the second game, Northshore is about to wrap up a 20–7 victory over Pope John Paul II. The Patriots have arrived in the game's last minutes and start to loosen up and stretch.

Mike Walker's parents and grandparents, who come to every game, arrived early for a tailgate get-together with Andrew Nierman's mom and grandparents. Mike's mom, Donna, hands out a few of the popcorn balls she brings to every game, then joins other parents climbing into the grandstands to find a good spot. Tank's mom, Althea, is there, along with Joe's mom, Jennifer. Kyle's parents are worried about his recently healed collarbone. So are all the other Patriots fans, who will soon get their first glimpse of the team's new quarterback. They're more worried about him than the storm the news has been warning of.

Earlier in the day, the National Hurricane Center issued an advisory. A storm called Katrina had just passed to the west of the Florida Keys, where it suddenly gained strength and was now being designated a Category 2 hurricane, expected to grow even stronger in the next forty-eight hours. Local newscasters this afternoon said the storm may be heading toward the Louisiana coastline, and have issued warnings of heavy rains and possible tornadoes in the next few days.

The storm is still five hundred miles from New Orleans, though, and as usual, most New Orleanians have greeted news of her approach with a shrug. The hurricane season, which begins on June 1, is annually filled with dire warnings of monster storms that never quite materialize. Such warnings have simply become a way of life in the Crescent City, and this one certainly wasn't going to distract fans from the first night of the high-school football season.

As the last few plays of the Northshore–Pope John Paul game wind down, J.T. calls his team around him. Before each game, he subjects his players to a Q-and-A session on the importance of special teams, a key component of the Patriots' strategy. In contrast to the pageantry of the police escort, the bright lights, the bands, and the rowdy fans, his pregame talks are subdued. All business, he drills his players, asking them what their goal is on a punt return. "Score," they respond in unison. *On a kickoff return?* "Score." *On a kickoff?* "Inside the twenty." *Onside kick?* "Get the ball."

"Okay, good," J.T. says. "Now, remember, on the kickoff return— get the ball to the wall, and the wall to the ball. Let's go to work."

As his players head off toward the end zone to warm up, J.T. surveys this group of young men he's coached for so many months, many for years. Some, like Joe, he's watched grow for a decade, since they were scrawny kids at the John Curtis lower school. They've all worked hard to get here. J.T. came of age during an era when it was okay for coaches, notably Bear Bryant, to weed out the weak by pushing players so hard that they puked or passed out. He's learned to bring kids to the brink of physical exhaustion without crossing the line. And he's always amazed that they keep coming back for more.

Sometimes J.T. is downright humbled by how the kids commit themselves so selflessly to the team, even as some of them face an awful lot of trouble at home.

Since Tank English's father died, two years ago, Tank's mom, Althea, has struggled to run her day-care center, juggling the demands of life as a working single mother. Like her son, she's always warm and upbeat, and babies Tank as if he's her teddy bear. They live in a small, brick house, along with Tank's two aunts and an uncle, in Kenner, a suburb just west of River Ridge. The house is crowded but at least Tank's got his own room, now that his brother, nine years older, has moved out. Tank is trying to be the man of the house, and dreams of getting a business degree and some day becoming an entrepreneur. Already he's talking about turning half of his mom's day-care building into a snow-cone shop.

Tank never seems depressed, his baby face always smiling. But J.T. knows that, in addition to his family's troubles, he is worried about earning a college scholarship. Meanwhile, he's fighting to keep his hulking weight down, which has been a struggle ever since grammar school. As a kid, he couldn't play football for his local playground league because he was over the weight limit. Working at a chicken-wing joint this year to earn a few badly needed dollars hasn't helped.

Tank played a few varsity games as a freshman and, in his sophomore year, became a full-time starter. This year, even though he's still a junior, he's determined to play a larger role on defense. The other players adore Tank, who is as competitive on the field as he is lighthearted off it. This summer J.T. began letting him run a few of the defensive drills at practice. Tank tells the other defensive players that their goal on the field is "negative yards," not just preventing the offense from advancing, but actually pushing them *backwards*. His larger goal for himself is impressing recruiters so he can win that scholarship. Playing college ball is what his dad would have wanted for him.

Tank's good friend since the fourth grade, Andrew Nierman, always reaches midfield ahead of everyone else at practice, and he's usually one of the last to leave. The presumptive class valedictorian is always first at this, first at that. He's been a starter since he was a freshman and, as the only returning member of the offensive line this year, he feels and acts like the team's wise old veteran. He hopes to get into a top college, if not Harvard, and J.T. sometimes worries that he works himself *too* hard, both in class and on the field. Just as J.T.'s dad refused to let his kids talk about their grades at home, J.T. has mixed feelings about any obsession with straight A's. To him, straight A's can come at the expense of health and happiness and, while he's never been one to quash the aspirations of high achievers, he does try to remind kids like Andrew that there's more to life, and more to a successful high-school career, than grades. He tries to tell the kid to slow down, that he's doing just fine. But Andrew, who lives alone with his mom, seems driven by some inner engine that just won't quit. J.T. is amazed at his ability to do *everything* at once—he works at his church, he gets perfect grades, he lost weight and packed on muscle this summer. He's what J.T. considers the ideal player, which means a lot is riding on him this season.

Quarterback Kyle Collura is another of the team's hardest workers, which is a good thing, considering how much work he's got to do to improve his play. J.T. finds it hard to tell what the laid-back teen is thinking, because he never has much to say. He remembers first meeting Kyle, when he came to the John Curtis lower school as a chubby sixth-grader. Kyle grew up across the street from the Wentwood Playground, one of a dozen athletic complexes in the town of Kenner. As a toddler, he'd look out the window at the ball players, and couldn't wait to grow up and join them. When he got his chance, at six, his coach put him on the offensive line instead of at quarterback. As he grew older and lost weight, he was given a chance to play running back and, finally, quarterback. He wasn't as naturally gifted as some of the other kids, but he practiced hard and played with grit. After one of his games, a burly bald man approached Kyle's mother, Melody. He said his name was Corey Buttone and he coached the elementary school team at John Curtis Christian School. He told her Kyle had promise, and suggested that Curtis would be a good fit for him.

Kyle has since lost the baby fat, and J.T. has been impressed with his multiyear fight to become a starter. Like most coaches, J.T. has a wish list for the right size and speed for each player's position. In addition to a player's sheer physical attributes, though, J.T. has always been intrigued, as he puts it, by "a young man who is willing to work to accomplish the goals that you set in front of him, who's willing to sacrifice and pay the price." J.T. has no doubt about Kyle's willingness to pay the price. His bounce back from the broken collarbone is proof of his commitment. However, a quarterback needs more than just the desire to play, he needs a slew of intangible qualities, with leadership and confidence atop the list. Those are qualities Kyle needs to find, and fast.

Last year, J.T. put Kyle in for only a handful of plays as the third-team quarterback. He threw exactly four passes. In early 2005, Kyle got a phone call from Johnnie Thiel saying, "I'm through with Curtis, have a good season." Kyle stepped eagerly into his new role, but his collarbone injury kept him from practicing through the late spring and from lifting weights over the summer. He's seen limited full-contact action since rejoining the team, and J.T. isn't sure he's found the level of composure a quarterback needs. Tonight's game will reveal a lot.

The battle for the starting linebacker jobs has been especially tight this year. A promising player named Lincston Jones recently broke his thumb and will miss tonight's game. Another linebacker, Kenny Dorsey, probably the best of them all, is also absent tonight, but for different reasons. His religion, Seventh Day Adventist, prevents him from playing on Friday nights.

All of which helped Mike Walker get the starter's job. It's been a hard-fought route for Mike, who has worked his way back onto the field after being cut from the team at Archbishop Rummel High, near his home in Metairie, adjacent to the city's western border. The coaches at Rummel had seen him in playground games and encouraged him to come out for their team, so he enrolled. Then they told him he didn't make the cut, and goodbye. The message: You're just not good enough.

He was heartsick, but instead of waiting to try again next year, he decided to switch schools immediately. He'd heard about John Curtis and its no-cut policy, so the day after the 2003 Christmas break, he enrolled and became a Patriot. He's fit in well at the school, becoming something of a class clown. Eager to please, he likes to make teachers laugh and to impress his coaches. Most of all, though, he likes to inspire his teammates. His grandparents come to every game, and the players have adopted them as team mascots. Huge linemen come up after games shouting, "Maw-maw! Paw-paw!" and roughly embrace the older couple. J.T. considers Mike one of those players who doesn't necessarily have the natural abilities but may just have the grit and smarts to compensate. The coaches have all worked hard with Mike this summer, teaching him how to drop back on pass defense, and choose the right angles to cut off a runner. Mike has soaked up those lessons well, and beefed up his body, and he now believes that this will be his year.

Mike's fellow linebackers, Preston Numa and Jacob Dufrene, have also had to overcome a fair share of adversity. Dufrene's burden was dyslexia. He and his family live down on the bayou, on a farm in the town of Larose, where his dad runs a lumber business. When Jacob began having problems in school, his parents decided to send him north to John Curtis. There, the teachers subjected him to a lengthy testing process and determined that he had some visual perception problems. They established a program to help him adapt to his disability and catch up with his peers, and Jacob not only conquered his learning disability but is now a member of the National Honor Society. He's already talking about going to college, where he hopes to study veterinary medicine and maybe work with racehorses. His parents have decided John Curtis is such a good fit for Jacob that they recently rented him an apartment near the school so that he won't have to commute. On the football field, he's performed impressively in recent months. That's why J.T. is uncharacteristically torn: Should he play the kid on defense, at linebacker, or on offense, at tight end? He's decided, for now, that he's going to bend his own rules and let Jacob start at linebacker and rotate in at tight end.

Preston Numa, meanwhile, despite a lifelong love of football, only started playing the game two years ago. As a child, he had been too heavy to play in the playground leagues, just like Tank. After years of being home-schooled by a member of his church, Preston asked his mom, Shirelle Wiltz, if he could attend a regular high school and finally play ball. Shirelle visited John Curtis, got a "warm feeling" about the place, and allowed Preston to go there his freshman year. It was a bit of a sacrifice, as she's also a single mother, divorced from Preston's father, who now lives in California. She and Preston live alone in a modest section of the Gentilly neighborhood of New Orleans, a half-hour commute to River Ridge; tuition stretches her salary as an IRS worker. But Preston loved his new school right away, making friends fast, and last year as a sophomore he was already playing in a few varsity games. She feels the financial strain is more than worthwhile.

In a game against a bayou team last October, Preston broke his jaw, which had to be wired shut, and he missed the rest of the season. The jaw has since healed, and he has been working hard in the weight room and at practice. Just a few weeks ago, however, as part of the ongoing chess match of finding the right position for each player, J.T. decided to move him from defensive lineman to linebacker. He's still struggling to adapt to the new slot, but he's been so anxious for the season to start, he told his mom, "I can *taste* it."

Then there's Joe McKnight. He always gets off to a slow start before practices, taking his time in the locker room before dancing onto the field. J.T. cuts him slack, knowing about Joe's long-gone father and his rootless home life. He really only knows parts of Joe's story, and he's sure there are darker bits he may never learn. Joe doesn't like to talk about that stuff.

When Joe was just a toddler, his father, who was an amateur boxer, left home. Joe was never sure if he went to prison or just disappeared, and he claims that he never much cared. "Never knew him" is the most he'll usually say about his father. He was raised by his mom, Jennifer, along with Joe's older sister, Johanna, and younger brother, Jonathan. The family lived in Kenner, often at Jennifer's mom's house, while Jennifer tried to finish school. Just a kid raising kids.

His mom began dating a playground football coach named Elmo Lee, who noticed that Joe never played with toys, only balls, and was always moving. To provide an outlet for Joe's energy, he set up garbage cans in the back yard and trained Joe to carry a football as he zig-zagged through the cans. As Joe's footwork improved, Lee expanded the daily workout to include wind sprints, pushups, and situps. It was Lee who suggested to Joe's mom that she send her kids to John Curtis. It helped to have a father figure around for a while, but then Lee moved on, and other men rotated in and out of Joe's mom's life. That's when Joe began to roam.

His mother was busy working and going to school, and she gave Joe all the freedom he could handle, but tensions between them grew. He'd leave after a disagreement, and he'd spend a few days with his grandmother or with cousins or friends. Then he'd come back and live with her for awhile, until another disagreement sent him right back out the door. Joe feels that since he was eleven he's been on his own.

J.T. has never been entirely sure whether Joe's mom doesn't want Joe around or if Joe prefers to be a roving lone wolf. He has no doubt that Joe loves his mom: When Joe was eleven, he got her name tattooed on his right arm, above a picture of an angel and, beneath that, the word FOREVER. J.T. got a glimpse at the extent of Joe's complicated domestic situation last year, though, when Joe injured his neck in a game, lost all the feeling below his waist, and was rushed to the hospital for an MRI and CAT scan.

After a tense few hours of tests, the doctors said it was probably just a pinched nerve. But to be safe, Joe should be woken up every two hours that night. When they were all ready to check out, Joe's mom turned to Coach Tommy and asked, "Are you taking him to J.T.'s? Or is he going home with you?" She explained that she was living with her mother and that there was no room there.

Joe stayed with J.T. and Lydia, and they set an alarm clock and woke him up every two hours, until morning.

Joe can be quiet and moody, and he gets into simmering dark funks that sometimes explode into anger. J.T. worries that one day he'll just walk away, especially now that his best friend Johnnie Thiel has left the team. He is also never quite sure where Joe is living, though he knows that lately he's been spending time with a family friend.

Joe's the best player J.T.'s got, the best he's seen in years, and once Joe tightens his laces, pulls on his wrist bands and trots to the field, he plays harder than anyone. He always cradles the ball with two hands as he slams into the line, and is strong enough to prevent thick linebackers' arms from stripping the ball away. As soon as he hits the open field he lengthens his stride, effortlessly gobbling yards, and if a defender draws near, he'll reach out with one arm and slap him down like a bad dog. What J.T. admires most is Joe's "fluidity," once telling a sportswriter, "He's one of those players who doesn't look like he's running full speed, but no one can catch him."

Joe's as good on defense as offense and, at first, J.T. preferred playing him in the defensive backfield. At practices, Joe would sneak over to the running backs' and receivers' drills and J.T. would playfully chase him back to the defense. As a sophomore, Joe got more chances to play on offense, though, and through the season he scored more than a dozen times. J.T. now has him playing *five* positions, as defensive back, kickoff returner, punt returner, wide receiver and, Joe's favorite, running back.

USA Today and *Sports Illustrated* have both ranked Joe as one of the nation's best high-school players and, while Joe accepts his status on the team, he doesn't always wear it comfortably. He's a team leader, but in a quiet way; he leads by example. His teammates respect him, and are even protective of him. They all know Joe is good enough to reach USC or Notre Dame or Michigan. But he's also hard on himself, taking nothing for granted. "God blessed me with ability. But I could be a better player," he once told a sports reporter. "You have to be self-motivated."

J.T. just hopes he can keep Joe on the field long enough for the recruiters to come calling.

As one Curtis teacher put it, "Joe just wants somebody to love him for who he is . . . He's a good kid, he just doesn't realize it yet."

Once the Northshore and Pope John Paul teams have cleared the field, the Patriots charge out of the end zone under the bright lights. Patriot fans dressed in red, white, and blue wildly cheer their team, stomping on the metal bleachers, whistling and shaking their home-made shakers. Because the school is so small, typically far outnum-bered by their opponents' fans, Patriots parents have developed a noisemaker—pennies or dried beans inside a plastic milk jug—to compete against the roars of their larger opponents. The jugs make a respectable racket.

As the Patriots take the field, the coaches gather in a circle and hold hands in the end zone for a silent prayer. Tonight, for the first time in the team's history, they'll all be playing without their number-one fan cheering and hollering like a crazy man. And, for the first time in those thirty-six years, J.T. will coach his team without his father looking on.

The whole team feels his absence.

Ever since his pre–World War II days of amateur boxing among the wharves of the Irish Channel, Mr. Curtis had been a steely competi-tor, someone who viewed life's challenges as win-or-lose propositions. When he opened the school in 1962, he applied that competitive zeal to his near maniacal love of football, coaching the team for the first few years, though with little success. He handed the reins over to J.T. in 1969.

As his son grew into a remarkably successful head coach, Mr. Curtis's passion for the game flourished. He loved the outrageous spectacle of high-school football, the pomp and drama of noisy police escorts, the bands and cheerleaders, the purity of teenaged warfare waged on a grassy, muddy battlefield. He would throw himself into a traditional Mardi Gras second-line dance up and down the sidelines, wagging his *we're-number-one* fingers, leading cheers through a megaphone, and late in the game yelling, "Empty the bench 'cause this one's over, baby!" When his team made it to the championship game, as it so often did, he would unveil a preprinted championship T-shirt halfway through the game, taunting opponents with his obnoxious prediction of victory.

Just before the 2004 season, chest pains prompted Mr. Curtis to visit a cardiologist, who suggested heart valve replacement surgery. Doctors also found a polyp on his colon, and planned to operate on that before performing the heart surgery. Complications ensued: Presurgery medication dehydrated him, then his kidneys shut down, then his heart began to fail. For three months, doctors tried to get his system under control, battling infections and breathing problems and high blood pressure. More than once, his blood pressure soared and the doctors feared he was on the verge of a massive heart attack. The family braced for the worst but, ever so slowly, he recovered.

Finally, when Curtis's systems had all stabilized, the doctors were able to remove the colon polyp, which they found to be cancerous. After removing sixteen inches of the colon, and feeling confident that they'd excised all of the cancer, they did not recommend radiation treatment or chemotherapy. Mr. Curtis was back at school a few weeks later, though the ordeal had weakened him, turning him pale and thin.

During the season, Mr. Curtis insisted on attending every game. He was too weak to dance the sidelines but demanded to at least sit in a folding chair beside the field, right at the fifty-yard line. J.T. had to post two players beside the old man, with orders to whisk him to safety if a play barreled too close. Once, a few players rumbled out of bounds at the fifty-yard line and Mr. Curtis and his chair were knocked flying. "I'm okay, I'm okay," he said, refusing all offers to help him back into his seat.

J.T. led his Patriots to their nineteenth state championship that year. Two months later, doctors found that Mr. Curtis's cancer had spread aggressively to his lungs; they did not suggest radiation or chemotherapy and gave him only a few months to live. Mr. Curtis called his family into his office and gave them the news. "Don't be afraid," he told them, as they gasped and fought back tears. Despite the doctors' advice, he dove into an aggressive treatment program. "I've always fought for everything I wanted and needed," he told his family that night. "And I just can't sit here and not do something."

During the next two months of treatment, Mr. Curtis befriended his hematologist, an Indian woman and a devout Hindu. They would talk about their respective religions and quickly became close. At the end of the eight-week treatment session, Curtis visited the hematologist for a progress report. He walked through the front doors, made eye contact, and knew instantly the news was bad. In that unspoken moment, she lost her stoic, physician's composure and broke into sobs. Curtis walked to her and wrapped his arms around her.

"It's okay," he said. "Don't worry. You don't have to say anything."

That afternoon, he went straight to the school and limped through the atrium, past the sea nymph sculpture and toward his school's front doors, where he met his daughter Alicia. In typical fashion, he issued orders to track down his brother-in-law, Larry; his sister, Ruth; he also wanted J.T. and Leon; daughters Debbie and Kathy; his grandkids, nieces, nephews, cousins and in-laws. He wanted them all. After a flurry of phone calls, the family members squeezed into Mr. Curtis's office, and he sat behind his desk in his worn red leather chair. "Well, I got some good news today," he finally said. "It looks like I'm going home." At first, no one was sure what he meant. But then his blue eyes watered, his lips quavered, and he began to cry.

"I won the fight," he said, his voice shaky. "I won the fight, and I have no fear."

Two months later, he was at home, just a few blocks from the school and surrounded by family members, when he whispered his final words: "I'm going home." He died the next day, on Memorial Day. He was eighty-six.

In the weeks to come, the family would learn that Mr. Curtis had deep friendships and relationships with people they never even knew about. There were liens in his name, loans he had co-signed to help needy families buy a car or house. Or, there was the teacher whose father died; Curtis talked to her by phone every night for a year, closing each conversation with, "I love you." They discovered the projects he had still planned to pursue and found his prayer list of people in need.

Many hundreds attended the funeral; the pastor called him "the most generous man I've ever met." Others spoke of him as "my father, my coach" or "my mentor and my friend." The peak of the ceremony was a video made by a grandchild showing highlights of Mr. Curtis's forty-three years as head of John Curtis Christian School, which prompted tearful applause and a standing ovation. J.T. then told congregants that the date of his father's death had been appropriate: "For a man who loved his country as much as he did," he said, "it's certainly fitting he passed away on Memorial Day."

His father's death thrust J.T. into the role of acting headmaster, although he refused to take over his dad's office, preferring to stay in the smaller office he'd used for decades.

J.T. has been dreading tonight's game, knowing how desperately he'd be missing his father. Now, as he walks toward the sideline, he's greeted by a reminder that gives him a jolt. Officers Craig and Red saved the white folding chair that Mr. Curtis sat in last year and have turned it into a memorial of sorts, decorating it with J.C. stickers and American flags. On the back, they painted: JOHN T. CURTIS SR. 1919–2005. On the seat, they folded a Patriots jersey with a large blue 1 sewn on the front. They've placed the chair right at the fifty-yard line, and put small orange construction cones on either side.

The sight of the chair is eerie for both the players and coaches. Some walk past tentatively. Others touch it and cross themselves. J.T. is deeply moved by the gesture; he still finds it almost impossible to believe his dad is gone.

Because this is the last of the night's three games, fans of the first two contests have begun to depart. Patriot fans are only a few hundred strong and are outnumbered at least two to one by the opposition, but the Patriots' side is making an impressive amount of noise with its fortification of rattling milk jugs.

The Patriots win the coin toss and David Seeman and Joe Mc-Knight are back to receive the kickoff. It's short and David takes it on the right-hand sideline.

A laconic junior with surfer-boy looks, Seeman is expected to be something of a fill-in player this year, as both Joe's partner on kickoff and punt returns and as a running back. The coaches have been impressed by David's speed and skills, but worry that he lacks the passion and work ethic to be a dominant part of the team. They're anxious to see how he'll play in the heat of a real game, and he quickly provides an answer.

As the kickoff falls into his arms, David waits, just as he's been taught, allowing his blockers to form a moving wall in front of him. He then races down the sideline behind that wall. Helped by several nice blocks, including a crusher by Joe McKnight, David streaks untouched down the right side of the field for an eighty-nine-yard touchdown to open the 2005 season. The Patriots' fans erupt while the Bulldogs' stands fall deadly silent. The extra point fails but, just seventeen seconds into the season, the Patriots are up by six.

The Patriots defense then handily shuts down Fontainebleau's first drive, forcing a punt. The kick is short, and the Patriots' offense takes over at midfield. Kyle appears alert, but a bit tentative as he takes the field. After a three-yard run on the first play, David Seeman gains six more yards on a handoff from Kyle, who is slammed backward on the play and is slow getting off the turf. His parents cringe in the stands, worried about his collarbone, but he shakes off the cobwebs and earns a first down on the next play with a short quarterback sneak. Two more running plays move the ball down to the thirty-five. In keeping with the modest goals of the Patriots' old-school offense, Kyle is steadily grinding out the yards, working the veer.

In the huddle on third and two, Kyle calls a play-action pass known as a "380 Ride." As he fakes a handoff and drops back to pass, both his receivers are open on the left side, with Joe in the end zone, and another receiver, Scott Makepeace, at the ten. It is the perfect chance for Kyle to show he's got the same stuff as Johnnie Thiel. He cocks and throws, but the pass is too high for Scott and too short for Joe. The only one near the ball is the Bulldogs' cornerback, who leaps, picks it off, and runs it back a dozen yards.

Kyle has been feeling the pressure build for months. So many teammates, classmates, and alumni have been saying to him, "You're the man now" and "You have to lead us." He's been anxious to get out there and prove he could do just that. With a better pass, he could have had his first touchdown, and could have quieted all doubters. Now his first series as leader of the Patriots' offense ends in an interception.

He is furious with himself as he trots to the sideline.

Coach Jeff pounces on him, "Who were you *throwing* to?" But just as quickly, Jeff calms down. More pressure isn't what his quarterback needs now. Shifting his tone, Jeff tells the kid, "It's all right. Learn from it, forget it, we'll get better."

Fortunately, on the very next play, in Preston Numa's first play at linebacker, he strips the ball from the Fontainebleau running back, and the Patriots recover.

Kyle retakes the field, ready to redeem himself. On the first play, he almost turns the ball over again on a bad pitch out to David Seeman, who fumbles but quickly recovers. There's a five-yard loss on the play. On second and fifteen, Kyle completes his first pass, a strike to Joe who runs it fourteen yards down to the Bulldogs' twenty, just a yard short of the first down. On third and a yard, though, Kyle takes the snap, turns to make the handoff, and practically sticks the ball in the belly of a charging Fontainebleau defensive lineman. The ball drops to the turf and the startled Bulldog player falls on it like it's a gift from heaven.

In two offensive drives, Kyle has been responsible for an interception and two fumbles.

On the sideline, J.T.'s frustration is palpable, though he doesn't explode. He takes the headset off, then paces, then combs his fingers through his hair, grimacing as if he's trying to pull off his own scalp, then folds his arms, then puts the headset back on. As Kyle jogs off the field, J.T. avoids eye contact. Jeff rushes over to Kyle wielding a small white board and begins furiously diagramming plays.

During games, the Patriot coaches are constantly in motion. As players come off the field, they typically sit in half circles of chairs set up for them. The coaches crouch inside those semicircles, wildly scribbling Xs and Os on their white boards, deciphering what's happening on the field, and making suggestions for players to work on.

Thankfully the defense—especially the front line, led by Tank—has so far been impenetrable. Leon likes to tell guys to envision themselves making each play. "See yourself roll him up," he says. Tank is flat out swallowing the Bulldogs' ball carriers, his thick arms and legs all over them. The Patriots' linebackers are also playing well, notably Mike Walker, who seems to be a factor on every play. On the Bulldogs' next possession, the Patriots' defense forces another three and out.

On his next offensive drive, Kyle once again botches a handoff, which is fumbled, though an alert Patriot dives on the ball and recovers it for a lucky first down. Then, on first and ten, on another sloppy handoff, the ball pops loose yet again. The Patriots again recover, but lose three yards. J.T. is relieved when, on the next play, Kyle pulls off a nice swing pass to Joe, gaining back fifteen yards for a first down. Despite a shaky pitch out on the next play, David Seeman snags the ball, tucks it tightly into his gut, sweeps to the outside, eludes a few tacklers, and sprints forty-two yards for his second touchdown of the night.

Though his quarterback is flailing, J.T. is impressed with David's surprising performance. On the sidelines, the assistant coaches exchange looks that say, *that Seeman kid can move when he wants to.* There's a flag called on the play, though, and the run is called back. Joe has also been hurt on the play, and is limping off the field, nursing his ankle. The team seems to be falling apart.

On the next play, in a sign that he's settling down, Kyle makes a clean handoff to running back Scotty Encalade, who runs the ball twenty yards to the seven-yard line. The Patriots are poised to score. Kyle hands off cleanly to fullback Jerico Nelson, a small, quick sophomore who jukes and spins into the endzone, triggering a frantic celebration in the Patriots' stands. J.T. calls for a two-point conversion, to make up for the earlier missed extra point, but Kyle's throw is incomplete. Still, the Patriots have a 12–0 lead.

With the first half winding down, J.T. assesses his team's play so far. Some offensive players are stepping up, most notably David Seeman. The line's lone returning starter, Andrew Nierman, is also playing well. At one point, he hit a defender so hard that the kid's helmet went flying, and it looked as if Andrew had popped his head clean off. But Kyle is clearly having major jitters. The defense is not. As the last minutes tick down, Tank and his pack make one aggressive play after another.

On one run by a Bulldogs' fullback, linebacker Mike Walker slaps his blocker away like he's a cardboard cutout, then plows into the fullback, dropping him for a two-yard loss. Just as the Bulldogs' receiver is about to pull in a ten-yard pass, defensive back Colby Arceneaux lays the kid out, slamming him onto his back so hard that the ball pops loose for an incomplete. On a fifty-yard run, the Bulldogs' longest of the night, Robby Green, the Patriots' gazelle of a defensive back, drags the runner down from behind and saves a touchdown. The half ends with the Patriots up 12–0.

Because tonight's game is two short halves, not four quarters, the teams empty the field for an abbreviated halftime. In the Patriots' locker room, no expletives or insults are spat in the players' faces. The team breaks up into groups, each coach meets with his respective guys, and asks, "What's happening out there!?" and "What can we do to fix it?" Jeff talks calmly with Kyle about the "mesh point," the point on a handoff when the ball should hit the running back's gut.

For J.T., these are the moments when games are won or lost. It's not just about running play after play, it's about capturing the moments in between plays, or in between halves, and using those moments to fix the problems on the field. Halftime is when J.T. and his assistants are at their best. There's very little rah-rah talk, and rarely any shouting. The coaches get busy with their white boards as players gulp from water bottles.

The way J.T. sees it, if he and the other coaches have done their job over the past few months, the players know what's expected of them. Now, they just have to apply what they've learned to a real game, with angry red-suited Bulldogs charging at them.

Just before returning to the field, J.T. calls everyone around him. "It's not that difficult guys, it's not that difficult," he says. "Just relax and have fun. And remember, win, lose, or draw, you're *my* players, baby. *My* players. Now, let's go to work!"

• • •

When people ask J.T. if he's grown tired of coaching after thirty-six years, he says, "Do I *look* bored?"

He looks back with pride on how the low-paying job his father offered him in 1969 became his whole life. He not only built a perpetually successful football program, but infused his whole family with his love of the game. Joanna, Johnny, and Jeff were surrounded by football from birth, weaned on Friday night games and two-a-day summer practices, and bounced on the knees of giant linemen. As soon as they could read and write, they learned to write scouting reports on upcoming opponents.

Joanna grew up thinking it was normal for kids to spend Friday or Saturday nights scouting teams in some backwoods or bayou town. They'd make a night of it, getting popcorn and hot dogs. It wasn't until much later that Joanna realized other kids got popcorn and hot dogs, too—at the zoo or the circus, not at high school football games. The Curtis kids collected footballs after practice, filled water bottles, and rode the buses to games alongside players. The two boys hung out in locker rooms, sometimes more than the players would have liked. When he was six years old, Johnny was playing in the locker room, acting like he owned the place, trying on shoulder pads and helmets. The players got fed up, grabbed him, and stuck him in a locker, then ran onto the field to start practice. On the field, J.T. asked if anyone had seen his son, and finally, a couple of players confessed that they'd forgotten to release him from the locker. Fortunately, J.T. was in a good mood that afternoon. Instead of chewing out his players, he gave Johnny some advice. "Boy, be careful," his dad said. "You've gotta stay out of the locker room—or you've gotta run *fast*."

J.T.'s kids also learned to cope with the highs and lows of winning and losing, right along with their father. One year, when the Patriots lost 29–0 to crosstown rival Isidore Newman, J.T. came off the field and five-year-old Joanna was waiting for him with a bag of confetti. As J.T. bent down to pick her up, she threw the confetti at him. It had been a typically sticky New Orleans night, and the confetti stuck to his sweaty face and arms, got in his eyes and hair. Standing there caked in confetti, having just gotten trounced, and looking down at his little girl's smiling face, J.T. had to laugh. He realized that even after the worst of defeats, losing is never the end of the world. Of course, in the years ahead, the Patriots didn't do much losing. After a tough defeat in the championship game in 1982, J.T. found six-year-old Jeff crying inconsolably on the bench. He realized later that his son had only seen the team lose twice in the past fifty games.

What outsiders don't understand is the enormous satisfaction he's found, season after season, in watching kids cohere as a team and rise to their potential. He loves to see team leaders emerge from the pack, loves being surprised by some quiet, hard-working kid who suddenly explodes midway through the season to become a dominant force on the team. And, while he's got plenty of doubts about the 2005 Patriots, he's seen enough solid play in the first half of tonight's game to feel hopeful.

In the second half, though, Kyle's woes continue. On one option play, he turns to hand off to his running back, but can't find the mesh point, so he keeps the ball. He's immediately slammed by a Bulldog linebacker, who plows Kyle backward two yards and lands him flat on his back. Again, his parents have flashbacks to the day he broke his collarbone. No matter how long you've watched your kid play the game, it's always painful to see him take a hard tackle. The Patriots' drive stalls when Kyle fails to convert on fourth and short, and the Bulldogs take over.

Coach Johnny keeps rotating linebackers, trying to get a good look at how they stack up, and he likes what he's seeing in Mike Walker, Preston Numa, and Jacob Dufrene, each of them holding his ground against the Bulldogs' large blockers. The secondary is sloppy, but fortunately the Bulldogs' quarterback, under intense pressure from Tank, keeps overthrowing and underthrowing.

On the Bulldogs' next drive, the Patriots' defense again shuts them down, forcing the punt. But two plays later, Kyle bumbles the snap for his sixth fumble, which gives the Bulldogs a first and ten at midfield. They're down 12–0, and Kyle has just handed them a sweet opportunity to score.

As the Bulldogs quarterback drops to pass, though, he's flushed out of the pocket and almost sacked. He hurriedly wings a long pass down the sideline, and Joe times a leap perfectly to intercept the ball. The coaches had worried all summer that Joe might still be upset about his pal Johnnie's departure but, if he is, it's clearly not affecting his playing tonight. He sprints diagonally across to the other sideline, turns upfield and accelerates, reaching the end zone more than fifteen yards ahead of the nearest defender, practically walking the last five yards. The score is now 19–0 with just a few minutes remaining.

As the last seconds tick off the clock, J.T. heaves an enormous sigh of relief. He's gotten past the first game in thirty-six years of coaching without his dad acting like a caffeinated madman on the sidelines.

Thanks to the Curtis defense, which played a vicious and stingy game, the Patriots have shut out their first opponent of 2005. But the game was much closer than the score reflected, and the players know they were sloppy. If Johnnie Thiel hadn't defected, this might be a whole lot easier. There's no question that Kyle has a challenging season ahead. Most of the team has shown real promise, but there's much work to be done. The bus ride home is unusually subdued, the kids lost in reverie, replaying the game in their minds: the missed tackles and misread signals, the failed kicks, and seven turnovers. Kyle is seething at himself for the way he played. Others, though, feel good about the way they stepped up. Mike Walker, for one, knows he played well. Now he's setting some new goals for himself: to become a team leader and to make the All-District team.

Officers Craig and Red have decided to escort the caravan right through New Orleans. All the windows are wide open, but the night air can't fight the reek of grass, mud, and teen sweat. As the buses rumble over the twin spans that carry Interstate 10 across Lake Pontchartrain into downtown, the glowing white spaceship of the Superdome looms into view. The Dome taunts them with the memory of last year's glory, Johnnie Thiel's MVP performance, and the pressure of all that's expected of them this year.

Suddenly, Jeff's cell phone breaks the silence. It's his wife, Toni. He can barely hear her above the drone of the creaky old engine. He leans forward, sticks a finger in his ear, and, for the first time, hears the words "Hurricane Katrina." He and the other coaches had been so busy all day they haven't made time to listen to the news. On her way driving home from the game, as their two kids doze in the seat behind her, Toni has been listening to radio reports of the approaching storm. She's starting to get nervous.

"Yeah, right," Jeff yells into the phone, "it's not coming at us. Don't worry about it."

Decades of false alarms have instilled in many New Orleanians a casual disregard for hurricane warnings. They've heard it all before, talk of "the big one"—*bigger than Betsy*, the weathermen always say, referring to the 1965 hurricane that nailed the city, causing billions of dollars in damage. Hundreds of hurricanes have barreled toward the Crescent City over the years, only to swerve or weaken. Residents have dutifully boarded up their windows and evacuated as instructed—four times in the past five years—only to return the next day when the storm petered out or veered into Mississippi.

What Jeff doesn't know is that Katrina has been steadily growing in strength, and has just turned toward New Orleans. She's the eleventh storm of the twelve-week-old hurricane season, preceded by Arlene, Bret, Cindy, Dennis, Emily, Franklin, Gert, Harvey, Irene, and Jose. None of those storms were nearly as dreadful as Katrina is shaping up to be. Public officials and meteorologists have been warning for years that it would be just a matter of time before a monster hits New Orleans. And, tonight, they've begun to predict that Katrina is that monster.

As she left the Florida Keys, Katrina was a Category 2 hurricane, but quickly grew in strength to become a Category 3, and is now on the cusp of becoming a Category 4. Forecasters are now saying that, in the next few hours, Katrina will become one of the strongest hurricanes ever to tear across the Gulf.

According to the eleven o'clock news, Katrina is now turning north from the Keys into the Gulf. At eleven, Governor Kathleen Babineaux Blanco declared a state of emergency, and New Orleans Mayor C. Ray Nagin floated the "e" word for the first time this year, saying that if the storm continues to shift west he may call for mandatory evacuations by noon tomorrow. By the time the Patriots arrive back home in River Ridge, just before midnight, greater New Orleans has developed a serious case of late-summer hurricane jitters.

At the school, the buses park, and the team clambers off. J.T. gathers his team and reminds them about tomorrow morning's practice. The Patriots always practice on Saturday mornings during the season, and will do so tomorrow, even with a hurricane coming.

"I'll see you back here at eight-thirty. Don't be late," he says as he dismisses his weary players. They shower and walk off into the night and toward their homes, or to meet up with girlfriends, or gorge themselves on a late-night meal with friends at the Backyard Barbecue in Kenner.

The coaching staff isn't nearly done yet. They started their workday early this morning, and they'll start again in just a few hours. But the night won't be complete until they argue over the postgame wrap-up.

They climb the stairs to their sanctum sanctorum to start analyzing next week's opponent, the Colts of Cottonwood High, a school with 2,400 students, whose gymnasium is said to be the largest west of the Mississippi. The Colts are flying in from Utah for a much-anticipated matchup, being touted as the Battle on the Bayou. To handle the expected crowds, the game will be played at the stadium of nearby Nicholls State University.

They all grab sodas from the fridge and sit back in well-worn chairs. The offices aren't so much offices as long closets: two narrow, unadorned second-floor rooms next to the school library, one flight above the weight room, in one of the many ramshackle buildings that J.T.'s father built. The musky smell of sweat permeates the air.

There are three small windows in the room, but the shades are always drawn. A noisy air conditioner set to sixty-eight degrees sits crookedly in one window singing "ya-ya-ya-ya-ya." Long desks are covered in plastic cups and soda cans, ancient newspapers, deodorant sticks, footballs, gym shorts, and shirts. They have no locker room of their own, so they often get dressed here, and they're always forgetting socks and boxers. A garbage can overflows with doughnut boxes, fast-food bags, and energy drink bottles. Beneath the desks are overstuffed file folders, and stacks of videos and DVDs. An entire wall is covered with a white board smeared with hieroglyphic Xs, Os, and other scribblings.

They first pop in the DVD of tonight's game for a quick and heated play-by-play critique. Then they begin clicking their way through footage of the big, bad Cottonwood Colts. They fast forward and rewind, fast forward and rewind, obsessively analyzing which foot the linemen lead with, left or right; studying whether Cottonwood's gun-slinging quarterback drops back to his weak or strong side; arguing over which defensive alignment will best stop the run.

As usual, they have plenty of disagreements. Their wives are always amazed at how the boys never get tired of talking football, and can argue as loudly and angrily as Congress on steroids. Tonight, they all agree on this: They should pray for another sultry New Orleans night next Friday. The heat will be a distinct disadvantage for a team from the cool mountain heights of Salt Lake City.

They could all be at better paying jobs with vacations and benefits. They could all be home with their families. They could all be getting some sleep. But they love this part of the job, get lost in it, *crave* it: scheming for an edge on an opponent, wildly scribbling their Xs and Os, arguing about the best way to defend against the screen pass or the fake punt. At times like these, the passion for football overtakes them and, in no time, it's past midnight.

That's when the phone rings. It's Jeff's wife again, telling him to come home. Toni *never* calls the coaches' room after games. They're supposed to go to a wedding Saturday, then a baby shower on Sunday, and she's worried about the storm.

"It's still *way* off," Jeff tells her. "Don't worry." When he hangs up he walks to the other room and turns on the television. Switching to the Weather Channel, he sees the hurricane for the first time. "There it is," he calls back to the others, "big, nasty Katrina, heading right for us."

A couple of coaches come in to watch the report, but most, J.T. among them, keep their eyes on Cottonwood.

An hour later, J.T. tells his staff to go home, but to be back by eight the next morning.

3

The Maestro

Just walking outside during a New Orleans summer requires commitment. In only a few steps, you're wearing a second wet skin, as if wrapped in damp gauze. The air is sticky and dense, an invisible fog of humidity. Few New Orleanians voluntarily *run* outside in August, least of all teen boys, who'd rather be inside dominating their PlayStations, amidst the cool effect of a thermostat set low. But the Patriots of John Curtis Christian School know that late-summer Saturday mornings mean hours of grueling, grassy drills. Just one of many sacrifices they make to be part of a dynasty.

Despite escaping with a 19–0 shutout the night before, the Patriots know they played a game full of dumb mistakes. The victory was more the result of good luck than good football, and J.T. is determined to drill those mistakes out of them today.

The last Saturday of August is now eight hours old, and the River Ridge community is coming slowly alive. Lawn sprinklers chatter and cicadas buzz in the trees. Neighbors walk their dogs or stroll to P.J.'s Coffee to meet with friends, eat scones, and page lazily through the newspaper. A local early bird fires up his hedge trimmer.

Even though they didn't get home until after midnight, the coaches started arriving at the glistening, dewy practice field at six. Coach Rob is washing last night's filthy uniforms in the furnace of a laundry room. Leon chugs around the field atop his New Holland tractor, chopping the Tifway 419 Bermuda grass down to precisely half an inch. The others are gathered again in the coaches' room, sitting and drinking coffee or Coke and watching more DVD footage of Friday's opponent, Cottonwood.

Sections of the *Times-Picayune* are passed around, and the men fight over the sports page. They're eager to learn how other teams fared in their jamboree games last night. Coach Francis, the elder statesman, skims the front-page headlines. One reads, STORM'S WEST-WARD PATH PUTS N.O. ON EDGE, above an article warning that Katrina is headed straight at Louisiana. He asks if anyone has seen the weather reports. "It's coming," he says. The others just razz him, "Yeah, whatever, old man."

J.T. arrives and tells them that, even with the alleged threat of bad weather, he wants no distractions. "Just business as usual," he says. "Let's get ready to play Cottonwood."

One by one, the players arrive at the rectangle of green where their fathers, uncles, and brothers once practiced. They're dropped off by parents or drive up themselves and head straight to the cave-like locker room to soak up a few more minutes of air conditioning before practice.

A few parents opt to wait in their cars, sipping coffee and reading the paper. Others gather alongside the field or in the bleachers, a larger than normal group of spectators for a Saturday morning.

At precisely eight-thirty the coaches disperse across the field, moving blocking dummies into place or plucking weeds from the otherwise perfect carpet of green. A crew of team managers packs water bottles into ice chests, and the Patriots straggle out of their dank cave into the soggy heat, bleary eyed and dragging their cleats in the turf. Thankfully, today's practice is light. No pads—just shorts, T-shirts, and helmets.

Even during the season, even after Friday night games, the Patriots practice on Saturday mornings. They practice on Memorial Day, Labor Day, and Thanksgiving, too.

J.T. has run practices the same way for decades, since long before they were born, since their *dads* were Patriots. He warns newbies, right from the start, that being a John Curtis Patriot requires sacrifice. And no excuses. Players must come to every practice, regardless of family vacations, birthdays, fishing trips, or personal problems. The kids mope into the calm, sunny morning, stopping at a spigot to spray cool water into their helmets, which they then pull onto their heads before jogging onto the grass.

Despite his stringent demands, J.T. is always acutely aware of his players' personal issues. He strives to keeps a mental checklist of anything that might be bothering them. Trouble at home? Check. Trouble in class? Check. Trouble with girls? Check. J.T. is a tough disciplinarian, but he does take account of special circumstances, of kids with missing fathers, or parents who have died, or have flat out abandoned them.

J.T.'s tolerance is why Kenny Dorsey is still on the team, even though he misses every Friday night game and Saturday practice. Kenny is a hard-nosed linebacker and one of the team's best players. But, because his religion prohibits him from playing on Friday nights, he probably won't see a single down of action this season. The kid loves the game, though, and he's got the potential to be a real good player. J.T. made him a so-called starter the past two years, even though he only played a couple of Thursday night games. During the recent two-a-day and three-a-day sessions, he took on a leadership role, impressing his teammates, who are amazed that Kenny is willing to endure all the torturous training without actually getting to play games. Leon sometimes teases Kenny that it's "sort of like not showing up on pay day." But Leon is impressed, too, and is thinking of making the kid a team captain this season. Kenny is so committed to the school and the team that he endures a thirty- to forty-minute rush-hour commute from his home on the east side of New Orleans. His family is also committed. To offset Kenny's tuition, his mom drives a bus for the school, and his parents have decided to send his younger sister, Jané, to Curtis this year as well.

That kind of dedication shouldn't go unrewarded, J.T. feels, which is why he's allowed Kenny to suit up solely for weekday practices, hoping that maybe they'll find a Thursday night game or two again. This morning, he's been granted a reprieve from practice. He and his family are headed to a big church meeting near their home in the Lower Ninth Ward.

J.T. is all too well aware that a coach who isn't dialed into his players' off-the-field lives can lose a whole team, a whole season. Back in 1974, when his team went 3–3–3, it wasn't until after the season had ended that a player finally told J.T. the truth: They couldn't understand the quarterback in the huddle. "Coach, he was smoking that pot," the kid said. "He didn't know what was going on." J.T. was shocked. He'd had no idea. That was a terrible year, but it was the last time he missed the warning signs.

J.T. is there for his kids, but once he crosses that white chalk line and steps onto the perfectly cropped Bermuda grass, he is totally focused on football. There's no time for coddling at practice. Players know to expect *Coach* J.T., not the counselor or the father, the doctor or the guru.

"Ninety percent of a game is won on the practice field," J.T. likes to tell his players. "Only ten percent is actually won on the game field."

Which is why he babies his precious field like it's a rare Turkish rug.

J.T.'s practice sessions, fine-tuned across his thirty-six years of coaching, have become legendary. Meticulously choreographed, they are equal parts Broadway musical and football drill. College coaches who come to scout John Curtis are amazed at how efficient the Patriots are, how much they accomplish in two hours. It speaks to the Patriots' status within the NCAA that USC doesn't send a scout, head coach Pete Carroll comes himself, just as Notre Dame head coach Charlie Weiss does. The coaches at Louisiana State, Nebraska, Arkansas, and Miami all know J.T. and his Patriots.

"Watching his practice is like watching a college practice," says Nick Saban, who sometimes stopped by to watch the Patriots when he was head coach at LSU, an hour up the road in Baton Rouge. "Nobody is standing around. Everyone is accomplishing something."

J.T.'s practice schedule, written in longhand late last night, in his boxers and in bed, is broken down with exactitude: *8:35–8:42 stretching, 8:42–8:45 agility, 8:45–8:49 tackling.* Coaches and players all know just where they should be at every moment. Not a second is wasted. A water break lasts precisely five minutes, because J.T. wants players to get used to hydrating quickly, as they would during a quick time out in a real game.

J.T. stands in the middle of his field, bent at the waist or arms folded, a general in gym shorts surveying his troops. He shrieks at anyone who disrupts the choreography: "Where's your jersey, son?" he yells, incredulous at a player who has come onto the field without a shirt. He hounds another player who slipped off the line of scrimmage, gets nose to facemask, veins popping and barks, "What the heck was *that*? I can't have slipsies. Slipsies are what we play in *grammar* school." Minutes later he yells at another player, pleadingly, "What are you *doing*? Where are your *hands*?" Then, lowering his voice, he drapes an arm around the kid's shoulder, and says more calmly, "In high school, you've got to come off the ball and *run*, son."

Equal parts drill sergeant and orchestra maestro, J.T. stalks the field. He hates to wait, hates having players idle, even for a minute. He paces and constantly runs his fingers through his black hair, pulls at his chin, tucks his shirt in, then untucks it. More than anything, he hates to see tentative playing. "You don't want to baby yourself here and pay the price Friday night," he tells one young player. He then spends ten precious minutes with a sloppy freshman, showing the kid how to use his hands to shed a blocker.

It's easy to spot the ninth graders, who look like babies among giants, as if they're ballboys suited up on a dare. Some senior linemen weigh as much as three freshmen. Yet, in J.T.'s practices, every single player runs drills and gets coaches' advice. Even the pipsqueaks get the chance to run plays, though they're usually clobbered by the older players, and ordered by the seniors to retrieve stray footballs or to "get me some water, kid."

The field is partitioned into drill areas, with quarterbacks and receivers working on curl-and-out patterns here and offensive linemen working on off-the-ball routines there. In one corner, defensive linemen slam into the padded blocking sled while the linebackers work on explode-and-release drills and defensive backs run sprints backwards. Players know that three tweets of a whistle means they rotate quickly to the next drill. Assistant coaches scramble from quadrant to quadrant. Over time, the groups merge, first into six, then four. Toward the end, the intensity will rise into a crescendo, and the practice session will climax into a simulated game, with the first-team offense and first-team defense lining up on opposite sides. That crescendo is still two hours away.

• • •

J.T.'s coaching methods have evolved slowly over the years. And the lessons about persistence and hard work were mostly learned from his own youthful struggles.

When he accepted his father's invitation to become the Patriots' head coach, he was just twenty-two years old, and yet to graduate from college. He'd been a standout in high school, "A leader in a silent kind of way," recalled his coach, Bob Whitman. He then went on to play at the University of Arkansas. After starting only a few varsity games, he realized he simply wasn't as talented as he thought, and wasn't likely to reach the NFL. So, he left Arkansas in his senior year, transferring to his father's alma mater, Louisiana College.

There, he married his long-time sweetheart, Lydia Bryant, a former cheerleader and preacher's daughter from San Diego who was studying at Louisiana College to become a singer. Lydia's father and J.T.'s father had attended Louisiana College together and became close friends. In 1967, Mr. Curtis invited Lydia to sing at his school's graduation when J.T. was home from Arkansas. In just those few days, the two fell in love, realizing only later that their parents had conspired to set them up.

By the end of their senior year at Louisiana College, J.T. was still nine credits shy of graduating, due to his transfer from Arkansas, and Lydia was expecting their first child. That's when he got the call from his father, and his first job offer.

Over the years, Mr. Curtis had shared his love of the game with J.T. and Leon, encouraged them to play, and attended most of their games. Even before college, J.T. knew he wanted to play or coach football for a living, but was reluctant to become his father's employee. With a baby on the way, though, and no other job prospects, what choice did he have? The job didn't pay much, but it was a start, and he figured he could finish his college credits in New Orleans. He agreed and moved back to River Ridge.

While it was a relief to have found his first job, the next few years would be among the most difficult of his life. For starters, he was determined to get his college degree, and had planned to make up his final nine credits at nearby Loyola University. When he registered, though, he learned that to graduate he'd have to take *thirty* credits. Doing so would take four years of night classes and summer school, while learning to build a football team virtually from scratch, and raising a young daughter, Joanna, then a son, Johnny, born three years later, then another son, Jeff, born in 1976.

J.T. would follow the long haul of his undergraduate degree with more summer and night classes to eventually earn his master's degree in administration. Later, he'd refer to his seven-and-a-half-year route to graduation when advising his players on the value of perseverance. "It's not when you get it, it's *if* you get it," he'd say.

His early years of coaching were also an exercise in moxie.

For his first practice, in August 1969, he meticulously put together three dozen playbooks, laid them out on chairs, and waited. Only six players showed up. After practice, he walked into his father's office to ask for help. Without looking up from his desk, his father said, "Guess you better pick up the phone and make some calls."

J.T. managed to pull together a team, with just twenty-five players, whom he led to a disastrous 0–10 season. The Patriots were shut out in eight of those games, twice by fifty points or more, and outscored by their opponents 374 to 12. He realized he'd been ill-prepared and naïve, but at least he was on his own. His father was not going to hold his hand, but he was also not going to meddle. The Patriots were entirely his, and he would succeed or fail on his own terms.

After his inaugural 0–10 season, he put together an off-season running and weight-lifting program. With no money for fancy equipment, he went to a local junkyard and bought some heavy steel flywheels from abandoned cars. He weighed each one and wrote on the rusty flanks 37½ POUNDS and 48¼ POUNDS, and so on. He had his players do pushups with the flywheels on their backs and pullups with them hanging around their necks. At the end of a workout, they'd have rust-covered hands and arms and in the showers players would try to scrub out the indentations of flywheel teeth etched in their flesh. His team got stronger, finishing an impressive 8–2 the next season and making their first play-off appearance.

The Patriots won seven games each of the next two seasons, finally making it back to the playoffs in 1973, when the team finished with an 11–1 record. After the disappointing team of 1974, plagued by pot-smoking, the team rebounded in 1975. That year, J.T. stepped up his off-season training program, with more running, more lifting, and twelve players quit in protest. The 1975 team, including the former pipsqueak, Gary Greaves, was the first group of Patriots willing to pay the price, as J.T. once put it, and went 12–1–1. They won the school's first state championship in a nail-biting one-point victory over the defending state champs.

The Patriots won their second championship in 1977 in a 45–0 blowout. They won their third in 1979, and in 1980 went undefeated, 15–0, for the first time, en route to another championship and a 43-game winning streak. Fifteen more championships followed over twenty-five years. J.T. attributes that record mainly to the rigor of his practice regime.

At nine o'clock, a nearby church bell peals the time and, already, the mercury has hit ninety degrees. Swarms of dragonflies divebomb the players, who swat at them with arms sheened in perspiration. Sweat pours off their faces, down their legs. They sprint and stretch, pivot and pass, while sucking greedily on water bottles caked with grass clippings. Linemen practice over and over where their *first* step off the line of scrimmage will land. Running backs sprint through a pit filled with sand that plucks and grabs their feet, forcing them to high step. The best runners practically knee themselves in the chest.

J.T.'s guttural shouts are echoed by his assistants, each in his own distinctive style. Coach Jerry screams at an offensive lineman, "No, no, no, no, *no*, NO! Y'all are un-*real*. Do it again," while J.T.'s son Johnny hollers "Dad-*gummit!* What are you *looking* at?" His other son Jeff shrieks wildly at his group's miscues, and J.T.'s son-in-law, Tommy, shouts and gesticulates like he's on fire. They're all world-class screamers at practice, except for laidback Leon, who takes a different approach. He spits out sarcastic remarks in a calm voice that can cut more deeply than any shouts. "Number 62, you have a bad habit of falling to the ground when you should be making the play."

An unusually large crowd of parents, friends, and girlfriends have begun to fill the team's small grandstands. Midweek practices attract dozens, if not hundreds, who bring camp chairs and coolers and, when the small bleachers are full, gather in the end zone beneath the stingy shade of pine trees that J.T.'s father planted forty years ago. Saturday morning practices, though, rarely draw more than a handful. Today, the crowd is growing steadily. More parents arrive, standing with arms folded along the sidelines or clustered in the stands. Some have pulled up with their cars' back seats crammed with suitcases.

New sounds begin to puncture the practice: the shrill whine of circular saws cutting into plywood and the staccato *baps* of homeowners nailing plywood over their windows. J.T. knows why so many parents have shown up, knows his neighborhood is preparing for the storm, but he stretches the practice even longer than normal, intent on squeezing every last minute from the day. What he doesn't know yet is just how serious the warnings have become in the hours since he hit the sack so late last night.

Katrina began her raucous life a week ago as a rainstorm among the tropical islands of Hispaniola, Puerto Rico, the Turks and Caicos, then meandered west toward Florida. Just below the vacationlands of the Bahamas, she gulped up warm Caribbean waters that, like steroids to an athlete, turned her from a tropical storm into a full-fledged Category 1 hurricane. Beginning late Thursday, she stomped a six-hour path of vandalism across southern Florida, then weakened back into a tropical storm.

After that, she was expected to hug Florida's west coast and lumber north toward that state's panhandle. Instead, she left the Florida Keys yesterday morning and quickly escalated back into a hurricane, turned west, then northwest, passing over an area of warm seawater in the Gulf called the *loop current*—more steroids—and, early this morning, grew quickly into a Category 3 beast. She is now getting even bigger, *fast*, and will soon double in size, with her expanding eye focused right on New Orleans.

After issuing hurricane advisories over the past forty-eight hours, at ten that morning, while the Patriots practiced, the National Hurricane Center took the next step, issuing a hurricane watch for New Orleans, predicting that Katrina could make landfall as a Category 5 hurricane. The presidents of both St. Charles and Plaquemines parishes have already sent out mandatory evacuation orders, and parish employees have begun busing needy residents north toward safety. When Plaquemines parish ran out of employees, Parish President Benny Rouselle began deputizing citizens, ordering them to drive others "Out, out, out . . . I want everybody out of Plaquemines Parish."

Having last night declared a state of emergency, Louisiana Governor Blanco has now given National Guard General Bennet C. Landreneau the okay to call in two thousand troops, with another two thousand to follow. The state police are preparing to enact a contraflow plan, which turns all lanes of the major highways around New Orleans into one-way exits.

If J.T. had been paying attention to news reports this morning, he would have noticed there are fewer jets now flying overhead to and from nearby Louis Armstrong International Airport, which will close to all air traffic at one o'clock.

Tourists are being asked to leave the downtown hotels, and Mayor Nagin is preparing for a noon press conference to announce that the city may soon order a voluntary evacuation. Many residents aren't waiting to be forced to leave. Families are frenetically packing suitcases, bottled water, batteries, and flashlights. Lines are growing at gas stations, and traffic is starting to clog Interstate 10 east and west of the city. Inside the city, all sorts of precautions are underway. Animals are being evacuated from animal shelters, and the piranhas at the aquarium are being killed, so that they can't escape into the Mississippi and breed. Governor Blanco has scheduled a one-thirty press conference at which she plans to urge all of southern Louisiana to flee. And the mayor of Kenner, where many John Curtis students live, has issued a heavily capitalized press release, I AM BEGGING YOU TO LEAVE TOWN NOW! THIS IS A KILLER STORM.

The mayor, Phil Capitano, tells residents that if they decide to stay, "and again, we strongly urge against it," they will need to keep an ax, pick, or hammer with them, "Some type of device that will allow you to break through your roof and get away from flood waters . . . and we do expect much of Kenner to be under water."

And yet, even with the severity of the most recent warnings, there are plenty who remain skeptical of Katrina, remembering how just a year ago Hurricane Ivan—Ivan the Terrible, folks called it—raised similar alarms across southern Louisiana with threats of severe flooding. Weather experts predicted twenty feet of water would flood New Orleans, and hundreds of thousands played it safe, nailing plywood over their windows, packing the car, and leaving town. Then, as usual, Ivan weakened and swerved east into Alabama. New Orleanians smacked their foreheads, regretting the decision to flee, feeling faked out once more. Many seethed in anger as they idled on I-10, which had become a virtual parking lot, and got the word that they could turn around and come home. After the mismanaged Ivan evacuations, many vowed never to evacuate again.

That's why, even as so many are packing up, others are staying put and going about their normal Saturday routines: football games in the playgrounds; defiant wedding rehearsals and backyard barbecues; hurricane parties at Garden District mansions, and French Quarter bartenders wielding cocktail shakers filled with the rum concoctions called hurricanes. Even Mayor Nagin himself, following his midday press conference, has plans to go to a restaurant for dinner later with his wife and daughter.

New Orleans has never ordered citizens to evacuate, and Nagin isn't doing so now. Soon, he'll issue a voluntary evacuation order, and the reaction of many residents will be: If it's still just a *suggestion*, maybe Katrina's really not so bad after all. In a city proud of its independence and defiance, many are simply refusing to let Katrina ruin their day.

Bringing his practice to its rousing crescendo, J.T. calls the first-team guys together for a simulated two-minute drill, in which the quarterback has to run a hurry-up, no-huddle offense. Now, Kyle will get his chance to show he's not going to let last night's fumbles and interceptions trip him up. The frenzy of the offense surging toward the goal line lures the parents closer to the field. Mike Walker blitzes and sacks Kyle at the line. On the next play, running back Darryl Brister breaks through for a first down. The team's two best linemen—good friends Andrew Nierman on offense and Tank English on defense—scrum on each play at the line of scrimmage. In the Patriots' signature style, the offense is steadily moving the ball. With just a few seconds left in the drill, Kyle drops back to pass. He scrambles to his left, looks to his right, then looks left, and finds Joe McKnight slanting toward the corner of the end zone. Kyle lofts a beautiful spiral and Joe leaps nimbly over the safety to snare it by his fingertips. Maybe Kyle will be ready for Cottonwood on Friday after all, J.T. thinks. Maybe he just needed to work the kinks out.

The offensive players congratulate each other, and a few parents step onto the field. They assume practice is finally over. Then, J.T. yells, "Do it again," and the parents dutifully step back behind the chalk of the sideline. They're anxious to retrieve their kids, but they're not about to interfere with J.T.

Finally, at eleven, J.T. calls the team together in the middle of the field and tells them he wants a meeting in the gym. A few players groan. One heads to the sidelines to check his cell phone and says, "Coach, I gotta go—my dad just called." The kid lives in Lafitte, thirty minutes south on the bayou, and his father needs help stacking sandbags around their house.

"Just go," J.T. tells him, frustrated but knowing he can't keep him.

Kyle's father grabs his son as he walks off the field and tells him that his mom and sister are packed, the pickup truck is loaded with bags and dogs, and the family is leaving town as soon as he's done. He then waits with the other parents outside the gym.

In the gym, the players take seats in the wooden bleachers as J.T. and his assistants gather on the basketball court. J.T. reminds them that if the authorities call for an evacuation, it'll be the fourth time in five years New Orleans has gotten whipped into an evacuation frenzy, only to be spared in the end. He's more worried about Cottonwood's gun-slinging quarterback, he says, than this hurricane. But, if the weather does get rough and they have to miss practice on Monday, the first day of school, he wants them back on the practice field Tuesday, worst case Wednesday.

"So, don't anyone go freaking out about it," he says. "Get back as fast as you can."

The assistant coaches then skitter around collecting cell-phone numbers and e-mail addresses. At a few minutes past eleven, the players slink toward their cars or their awaiting parents, into a high-noon Saturday whose clear, blue skies look anything but menacing.

• • •

During the football season, J.T. always gives his coaches a twenty-four-hour break after Saturday practice, asking them to come back to the offices on Sunday afternoon. He wants them to spend time with their families, go to church, refresh themselves. With a return on Sunday afternoon now in question, he wants to squeeze the most from what's left of today. So, after the players leave, he turns to his staff and says, "Let's go to work." Not that he has to twist anyone's arm. There's no place they'd rather be than climbing the steps back upstairs to their musty, second-floor boys' clubhouse.

The coaches' jobs don't end with practice. First, they have to *analyze* practice. They drop into their chairs and prop muddy feet on desks, right back to the DVDs and the white board and the secret language of coaching, with talk of foot plants, hand placement, off-the-ball leg drive, and shoulder turns. Even in miniature format on the TV screen, the coaches can pick up on the smallest imperfection. "Look at Chris. What's he doing with his left foot? I've told him a hundred times," one coach complains. "Rewind that, rewind that," barks another.

Late summer is when the time-tested Curtis training regimen should pay off, when the minute details of the game converge, when footsteps and blocking schemes that once required concentration become second nature. That's what happens when you do something again and again and again. There were some promising signs at last night's jamboree. Then again, there were too many penalties and turnovers.

That, of course, is the inexhaustible topic this Saturday afternoon.

But the storm has become their nemesis. As they hunker down to review more Cottonwood footage, Jeff's cell phone rings. It's his wife, Toni, again.

Leon doesn't carry a cell phone for just this reason.

Toni has been watching both the Weather Channel and the local station all morning and the news keeps getting worse. Her *parraine*, Cajun for godfather, has called and offered them a bed once they evacuate. She's also spoken with Johnny's wife, Dawn, who is six months pregnant and at home with her two kids, so she knows that Johnny isn't home yet either.

"When are you coming home?" she asks Jeff. She never asks that question. Now it's twice in two days.

"Soon," he tells her. "Soon."

He goes down the hall to the other television and turns on CNN. Satellite images show an angry gray-white swirl filling the entire Gulf of Mexico. CNN has superimposed a fat, angry red line indicating the storm's intended path, directly into New Orleans. Toni tells him she doesn't think he realizes just how bad the storm has become.

"I know," he tells her, "I'm *looking* at it."

When Jeff hangs up, he calls out to the others.

"Hey, y'all better come look at this. It's looking *ba-a-d.*"

They don't pay him any heed. "I'm *tellin'* ya," he tries again, yelling above the old air conditioner and their noisy arguing. "It looks for real this time . . ."

Then Johnny's cell phone rings, and the other coaches exchange looks. Dawn never calls the office, either. She wants to know if she should book a hotel room somewhere. "Why are you calling me to ask such a silly question?" Johnny responds. "We're practicing."

The other coaches grow quiet.

"I don't care what the news says, we're practicing," Johnny tells his wife.

But soon, the gig is up. One by one, office phones and cell phones begin to ring and bleep. It's time to head home to their families, and they know it.

4

The Birds Are Gone

When Ivan the Terrible caused so much stir a year ago, most members of the Curtis family once again pulled out the custom-cut sheets of plywood they keep stored in the garage or at a relative's house or at the lumberyard. They nailed or screwed the plywood over their windows, put away all the lawn and deck furniture, packed some valuables into the car and fled, then quickly wished that they hadn't.

The contraflow system collapsed into such a confusing mess, and the Curtises, like many of the tens of thousands of evacuees, sat in frustration, inching west along Interstate 10, some of them stuck for eight hours or more. All lanes of I-10 were supposed to be one-way egresses, but state and local police failed to implement the plan with consistency, and some sections of the interstate remained in two-way mode. All around them, cars overheated or ran out of gas. Some drivers simply abandoned their cars and walked. Many of the Curtises were still in their cars at dawn the next morning when they learned that Ivan, like every other hurricane, had spared New Orleans.

The experience was maddening and, feeling duped by yet another false alarm, only contributed to the cynical disdain so many New Orleanians have for hurricane warnings. Tommy at the time declared that he was never again going to evacuate for a hurricane and, instead of storing his plywood, tossed it out in disgust.

Ever since, the Curtises have joked around the dinner table that next time they're advised to evacuate, they'll just park a big school bus in J.T.'s front yard and all pile aboard. If the water rises too high, they'll drive over to the school and climb to the second-story library to wait out the storm.

But Saturday afternoon, as J.T. and the other coaches get home from practice, the news bulletins are suddenly shrill and troubling, and the school-bus idea is not an option.

Just before noon, in an interview with CNN, the head of the Federal Emergency Management Agency, Michael Brown, urges residents to evacuate today or tomorrow and warns those in low-lying areas "to make your preparations to keep your family and to keep your business safe. You've got to do that *now* . . . Monday is going to be too late."

Mayor Nagin still has not issued evacuation orders, causing many New Orleanians to take a wait-and-see approach. Those tuned into the Weather Channel or the local TV stations are convinced that Katrina is coming fast.

Despite Nagin's hesitance, Governor Blanco seems unwilling to take any chances.

At one-thirty, she appears in a televised press conference with Jefferson Parish officials and announces that the contraflow will go into effect at four that afternoon. At that time, all the highway lanes will become one-way exits out of the city. Blanco assures residents that she has worked out the kinks since last year's Ivan evacuation. She also announces that after declaring a state of emergency last night, she wrote to President George W. Bush this morning, asking him to declare a federal state of emergency for southern Louisiana. Bush, vacationing at his ranch in Crawford, Texas, has agreed to Blanco's request. Further, Blanco has activated the state's three-year-old Emergency Operations Center, a high-tech command post where local, state, and federal emergency and military workers will meet to monitor the storm and subsequent rescue operations.

Blanco urges all of southern Louisiana to flee, and to go door to door to encourage their neighbors to leave as well. "We have been very blessed so far. We've escaped the brunt of most of the hurricanes," she says, "but now it looks like we're going to have to bear some of the brunt of this storm."

Forecaster are now saying Katrina will be a storm of unprecedented strength, possibly as strong as Hurricane Camille. For those who lived through 1969's Camille, and, four years before that, Hurricane Betsy, those two storms are the benchmarks of destruction. Camille's 190-mile-per-hour winds flattened the southern coast of Mississippi, killing more than two hundred, while Betsy's storm surge sent the waters of the Mississippi River and Lake Pontchartrain spilling over the levees and flooding several New Orleans neighborhoods with ten of more feet of water. The fast-rising waters drowned dozens in their attics, killing seventy-five overall. Because New Orleans seems to have almost magically been spared by every hurricane since the 1960s, most residents have become stoically inured to the annual rites of hurricane threats, but those who survived Betsy and Camille always pay attention when those two terrible names are mentioned.

In his press conference with Governor Blanco, Jefferson Parish's emergency management director, Walter Maestri, states it unambiguously: Katrina is as strong as Camille, and is following the same course Betsy did forty years earlier.

At the same press conference, Jefferson Parish President Aaron Broussard tells residents of low-lying regions to leave immediately, and issues a voluntary evacuation order for the rest of the parish. All parish schools will be closed Monday and Tuesday.

As Blanco is wrapping up the press conference, the Curtis family members are preparing to jump into evacuation action amidst a flurry of phone calls. First, having driven straight home after practice, Jeff is trying to eat a late lunch, his first meal of the day, with Toni and their two girls, Anna, two, and Abbi, eight months. While Jeff prepares a sandwich, they come up with a plan: They'll abandon Toni's cousin's wedding tonight, cancel tomorrow's baby shower, and start loading up their Chevy Suburban right away. Tonight, after midnight, they'll start driving toward Eunice, Louisiana, taking Toni's godfather up on his offer of a place to stay.

As he begins to eat his sandwich, though, the phone rings. It's Johnny, asking if Jeff's going to board up. Jeff says he is, but Johnny decides he won't. They hang up. Jeff takes another bite of sandwich, and gets another call. It's his brother-in-law, Tommy. Despite his earlier predictions that the storm was nothing to worry about, he's now decided that it looks so big it's not even worth boarding up. "No boards are gonna stop the inevitable," he says to Jeff. Anxious to get started, Jeff abandons lunch and calls his best friend, Coach Jerry, who comes over to help him screw plywood panels over his windows. After a trip to Home Depot, they do the same at Jerry's house, a job that leaves Jeff with a broken, bloody nose when a hanging flower pot falls on his face.

Toni, meanwhile, drives to the bank to withdraw some cash. The local streets are already congested, and the ten-mile round trip takes an hour. Back home, she starts packing up valuables, bills that are due, videos, photo albums, financial and medical papers, toys, clothes, and food, cramming it all into the Suburban. The girls start crying; Anna wants to know where her toys are going and Abbi just wants to be held. On the other side of town, Johnny's wife, Dawn, is waiting in a long line for gas. As Jeff, Johnny, and the others scramble to button up their homes and pack their cars, various Curtises exchange phone calls to come up with a group exit strategy.

J.T. and Lydia, Jeff and Toni, Johnny and Dawn, Tommy and Joanna, all decide to stick together. Late last night, despite Johnny's skepticism, Dawn had managed to reserve a few hotel rooms in Houston, and that's where they're all headed. Instead of getting on the road immediately, however, the plan is to convene at three tomorrow morning at the school, hoping to avoid the worst traffic, and caravan together toward Texas. Jeff and Toni will peel off I-10 in Eunice, near the Texas border, to stay with Toni's godfather. Other branches of the Curtis family make similar plans, reserving hotel rooms or calling on friends or relatives in Mississippi or Alabama in search of a safe haven.

According to the contraflow, those on the east side of the city will have to exit to the east or north, along Interstates 10, 55, or 59, and those to the west, including River Ridge, must head north across the Lake Pontchartrain Causeway or straight west on I-10, toward Baton Rouge and beyond, into Texas. Most of the Curtises decide to head west, while a few others decide to evacuate north across the causeway to Mississippi.

J.T. and Lydia spend Saturday afternoon stowing the patio furniture in a shed and under the porch, taking framed photographs of the kids and grandkids and news clippings about Curtis victories off

the walls. Lydia wraps them all in black garbage bags, tapes them shut and stacks them atop their king-sized bed, then covers it all with blankets and comforters, in case the ceiling caves in or the roof leaks. Then, like a pro, she fills up the bathtub—it'll help them refill toilets later, if the water goes out. They've all been through this before, and they all know the tricks of evacuation.

Lydia has been saving cash to pay their home and car insurance, which is due in September. She packs that money, along with her jewelry, the display case holding J.T.'s nineteen championship rings, a couple changes of clothes, and some toiletries.

Meanwhile, parents have started calling, asking J.T., "What are you going to do?" Parents had come to the school for an open house and orientation session on Friday and are now worried about whether school will be open on Monday. J.T. tells them to follow the advice of public officials, but that he expects the school to be open on Monday.

At four in the afternoon, the contraflow gets underway, with state police stopping all inbound traffic and diverting it across the highway and in the other direction. The initial transition causes thick backups and plenty of confusion all across the city. Surprisingly, at the end of the first hour, traffic begins moving again. State police are pleased that the modifications to the contraflow plans appear to be working. Yet they can also tell that the cars are moving so well largely because not everyone is evacuating yet.

At five, the governor appears at another press conference, this one in New Orleans with Mayor Nagin and other city and police officials, and together they announce a voluntary evacuation order.

"We strongly advise citizens to leave at this time," Nagin says, adding that residents of low-lying areas, such as the Lower Ninth Ward, should "take this a little more seriously and start moving, right now, as a matter of fact." He says all the projections still show Katrina hitting New Orleans "in some form or fashion," and announces that he may decide to use the Superdome as a shelter for those who can't get out of town. "This is not a test," he says. "This is the real deal."

St. Bernard Parish, adjacent to the east side of New Orleans, and St. Tammany Parish, to the northeast, decide not to wait any longer

and, following the lead of St. Charles, Plaquemines, and Jefferson parishes, issue mandatory evacuation orders.

At the same time, Katrina seems to be gaining strength.

Hurricanes are classified in five different categories on the Saffir-Simpson Hurricane Scale, developed in 1969 at the U.S. National Hurricane Center to measure a storm's intensity. (Elsewhere on the globe, storms are categorized as cyclones and typhoons.) Category 1 hurricanes are a watery nuisance, but Category 2s and 3s grow progressively more deadly. The best-known Category 4 storm was the unnamed hurricane that hammered Galveston, Texas in 1900, killing at least 8,000—the deadliest natural disaster on U.S. soil. The worst hurricanes, Category 5s, like Camille in 1969 and Andrew in 1992, pack screeching winds of 150 miles per hour and push ashore storm surges taller than a two-story building, which can inundate coastal cities.

The latest advisory issued by the National Hurricane Center states that Katrina is currently a Category 3 hurricane but will get stronger over the next twenty-four hours and "could become a category four hurricane later tonight or Sunday."

The Hurricane Center director, Max Mayfield, worried that government officials still aren't taking the advisories seriously enough, begins calling scores of officials at the state, local, and federal levels, to personally warn them of the storm's severity. He tells FEMA director Michael Brown that the storm is "really scary," and tells Governor Blanco the same. Mayfield also tells Blanco he can't reach Mayor Nagin, and she offers to call Nagin's cell phone and have Nagin call Mayfield back, which he does, at eight in the evening.

Mayfield is unnerved to learn that the mayor is at a restaurant with his wife and daughter, and tells Nagin in an insistent, impassioned voice, "I've never seen a storm like this . . . This is going to be a defining moment for a lot of people."

But Mayfield isn't finished. Shortly after hanging up with the mayor, he tells a CNN reporter, "Well, it's very serious. And it can not only cause a lot of damage, but large loss of life if people don't heed the advice of those local officials.

"This could be stronger than Hurricane Betsy in 1965."

Mayfield also warns that the levees will not likely hold back

Katrina, that the anticipated storm surge will probably top the levees and the water will inundate the city. This is the first time anyone has issued such a dire prediction.

Nagin will later say that Mayfield "scared the crap out of me."

By Saturday night, all the day-in-the-life plans, the barbecues and baby showers, weddings and video game sessions, shopping and movies and job shifts are grudgingly abandoned. Across New Orleans, southern Louisiana, and southern Mississippi, families act out the same scene. Millions of tiny decisions are being made: what to take, what to leave, where to go. Even the most cynical, best-prepared evacuees expect a few days of disruption at most. Many last-minute preparations, therefore, have the feel of going through the motions. Families put valuables atop the fridge *just in case*. They leave the cats but take the dog *just in case*. Maybe they wrap the computer in plastic or bring along the wedding album or dig out that insurance policy or turn off the gas or roll up and stow the oriental rug, *just in case*. But there's only so much they can carry, and all they can do is hope the levees will hold and the plywood on the windows will hold and that their life's belongings will be intact when they return.

Later, an entire city will mournfully review those final just-in-case decisions, wishing they'd taken an extra minute to do this or grab that.

All across the city, hospitals are evacuating patients who aren't seriously ill, and some nursing homes are evacuating residents. Businesses, including national chains like Starbucks and Wal-Mart, are shutting their doors. The city's colleges—Tulane, Xavier, Loyola, and the University of New Orleans—have closed their campuses. The Coast Guard has issued a bulletin ordering all oceangoing vessels to leave port immediately, and warning that all area waterways will be closed by two Monday morning. The last Amtrak train has left New Orleans and, sadly, there are no passengers aboard.

Yet, for all the preparations, time is quickly running out.

At ten that night, the National Hurricane Center upgrades the hurricane watch it had issued twelve hours earlier to a hurricane warning for the whole Gulf Coast, a bit of a technicality at this point, but a message nonetheless that the storm is getting worse by the hour. A more insistent reminder comes from the Hurricane Center's latest advisory, also issued at ten, which states that Katrina "could become a Category 5 before landfall."

"Preparations to protect life and property should be rushed to completion . . . this has to be taken very seriously."

The city's highways are all fairly congested, but the contraflow seems to be working and traffic is actually moving along. Once outside the city limits, traffic in some sections is even cruising at fifty to sixty miles per hour. This concerns some public officials, however, who realize that the smooth-running contraflow is a clear sign that all too many citizens are still waiting until tomorrow to decide whether to evacuate.

Worse yet, many of them may not be evacuating at all. "Unfortunately, this is an economically depressed city," Tulane-based historian Douglas Brinkley tells FOX News. "And a lot of poor people living in shotgun shacks and public housing don't have the ability to get in a car and just disappear."

So, while many precautions seem to be in place, Governor Blanco frets that it may not be enough, and tonight she is penning another letter to President Bush, asking him to expedite all federal assistance to the region because the expected severity and magnitude of the storm will surely be "beyond the capabilities of the state."

The Curtises all make final sweeps through their homes, and J.T. and Lydia try to catch a couple hours of sleep before meeting their kids at the school at three.

At midnight, Jeff goes outside to videotape the outside of his house and the neighborhood—who knows what it'll look like when they get back? He chats with his neighbor, a police officer, who is staying behind and promises to watch over Jeff's house. Then, the guy holds out his hand. "Here," he tells Jeff, giving him a gun. "There are crazy people out there," he says. "You're traveling alone with the girls. You never know what people might do to get a ride out of town."

Katrina is still three hundred miles to the south, crawling at eight to ten miles an hour. Just past midnight, she is upgraded to a Category 4.

At three, just as planned, J.T. and Lydia and their children and grandchildren meet in front of the school and, after one last look, begin their journey west toward Texas. Other Curtises have begun their own journeys, most of them managing to get on the road before dawn. They are soon thankful to have escaped when they did.

At dawn on Sunday, as predicted, Katrina is upgraded to a Category 5 and already forty- to fifty-foot waves are churning up the Mississippi River.

At eight-thirty, FEMA director Michael Brown again appears on CNN, telling New Orleans residents to "leave now." Shortly after nine, President Bush calls Governor Blanco, asking her to "ensure that there would be a mandatory evacuation." Whether it's in response to Bush's call, or of his own volition, Mayor Nagin at a nine-thirty press conference officially orders New Orleans to evacuate. It is the first mandatory evacuation ever for Orleans Parish and the city. "We're facing the storm we feared most," he tells radio listeners and TV viewers.

"I do not want to create panic. But I do want the residents to understand that this is very serious. This is going to be an unprecedented event . . . The storm surge most likely will topple our levee system."

As he had first mentioned yesterday, Nagin has opened the Superdome as a shelter of last resort, designated for people with special needs. Residents are supposed to call ahead to reserve space at the Dome, and to bring three to five days worth of food and water. "I want to emphasize, the first choice of every resident should be to leave the city," he says. Nagin acknowledges that many people without cars—more than one hundred thousand, according to the census—will be unable to evacuate, which is why the city has established ten pickup areas. Buses will transport residents from the pickup areas to the Superdome. What he doesn't mention is that the city is having a difficult time finding bus drivers.

In conclusion, Nagin states: "This is an opportunity in New Orleans for us to come together in the way that we've never come together before. This is a threat that we've never faced before. And if we galvanize and rally around each other, I am sure that we will get through this. God bless us."

News of the mandatory evacuation and the increased strength of the storm triggers a midmorning rush of panicky residents fleeing toward the highways, primarily I-10, which in no time becomes overwhelmed and sluggish. As residents search for alternate routes, secondary highways and backroads also quickly become clogged.

And the news keeps getting worse. At ten the Hurricane Center issues a new warning, Advisory 23, which predicts that the storm will lash the city and the surrounding coastline with shrieking winds, tornadoes, and a storm surge of eighteen to twenty-two feet. Katrina has now become a full-fledged Category 5 hurricane, five hundred miles wide and propelled directly toward New Orleans by 175-mile-per-hour winds. The storm surge may be as high as twenty-eight feet at the spot where the hurricane makes landfall. With so much of New Orleans below sea level, and many of the levees at less than twenty feet, the news sends new ripples of anxiety through the city.

Until now, many New Orleanians have counted on the U.S. Army Corps of Engineers' levees to do their job. Though the city's levee system is centuries old, many new levees had been built and others refortified after Hurricane Betsy. Some of the earthen levees were topped with concrete flood walls, others with interlocking steel panels, raising the height of the levees along Lake Pontchartrain to an average of roughly fifteen feet, and those along the Mississippi to an average of about twenty feet. There's been much debate in recent years among scientists, academics, and journalists about the true strength of the levees, which are far more vulnerable than most citizens realize. The Orleans Levee District is supposed to assist the corps with levee improvements, but is often accused of wasting and mismanaging funds, and spending frivolously on gambling boats, parks, and boat docks. The corps has also been accused of failing to follow through on improvement projects, with some projects languishing for decades.

It's not just the imperfect system of levees that makes New Orleans so vulnerable. Massive amounts of wetlands and bayous to the south have disappeared over the decades, caused by numerous actions, from coastal construction to oil drilling to dredging projects designed to channel silt from the Mississippi River deeper into the Gulf of Mexico. The result: There aren't enough spongelike wetlands left to absorb storm surges.

In short, downtown New Orleans is now closer to the Gulf than it has ever been.

While most residents have been confident that, even if a hurricane hit their city, the levees would hold, experts have estimated that the New Orleans levee system is only strong enough to hold back Category 2 or Category 3 hurricanes. *Maybe.* Even if the levees are as strong as some claim, Katrina is promising to defy them. If she stays at Category 5 strength, none of the experts hold out any hope that the levees will withstand a direct hit. The only hope is that the storm will still veer away from the city.

This morning, the *Times-Picayune* has printed a map, based on the predictions of hurricane experts, showing what the city will look like if the levees fail. According to the map, levees will be overtopped in Kenner, Metairie, New Orleans East, and in other outlying parishes. Most of downtown will likely be under ten feet of water.

Including the refuge of last resort, the Superdome.

The Dome is a problematic choice for a refuge, as it sits twelve feet below sea level. If the city floods, the supposed safe haven may flood, too. But because so many residents have not yet, and may not ever, leave the city, Nagin decided they need a large enough shelter to temporarily protect the large numbers of expected evacuees.

The Dome has been open since eight, staffed by a few hundred National Guard troops—subsequent reports will put that number anywhere from 150 to 900. Already lines are growing outside, as troops confiscate knives and guns from edgy evacuees. The Saints played a preseason game against the Baltimore Ravens two days earlier and are scheduled to play the Carolina Panthers in two weeks. The artificial turf is in pristine shape for opening day, a synthetic electric green that almost glows beneath the feet of residents pouring onto the field with their blankets and supplies.

Even with Nagin's evacuation order, meteorologist Robert Ricks is gravely concerned for the city's residents. He is based at the National Weather Service office in Slidell, where the Patriots played on Friday night. Ricks, who grew up in the Lower Ninth Ward, an area especially vulnerable to flooding, is worried that government officials and residents still aren't taking the hurricane warnings seriously enough. He thinks Nagin waited too long to enact a mandatory evacuation and that the wording of the advisories isn't getting through to people. The magnitude of the probable devastation hasn't sunk in. No one knows for sure how many people are still in the city, but Ricks is sure that it's still far too many. He thinks the airwaves should be filled with shrill "Get out of town!" appeals from public officials, but there's been too much Big Easy nonchalance and not enough panic. So, he decides to risk being accused of crying wolf and, as he puts it, to "pull the trigger" by penning a more urgent message, in fact calling it URGENT WEATHER MESSAGE. He releases it to the media and to government officials shortly after ten that morning.

In all capital letters, beginning with DEVASTATING DAMAGE EXPECTED . . . ," the message is unambiguous:

Most of the area will be uninhabitable for weeks . . . perhaps longer. At least one half of well constructed homes will have roof and wall failure. The majority of industrial buildings will become non functional. Partial to complete wall and roof failure is expected. All wood framed low rising apartment buildings will be destroyed. High rise office and apartment buildings will sway dangerously . . . a few to the point of total collapse. Airborne debris will be widespread . . . and may include heavy items such as household appliances and even light vehicles. Persons . . . pets . . . and livestock exposed to the winds will face certain death if struck. Water shortages will make human suffering incredible by modern standards.

Katrina is still more than two hundred miles away, but moving steadily now, at ten to twelve miles an hour. Her course seems straight and true, and she'll make landfall in less than twenty-four hours, probably by early morning, apparently passing right through the Crescent City, right over the Superdome, right through the French Quarter, where a bar or two remain open, where some evacuation holdouts are still partying on Bourbon Street.

TV news producers all around the country take note of Ricks's blunt words. They begin to realize for the first time just how bad Katrina has become, and they start sending crews to the Gulf Coast. In one of the more vivid pieces of news that morning, a spokesman for the Louisiana state health and hospitals lets slip that they've ordered twenty-five thousand body bags. In Jefferson parish, emergency director Walter Maestri orders the fire department to start patrolling the streets, with the loudspeakers blaring from atop their fire trucks: "Alert! Alert! You live in a low-lying area that is highly prone to flooding. And it is the recommendation of your parish government that you immediately evacuate."

The reality has finally hit: The Big One isn't just coming, it's here.

All across New Orleans, John Curtis players are making their own escapes.

Some managed to leave yesterday. Kyle left practice, got into his father's truck, and his family got right on the highway. Mike Walker and a teammate first drove to Cici's Pizza, as they always do on Saturday afternoons but, when they got home, their parents, who had been glued to the television, were packed and ready to go.

Kenny Dorsey, the linebacker and Seventh-Day Adventist who always skips games and Saturday practice, has left his home in the Lower Ninth Ward. A large church convocation was cut short Saturday afternoon to allow the congregation to go home and start packing. The Dorseys live on Jourdan Avenue, right across from the Industrial Canal, which is a mere fifty yards from their house. This morning, Kenny and his dad quickly packed the family van. Kenny, his sister, and his parents then picked up Kenny's great-grandparents from down the street. They're now on their way to Kenny's aunt's house in Lake Charles, two hundred miles west of the city.

The Dorseys drive right through Kenner, where Tank English and his mom are ready to leave by midmorning, planning to drive north to Tank's grandfather's house in central Louisiana. Tank and his mom, Althea, initially planned to stay at a Quality Inn near the French Quarter with Preston Numa and his mom, Shirelle. That's what they'd done last year for Hurricane Ivan, and it worked fine. When Althea hears the mandatory evacuation order, though, she calls Shirelle and they agree to cancel the reservation and leave town. "It's going to be horrible," Preston's mom says. Tank is actually relieved, and quickly packs a small duffle bag of clothes. He then helps his mom take pictures off the wall—pictures of his deceased father and his parents' wedding—and puts them atop the fridge. They stow photo albums and his parents' wedding album up there, too.

Tank's mom then decides to check on some of her elderly friends and relatives. She calls her friend Miss Dee, who's eighty-three and lives in the Ninth Ward. Miss Dee says she isn't going to evacuate. If her neighborhood floods, she'll just go upstairs; if it floods real bad, she'll go to the attic. Tank's mom tells Miss Dee, "We're coming to get you." Next, she calls a friend's eighty-five-year-old father, who is also planning to stay put. She argues with him back and forth and he finally agrees to come with her. Next, she calls her brother, who says, "You all go on, and I'll meet you up there." She knows he won't come, so she stays on the phone, pressing him, until he finally relents. Tank is anxious to get on the road but can't get his mom off the phone. Finally they take off, first to pick up the three passengers, then to head west on I-10 and, eventually, north on I-49 toward Tank's grandfather's house, two hundred miles away in Alexandria, in central Louisiana.

They get on the road just before noon, but the highway is choked, and will remain that way for the next eighteen hours. Occasionally, Tank stares into the wide-eyed faces of passengers inching along beside him. Tank is thinking, "This is something I pray I never have to experience again in my life."

Midday Sunday is when the contraflow, which had been working fairly well yesterday afternoon, becomes totally overwhelmed by evacuees, creating hellish scenes of broken-down and out-of-gas cars, many of them idled on the shoulder and more than a few of them on fire. The *Times-Picayune*'s Web site has begun a Katrina blog that contains reports called in by cellphone from drivers stuck on the highways. One driver, heading east on I-10, has been on the road for four hours but traveled only eighteen miles.

Preston Numa and his mom join Preston's uncle, Stanley, who is evacuating his family from New Orleans East, bound for Texas. Preston and his two cousins squeeze in the back seat of his uncle's Ford Expedition. Preston tries to sleep, but the herky-jerky motion of the stop-and-go traffic keeps waking him up. The drive has just begun, and Preston's mom is worried about relatives who stayed behind in their homes in low-lying areas, such as Gentilly and New Orleans East.

The instinct to be with family is strong, which is why Andrew Nierman opts to stay behind, heading to Ochsner Medical Center with his mother, a nurse, who will begin a lockdown shift in the hospital's emergency room. Andrew doesn't have a relationship with his father, so it's just him and his mom, and no way is he going to evacuate without her. When Andrew joined his mom for a lockdown during Hurricane Georges in 1998, it was actually fun. He was ten at the time, and there were other nurses' and doctors' kids to play with, so he figures maybe he'll make a few new friends this time, too. And if they get stuck for more than a day or two, he has his school books and his ACT study guide with him. The ACT test is a few short months away, but Andrew is studying hard, determined to do everything he can to get into a good college.

When they get to the hospital, Andrew says goodbye to his mom, who suits up to start her shift, and he finds his way to the hospital chapel for a quick prayer. He then searches for a spare cot in an empty lab and, in no time, he's fast asleep.

There are nine major hospitals in New Orleans, and a handful more in Jefferson Parish. They had all been able to evacuate the majority of their patients, but some of those in critical condition, those hooked up to life-support machines, could not be moved. The hospitals have decided to stay put with those patients, numbering in the hundreds at each hospital. In the event of power outages, the backup generators should keep the life-support machines running. To help with these seriously ill patients, the hospitals have called in teams of doctors and nurses and committed them to such lockdown shifts.

Patriots' wide receiver Scott Makepeace's mom also works as a hospital nurse and has also been called in for a lockdown, at downtown's Memorial Hospital. Scott's not leaving either. He decides to take his dog and stay with his mom. In no time he's thinking, *worst decision of my life.*

All over the city, holdouts who'd decided to stay behind have frantically joined the evacuation. Highways that yesterday were merely congested are now parking lots. Some evacuees try alternate routes and backroads, heading east along the coast toward Florida instead of west or north, where the traffic jams are worse. Well-thought-out plans are scrapped for instinct and a prayer. Even those who left earlier today or even yesterday aren't putting enough miles between themselves and Katrina to feel at ease.

Mike Walker, his sister, and their parents left their home in Metairie last night, after putting the television on a dresser and stereo equipment on the fridge. They've found a $169 hotel room in Dallas and, after spending last night with relatives in Mississippi, got back on the road toward Dallas this morning. The only nagging concern is Mike's grandmother, Maw Maw Teddy, who is at Kenner Regional Hospital, where she's being treated for pneumonia. Mike's dad keeps trying to get through to the hospital, but gets either a busy signal or an endless series of rings. He doesn't know it yet, but his mom's doctors have determined that she's too sick to evacuate.

Kyle Collura, who left yesterday after practice with his parents, sister, a cousin, and two dogs, spent the night in a motel and is now squeezed once again into a pickup truck with the family's suitcases and supplies, still driving slowly toward Mississippi.

Robby Green's dad picked him up from practice and told him the plan: He'll stay with the house, in Algiers, on the west bank of the Mississippi across from the French Quarter; Robby will evacuate with his mother, brother, aunt, and cousins. Robby wanted to stay, but his father said *no*. At home, the car was already packed. An hour later, Robby's mom and little brother began to cry as they prepared to leave without Robby's father, who pulled his sixteen-year-old aside. "Son," he said. "Are you paying attention? You need to become a man—*fast*."

Joe McKnight, meanwhile, left yesterday afternoon's practice, stopped for a quick trip to the store to buy school supplies, crawled into bed, and then fell into a deep sleep.

Joe loves sleep almost as much as football, even if he doesn't have a bed or bedroom of his own. For the moment, Joe has been staying at the home of his mother's cousin, who lives in Kenner and has two sons. Joe hadn't been too worried about Katrina. "The storm isn't coming," he told friends at practice. When he awakes from his nap, he realizes he's all alone at his mom's cousin's house, so he picks up the phone.

Joe likes to think he's been on his own for years. The self-sufficient lone wolf image can be an empowering one, and helps him deal with the insecurities and instabilities of his rootless life. The truth is, Joe is never entirely alone. People take care of him. They feed him and give him a bed for a week or two, a month or two, whatever he needs. They give him a few dollars spending money, buy him a meal or some clothes. It makes them feel special to help this kid who might just be the next Barry Sanders, the next Reggie Bush, and maybe someday they'll be able to boast, *Joe McKnight slept here.*

One of those who has tried to care for Joe over time is Mike Tucker. Joe became friends with Mike's daughter in seventh grade, when they were classmates at Curtis, and he started hanging out with the family on weekends and sometimes staying a few nights. Mike was a talented athlete himself, who grew up in East St. Louis raised by a single mom. He's sympathetic to Joe's plight, and has tried to help over the years when he can.

Joe calls Mike and asks if he can come spend the night with them, and Mike agrees to come pick Joe up. At eleven this morning, they leave town and are headed for Shreveport. During the drive, which will last well past midnight, Joe keeps trying to call his mother. He has no idea where she and his younger brother are and can only hope that they've evacuated.

By nightfall, eighty percent of New Orleanians have left, as have more than half of the residents in the suburban parishes. Mayor Nagin will boast of the impressive evacuation rate. Yet, with twenty percent of the half-million city residents staying behind, and larger percentages of the nearly one million suburban residents, hundreds of thousands across greater New Orleans have decided to stay and face Katrina.

Some of the holdouts are staying out of a wicked New Orleans streak of independence, defying the odds and risking their lives. Many others are staying because they have no choice.

The city's poor can't afford transportation or a hotel room, and city officials say more than one hundred thousand don't own a car or have access to one. Many of those without cars live in the predominantly African-American enclaves of New Orleans East and the Lower Ninth Ward, which also happen to be two of the areas most susceptible to serious flooding. Both sections of the city are essentially surrounded by water, but the Lower Ninth Ward is especially vulnerable, with the Intracoastal Waterway, a small bayou, and a canal to the north, with the Industrial Canal to the west, and the Mississippi River to the south. When Hurricane Betsy hit in 1965, homes in the Lower Ninth and New Orleans East flooded to the rooftops, and many thousands were stranded.

In addition to those who can't afford to evacuate, others are stuck behind because they are old and alone. They can't drive or walk away, or are too sick to be moved, including Mike Walker's grandmother and others in hospitals and nursing homes.

Unfortunately, among the evacuees are some who should be staying, including scores of New Orleans police officers and the mechanics who operate the massive pumping stations in Jefferson Parish. Many parts of the parish—Metairie, Kenner, and a portion of Lakeview—sit below sea level and typically fill quickly with storm waters. The 130 pumps are designed to send that water back into Lake Pontchartrain or the Mississippi. However, the pump operators, along with other parish employees, have been ordered by Parish President Aaron Broussard to save themselves and leave town.

During their bumper-to-bumper drives away from home, many evacuees tune in to WWL 870 on the car radio. Over the past two days, mixed in with the messages from public officials to leave town have been messages urging calm. Don't panic, Broussard and Nagin and others have said. But today WWL radio host Garland Robinette is telling listeners it's indeed time to panic. Garland explains that he's just come into the studio from the streets of downtown and noticed a creepy, ominous lack of birds.

"The birds are gone," he says. "I know the powers-that-be say not to panic. I'm telling you, panic, worry, run. The birds are gone. Get out of town! Now! Don't stay! Leave! Save yourself while you can. Go . . . go . . . go!"

Not everyone is tucked into some distant motel bed or into a foldout couch at grandpa's house. For some, it's either impossible, or too late, or they've already decided to gamble. They're taking stock of their bottled water, their batteries and flashlights. They're scrambling around the house lifting valuables up to higher spots. And they're waiting.

At dusk on Sunday, a gentle rain starts to fall upon New Orleans.

Having left so early, the caravan of Curtises managed to avoid the terrible traffic that began in late morning. Jeff and Toni and their kids peeled off at the exit for Eunice, headed to Toni's *parraine's* house. The rest of them—J.T. and Lydia, Johnny and Dawn, Joanna and Tommy, and the gaggle of restless grandkids—reached Houston by late morning, driving straight to the hotel where they'd made reservations. The hotel was overbooked and the lobby was chaotic but, after a long wait amidst the constant shouting of frustrated evacuees, the Curtises piled into their two rooms by early afternoon.

Exhausted and irascible, they collapse onto their respective beds, most of them intent on staying up late to watch news reports of Katrina's approach.

For the Curtises and many hundreds of thousands of evacuees, the night ends with a tense session in front of the television, hoping and praying to hear a few magic words: *shifted east* or *downgraded* or *dodged a bullet.* On the evening news, CNN's grim-faced anchorman Aaron Brown isn't holding out hope: "The potential for destruction is enormous. And that is not an exaggeration, that is not hype . . . It's hard to know when people will be able to come back. Will it be days or weeks or months? And what is it they'll come back to?"

At nine, the wind and heavier rain of the forward edge of the storm nears the city, looming just to the south, where the street signs and traffic lights and motel signs of small towns out in the bayou of the Mississippi River Delta are all struggling to cling to their moorings, where roads are beginning to turn to rivers. At ten, the storm is less than a hundred miles away. CNN correspondent John Zarella, reporting from the French Quarter, describes a light drizzle, a gentle breeze, and an "eerie feeling."

A few holdouts in the French Quarter are thumbing their noses at Katrina, tossing back rum drinks and beer, and someone has displayed a defiant, homemade sign that reads, GO HOME MISS THING.

Then, as Sunday night approaches Monday, as if on cue, Katrina seems to be graciously easing from a Category 5 to a Category 4. She is still a deadly beast, with treacherous winds, and is hulking her way northwest at twelve miles an hour. But those who stay awake well past midnight are encouraged, finally hearing at two that the storm has been downgraded; they hope this is the first sign that she'll exhaust herself further by tomorrow. Katrina also makes a middle-of-the-night eastward shrug, a slight last-minute veer away from New Orleans, with her eye now aimed at Biloxi, Mississippi.

J.T. and Lydia embrace the apparent good news and relax, finally turning off the television and nodding off with visions of a long drive back home in the next day or two. As he waits for sleep to come, J.T. is already planning Tuesday afternoon's practice session.

5

Storm Surge

As Katrina lashes her way toward the city early Monday morning, roaring across the fragile bayou towns and fishing villages of the Mississippi River Delta Basin, Colby Arceneaux is holed up within striking distance of the eye of the storm, with just a window between him and Katrina.

Colby is a junior Patriots' defensive back, whose family lives on a farm in Larose, a bayou town forty-five minutes south of New Orleans. He stays at a small apartment in River Ridge during the school week and comes home on weekends. After Saturday morning's football practice, he and his dad moved their horses and cows into a barn on higher ground and boarded up windows. They were going to stay.

Colby's father owns a business whose 260-foot supply ships transport mud, oil, and other bulk items up and down Bayou Lafourche (pronounced la-FOOSH), a deep-water channel that runs right past the Arceneaux home north toward Baton Rouge and south to the Gulf, one of many such channels that slice through the region. The bayou once served as a shortcut, known as a *cut-off*, from the Mississippi River south to the Gulf, but was dammed shut in 1904. Colby's dad knows these waters well, having spent his life on the bayou.

He also knows storms, and he knows his big boats can handle Katrina.

Colby's dad has convinced several family members to join them, including most of his in-laws, from St. Bernard Parish, to ride out

Katrina on the banks of the bayou. He's told them all that a big boat is the safest place to be in a hurricane. Almost everyone agreed, except for Colby's grandfather and uncle, who refused to leave their homes in the town of Chalmette on the east bank of the Mississippi.

Yesterday, Colby and his dad lashed two of the supply boats together, then tied them to the thick wooden pilings that are driven deep into the floor of the bayou. Next, they ran extra ropes to four heavy, eighteen-wheel tanker trucks, which they had filled by hose with water and then parked on shore. Last night, more than two dozen aunts, uncles, and cousins climbed on board and settled down in the crew quarters. The boat's growling generators powered the lights and the radio murmured all night.

They all awoke this morning to Katrina's awful howling. The family knew the storm was coming straight at them, but now that it's arriving, it seems unreal. Colby keeps whispering, *unbelievable*, even though he feels surprisingly serene about the storm's approach.

He is standing beside the wraparound windows of the wheelhouse atop the boat, a few stories above the churning waters of Bayou Lafourche, hoping that he and his dad moored the ships tightly enough. As Katrina whips her way closer, the vibrating windows of the circular wheelhouse offer a 360-degree view of the storm. It's like being inside a protective bubble.

The winds pick up speed and screech all around, and uprooted trees, fence posts, barbed wire, and power lines start flying past as if they're bits of twig, paper, and string. The gray-black sky is a whirling menace, like some phantasmagoric beast, barking and snarling. Colby's dad was right, though; he feels safe, even as he realizes, *people's life-long ambitions are being destroyed*. He just hopes that his uncle and grandfather are safe in Chalmette.

Colby peers through the storm at his house, a few hundred yards away, relieved that it's so far withstanding the hurricane's force. He's relieved, too, that the ship is barely moving, except upward, as the storm surge raises the level of the bayou and begins pushing the ship toward shore. As the guide ropes slacken, Colby and his dad must venture outside to tighten them. Colby's dad orders his younger son to stay inside, knowing he'll get swept overboard. Outside on the ship's deck, the angry, relentless winds push and pull Colby and his father, who hold tight to the railings and are soaked to the bone within seconds.

The strength of the storm is both terrifying and awesome.

As Colby watches the hellish effects of the storm's western flanks, Katrina's center is passing just east of the small bayou town of Grand Isle, forty miles to the southeast of the Arceneauxs, and fifty miles straight south of New Orleans as the crow flies, though twice as far by the snaking roads. Katrina is heading to the northeast across Barataria Bay and Bastian Bay toward the hardluck towns of Port Sulphur and Buras.

Grand Isle and Buras are part of southeastern Louisiana's vast Mississippi River Delta Basin, which sprawls out for many miles to the south, southwest, and southeast of New Orleans, an ecologically fragile area of wetland marshes, swampy islands, and waterlogged lobes of land, home to sugarcane fields, citrus groves, and abandoned oilfields. The delta land was created over many centuries by the silt carried downstream for more than two thousand miles by the Mississippi River. As the silt was deposited into the Gulf over time, it continued to build up and dry out, and tentacles of land grew further and further into the Gulf. The deposits of clay and sand now terminate in a splayed-out series of peninsulas resembling a chicken foot, which is, in fact, referred to as Birdfoot.

Dotted up and down the chicken's leg are shrimping villages and oyster farms, set atop marshy ground that can barely be called land. Viewed from the air, it has the consistency of fine lace. The Mississippi runs like a vein down the length of that leg.

Manmade efforts to channel and control the river—by building levees and dikes, by damming the river's natural outlets, including Bayou Lafourche, and by draining swamps to create farms—have in modern times impeded the river's ability to create new land. In fact, the delta is disappearing at a rate of a football field every thirty-eight minutes, by some estimates. Some towns are losing elevation by as much as an inch a year. The vast region below New Orleans is literally getting swallowed up by the Gulf and, in the words of one scientist, is "living on borrowed time."

This is not only bad news for those towns and their citizens, but for New Orleans. The disappearing delta means there's less of a buffer zone of earth, grass, and trees left to absorb the waters that Hurricane Katrina is now pushing toward the Big Easy.

It is dawn on Monday morning as Katrina skirts past Grand Isle, pummeling the small, gulfside fishing and tourist community, home to the annual International Tarpon Rodeo. Winds are racing at 150 miles per hour, sending huge, crashing waves across the streets and into vacated homes. Mobile homes, shotgun shacks, and fishing cabins are crushed, flooded, literally exploded, then swept away.

After crossing Bastian Bay, the eastern edge of Katrina's eye slams full force with 160-mile-per-hour winds into the tiny town of Buras, just north of the Birdfoot. Fifty-foot fishing boats are tossed across the lone highway and cows are flung into trees, where they become stuck in the limbs to die. Uprooted carpets of marsh grasses are tossed around like tumbleweeds. Katrina's storm surge, upwards of twenty-eight feet, obliterates Buras, the adjacent town of Triumph, and a score of other nearby villas and fishing villages—Empire, Tropical Bend, Boothville, and Venice—along lower Plaquemines Parish. Even in Port Sulphur, thirty miles north, houses are lifted off their foundations by the storm surge and shoved into the street or into the Mississippi.

While most of Plaquemines Parish has been evacuated, Parish President Benny Rousselle is hunkered down with a few others in an emergency operations bunker. At seven-thirty that morning, he manages to get a call through to New Orleans officials to report that his operations center has lost power, that the roof is being peeled off, and that whitecaps are crashing against his windows. "We're catching hell right now," he says.

The storm continues her arc north and east, leaving behind the Mississippi River and the long, narrow stretch of vulnerable bayou lands that border the river, and begins to cross the open waters of Breton Sound, smashing hundreds of oil rigs. She skirts the far eastern edge of the Louisiana bayou, across Morgan Harbor, ravaging the uninhabited Chandeleur Islands, on track for a cruel midday battering of the Mississippi coast.

Two days earlier, on Saturday afternoon, a Patriots' defensive tackle named Mike Klein, along with his dad and two brothers, drove from their home in Metairie out to their fishing camp east of New Orleans on Lake St. Catherine, near the Mississippi border. The camp has been in the family for generations. Aunts, uncles, and cousins came out from Chalmette and they pulled up all the crab traps, boiled the crabs in the kitchen of one of their two cabins, and stuffed themselves with crab meat until dark. Finally, at nine, they packed up everything worth salvaging and drove back home to Metairie.

Mike's dad said, "It'll probably be the last time we see this place."

Indeed, the fishing camp, along with scores of camps, towns, and villages scattered throughout the ancient bayou, is now being wiped off the face of the earth.

Due to her early morning tick to the east, the storm is racing in a northeasterly direction, rather than heading straight north toward New Orleans, and it's become clear that the center of the storm will slam into the coast of Louisiana's next-door neighbor, Mississippi, whose governor, Haley Barbour, issues an urgent, last-minute warning of "a thirty-foot wall of water. Take this seriously."

At about nine, shortly after passing over Mike Klein's fishing camp, Katrina charges into Mississippi with the howl of a freight train and her wind-pushed wall of water begins to disassemble the towns of Waveland, Bay Saint Louis, Pass Christian, Gulfport, and Biloxi, shredding the coastline, flattening homes and apartment buildings, turning all neighborhoods into nightmarish mounds of twisted debris.

Until now, all the meteorological predictions had showed Katrina passing over New Orleans, so the storm's last-minute eastward shift has caught many Mississippians by surprise. The surge arrives so suddenly, so violently, that for many there's no time to escape. The lucky ones find their way to the roofs of tall buildings or into the limbs of high trees. In Waveland, police officers are washed out of their headquarters and will spend hours clinging to a bush, fighting not to get swept away by the storm's insistent current. All around them, as in other coastal towns, floating refrigerators and soda machines and garage doors and tree trunks and dead animals and cars have become the deadly flotsam of the surge.

Even the casino boats of Biloxi are being yanked free of their moorings and sent flying inland. Before the day is done, many hundreds of boats will be blown across highways or into the trees, and thousands upon thousands of homes will be shredded into unrecognizable shards of mulch, as if run through a giant blender.

Johnny's wife, Dawn, is relieved that she convinced her parents to evacuate. They live in Louisiana but own a beach house in Bay Saint Louis, and had initially planned to stay in their cute little vacation house during the storm, which was supposed to pass further to the west. The flood waters rose fifteen feet in half an hour in Bay Saint Louis, demolishing even the homes that were designed to be hurricaneproof, including Dawn's parents' house.

Later, when officials are able to tally the destruction, they'll find that nearly three hundred thousand Mississippi homes have been destroyed and at least a hundred residents have drowned, trapped in their attics, or been killed by flying debris.

In the coming days and weeks, most of the nation will focus on Katrina's devastation in New Orleans, but Mississippi is experiencing the equally horrific pain of losing so many loved ones, watching the corpses of relatives and neighbors get swept away. In the aftermath, many survivors and public officials there will use the same word to describe the destruction: *Hiroshima*.

Katrina is now a Category 3 storm, though the meteorologists don't know that yet and are still calling her a Category 4. She's still a terrifying banshee, nearly two hundred miles wide and carrying screaming winds of one hundred fifty miles per hour or more. Though the center of the storm is slamming into the coast fifty miles east of New Orleans, Katrina has begun to hurl plenty of fury at the city.

And, as feared, she's pushing her storm surge straight at the levees of downtown.

As the storm descends on New Orleans, deafening winds begin peeling off roofs and punching in windows, all across the region. The first reports of power outages, fires, building collapses, and wind damage begin between five and six in the morning, and continue to escalate as the long morning wears on.

Scores of tornadoes tear up century-old oaks and maples and shred centuries-old homes. The famous canopies of oak trees lining St. Charles, Calhoun, Nashville, and State streets have toppled like dominoes. The root-beer mug on top of Ted's Frostop, a landmark in the Uptown neighborhood, has crashed to the ground. And the popular Sid-Mars seafood restaurant in Bucktown is smashed and whisked away.

Katrina's winds and waters attack the causeway that carries Interstate 10 across the eastern lobe of Lake Pontchartrain, connecting Slidell with New Orleans, the twin spans over which the Patriots made their return to the city last Friday. The storm's assault washes thick concrete slabs of roadway into the lake and demolishes or knocks askew other slabs, severing the link between St. Tammany and Orleans parishes.

Brick facades are peeled from buildings like wallpaper. In downtown hotels, those who chose not to evacuate stand back from walls that are moving as if they're breathing. Down on the street, cars are tossed about like bath toys and the *pow . . . pow* of exploding windshields sounds like bombs. Street signs become deadly Frisbees that whiz down Bourbon Street and Esplanade and lodge in buildings. Electrical poles snap like twigs and power lines become flying spaghetti strands shooting out sparks. Thick poles holding up the traffic lights bend like willows and out on I-10 the concrete posts holding up highway lights are snapping in half, as billboard signs are shredded to pieces. Manhole covers cough up water that begins flowing drunkenly through downtown. The wind and rain is incessant, and the water is everywhere.

At nine, state officials learn there are reports of unexpectedly high floods in sections of the city, up to nine feet in parts of the Lower Ninth Ward and Lakeview. The officials aren't yet sure if the flooding is the result of storm waters overtopping the levees or if the levees might be failing, their walls crumbling under the weight of the surge.

Hundreds of 911 calls come crashing into police headquarters from Lakeview, the Ninth Ward, and New Orleans East, flooding the police dispatchers on duty. People are shrieking that the water just keeps rising, that it's up to the roof. One call is from one of their own, an officer trapped in the attic of his Lakeview home, with the water up to his neck. He is advised to shoot his way through the roof (successfully, they'll learn a few tense hours later). More and more horrific calls come in from parents screaming that their child is going to die, that they're drowning in their own home.

At times the 911 lines are overwhelmed and callers can't get through. At nine-thirty, the city's entire phone system begins to fail. Dozens desperately phone the Coast Guard to report that they are stranded on their roofs by fast-rising floodwaters. In St. Bernard Parish, the 911 center has been evacuated, and residents have no one to call.

Many callers begin to rely on WWL radio and the *Times-Picayune* Web site, calling in to report flooding or injuries or damage, information that WWL quickly airs as part of its heroic coverage of the storm, and which the *Times-Picayune* posts online. Some callers report that they're looking out at neighbors who are clinging to porches or hanging in the limbs of trees. With the extensive media coverage of the storm's approach in recent days, everyone expected flooding. But no one expected a deluge of this magnitude. For most, there's no place to go but *up*.

With New Orleans on the west side of Katrina's eye wall, the force of the storm's counterclockwise swirl is pushing the waters of Lake Pontchartrain and Lake Borgne south and west into the city's numerous waterways, and onward into the city itself.

The force of the surge, combined with unprecedented amounts of rain, quickly fills Lake Pontchartrain to the brim. Katrina's winds, spinning in their counterclockwise rotation around the storm's eye, begin to push those waters over the levees that separate the lake from the city. The lake's waters flush into the canals that run south into the city, including the levee-rimmed Industrial Canal along the east side of the city, beside the Lower Ninth Ward. An undulating surge also flushes out of Lake Borgne, which is east of downtown, and that wall of water barrels westward down the manmade shipping lane known as the Mississippi River Gulf Outlet, a portion of the Intracoastal Waterway that links at a T with the Industrial Canal at the Lower Ninth.

Waters begin coursing through the streets, knee-deep here, chest-deep there. Officials had warned for days about a surge, and the chance that it would likely overtop the levees. Those who witness it are surprised at the strength of the initial surges of water, which strain against the levee walls, punch fists of water up and over them, then march through the city's network of canals, straight into downtown and the adjacent neighborhoods, pulsing and gushing all across the nation's thirty-fifth-largest city.

Amidst the bedlam, one resident, unable to get through on the city's overwhelmed 911 system, manages to call the Army Corps of Engineers to report what seems to be a breach in the 17th Street Canal, a waterway that creates a border between the western edge of New Orleans and the eastern edge of Jefferson Parish, cutting south from Pontchartrain through a neighborhood known as Lakeview. The canal is essentially a glorified ditch that's supposed to help New Orleans drain its excess waters north into Pontchartrain, but the canal has been flooded like never before.

Some time during the turbulent morning hours, a weakness in the 17th Street levee gave way and a section of the concrete wall collapsed. City, state, and federal officials holed up at the downtown emergency command post soon learn that the breach is a football field long and is growing larger, forcing water in among the million-dollar homes of Lakeview. The water is flooding south from the breach into the heart of the city, as well as west into Jefferson Parish and Metairie. It's the first of an unthinkable series of similar reports.

Oily-black waters are rising unnervingly fast around the homes east of downtown, in Tremé, in Mid-City, in Broadmoor, in Gentilly, in New Orleans East, and especially in the Lower Ninth Ward and further east from that, in the St. Bernard Parish towns of Arabi and Chalmette.

By ten, more than an hour after making landfall against the continental mainland in Mississippi, even as the winds begin to die down, Katrina's raging waters continue to pummel the fragile canals and levees of New Orleans.

In some parts of the city, including the touristy French Quarter and Garden District, a few optimists are actually heaving sighs of relief. Except for some trash in the wet streets, everything seems fine. Elsewhere across the city and its parishes, things are only getting worse.

Ten miles west of downtown, in Jefferson Parish, where River Ridge butts up against the Mississippi River, streets in many neighborhoods are becoming rivers, and Swiss-cheesed rooftops look as if they've been attacked by a meteor shower. In Kenner, on the west side of the parish and just a few miles from John Curtis, the top half of the Backyard Barbecue restaurant, a popular spot among Curtis students, has been flipped off. Fires are raging in at least two residences and at a day-care center, forcing Kenner firefighters to drive out into the storm. At Louis Armstrong International Airport, on the south side of Kenner, the roof of a parking deck has collapsed, crushing scores of cars. All across Kenner and other parts of Jefferson Parish, roofs have been popped off houses like bottle caps. The destruction is oddly random, with some houses sustaining irreparable damage, while others on the same block remain unscathed.

Elsewhere in Kenner, streets that hadn't flooded for decades, if ever, are filling with water. It seeps into thousands of basements, under thousands of front doors, filling living rooms and kitchens and bedrooms. Trees have torpedoed through roofs, and the rains are cascading onto people's beds, trashing the valuables they thought they'd saved by moving them upstairs. Cars are being crushed by fallen trees and limbs. And the rising flood waters are making an island of East Jefferson Hospital, in Metairie, whose three thousand patients and their doctors and nurses are now trapped.

Reports are pouring into the Jefferson Parish 911 lines of scattered building collapses, power outages across the entire parish, and buildings afire everywhere, apparently caused by breaks in gas lines. Although waves from Lake Pontchartrain are washing over the levees on the north side of the parish, the levees appear to be holding, keeping Pontchartrain to the north, and the Mississippi to the south, in their places.

In Metairie, however, at the eastern edge of Jefferson Parish against the New Orleans city line, National Guard crews have started dumping piles of rocks at the border between city and parish, attempting to create a makeshift dam to block the flow of water cascading west from the 17th Street Canal.

In other parts of Jefferson Parish, including Kenner, the giant pumps aren't draining off the rapidly rising flood waters because they haven't been turned on: The pump operators had been told to evacuate.

By late morning, rescue operations have gotten underway, but the rescuers are instantly overwhelmed by the pleas of those who are trapped and, in too many cases, dying. Elderly or infirm residents who had been unable to evacuate their homes or had not been evacuated from their nursing homes are helpless. In one St. Bernard Parish nursing home, would-be rescuers chop holes in the roof amidst the dying screams of trapped residents. Thirty-four are killed in an instant, as the waters reach the ceiling.

At the city's hospitals, thought to be impregnable, there is bedlam. In downtown New Orleans, Memorial Medical Center's windows have been blown out and floodwaters are lapping at the hospital's front steps on Napoleon Avenue. Five floors of windows at Charity Hospital have been smashed, and the first floor is taking on water. When the windows shattered at West Jefferson Medical Center, south across the Mississippi River from New Orleans, nurses and doctors rushed to move patients into the hallways.

While doctors and nurses struggle to save their patients, they suddenly must also deal with the arrival of the desperate and the waterlogged, citizens who have fled their homes and are frantically searching for safety, warmth, and dry land.

Doctors at a few hospitals must resist every life-saving instinct and, in the interest of the safety of their current patients, turn away the new arrivals, sometimes at gunpoint. Most of the homeless are pointed toward the refuge of last resort, the Superdome.

By midday Monday, even as Katrina begins to weaken and skulk away to the northeast, residents of the Lower Ninth Ward and New Orleans East and Lakeview and other flooded neighborhoods are realizing that their homes are no refuge against the still fast-rising tide, and reluctantly they flee toward the alleged safety of the Superdome.

Their desperate migration, the likes of which has never been seen in modern America, entails a treacherous walk/swim into the city's heart. Residents grab a necessity or two, a water bottle or a cooler to use as flotation, and start heading toward the corner of Poydras Street and Loyola Avenue. Many of the escapees must travel awful distances—at least four miles from Lakeview, Gentilly, and the Lower Ninth.

In all too many cases, they are carrying children on their shoulders or attempting to tow elderly or infirm relatives atop air mattresses.

For those who complete the trek, the arrival at the Superdome is of little comfort.

The Dome was the largest structure of its kind when it opened in 1975, the same year J. T. Curtis won his first championship. Thirty years later, it has become the destination of last resort for a growing number of terrified New Orleanians.

On Sunday night, roughly ten thousand people showed up, many of them unable or unwilling to evacuate, realizing only on the eve of Katrina that home was no place to stay. When the storm hit at dawn this morning, more arrivals quickly began pouring inside, and the number continues to grow as the day evolves toward night.

With more than a third of Louisiana's six thousand five hundred National Guard troops now serving in Iraq, Governor Blanco has called in as many as she can, about two thousand, which will grow to four thousand in the days to come, as they're mobilized at posts as far off as Memphis. Of the troops able to get into the city before Katrina, about four hundred (some estimates will later say the number is twice that, others will say half that) are stationed at the Superdome, and have brought three trucks of water and enough MREs (meals ready to eat) to feed fifteen thousand for three days.

The number of those who've fled their homes grows to twenty thousand by dusk. As the brutal day wears on, some estimates will place the number of Monday night evacuees at the Superdome at or above twenty-five thousand. Because so many have trekked from lower-income neighborhoods such as the Ninth Ward, the majority are African American. Most of the National Guard troops are young, white males. There are too many people, and there's not enough food.

It's a big problem waiting to happen.

Even before the late afternoon surge of people, the crowd at the Dome had become irritable and skittish. The lights had flickered and gone black before dawn, as Katrina's first winds hit the city. For too many minutes, the enormous Dome was shrouded in darkness as families huddled in cliques with their meager belongings. Backup generators finally kicked in to power faint emergency lighting, but the generators couldn't power the air conditioning, and the Dome quickly heated up, becoming a sticky sauna. In no time, temperatures soared into the midnineties. An hour or two later, evacuees were assaulted by the haunting, groaning sound of roof panels being sheared off by the winds. People ran for cover as storm water poured through two six-foot holes torn open, the water gushing onto the field below.

When it was built, the dome's architects said it could handle two-hundred-mile-per-hour winds. With two holes pried open by winds half that strong, terrified evacuees scramble into the tiered grandstands, fretting that the whole ten-acre roof is going to collapse. Guardsmen do what they can, but when the plumbing fails and overflows, turning bathrooms into sewage pits, the mood becomes as fetid as the air, and the uneasy atmosphere becomes a breeding ground for rumors, some true (a man has killed himself by diving off the upper deck) and some not (roving bands of thugs are raping and killing). Nervous families cluster together in circles, taking turns on the lookout for rapists and murderers.

As horrific as the Superdome has become, many residents decide it's a better alternative than risking their life in the dangerous, flooded streets and neighborhoods.

In the Lower Ninth Ward, the water has risen to eight feet, higher in some spots, and many of the single-story homes are flooded to the rafters, with residents trapped inside the attics to which they've desperately climbed. It will take weeks and months before officials can even begin to tally how many have died inside those attics. The lucky ones are still breathing, a foot or two above where the flooding stopped, many hundreds of them chopping holes in their roofs or eaves, trying to escape the festering attic prisons.

Late in the day Monday, some of the awful puzzle pieces begin to come together.

The London Avenue Canal, running south from Lake Pontchartrain along the west edge of Gentilly, has breached in at least two places. Combined with the earlier breach in the 17th Street Canal levee and breaches in the London Avenue Canal, waters from Pontchartrain rush south into the city. The scenario New Orleans had long feared is coming true. The city is filling up like a bathtub.

At the same time, the flooding of the Lower Ninth has resulted from an enormous storm surge that came from all directions at once. The Mississippi River–Gulf Outlet (the shipping channel known as MR-GO, or Mister Go), is part of the Intracoastal Waterway system and runs straight west from Lake Borgne. Katrina sent a wall of water rushing west down the Mister Go, coming to the T at the Industrial Canal, the five-mile, north–south waterway that links Pontchartrain to the Mississippi. Like a battering ram, it punched a hole in the Industrial Canal levee, and the waters exploded out in all directions, crashing over and through levees into the Lower Ninth and then rushing further east, overwhelming the canals beside the St. Bernard Parish towns of Arabi and Chalmette, which are inundated beneath ten to twenty feet of water.

By late afternoon, the last of Katrina's high-powered winds have raced on, heading toward an inland finale, an elongated exhale that will last three more days. As an eerie quiet descends on the city, the storm's havoc is yet to be fully realized.

Toward nightfall, most of the Ninth Ward is a lake, with only rooftops poking above the water, and many desperate, frightened families lying exhausted atop those roofs. Some of the stranded have been rescued by Coast Guard helicopters, who deposit them on I-10 or I-610, among growing hordes of people who've escaped the flood. But the rescue efforts have only just begun, and will last deep into the week.

In areas where flooding is less severe, parents lead children away from their ruined homes, wading through foul-smelling water up to their chests and necks, feeling gingerly with their feet for hidden dips in the unseen streets below. They lug personal belongings in backpacks or pillow cases and carry pets on their shoulders. Some drag children sitting inside large, floating coolers. One group pushes a floating table with two elderly women sitting on top. Underneath somber, gray skies, they walk—past neighbors, young children, dogs, and old women in wheelchairs who are still stranded atop their porches and rooftops—toward the Superdome, hoping to get there by dark.

Once there, the terror hardly subsides.

To those as yet unaware of the extent of the flooding, Katrina's fateful, last-minute turn toward Mississippi seemed to have spared

New Orleans the horrific effects of a direct hit. There is already talk of New Orleans *dodging a bullet*. The city is an absolute mess, no doubt about it. The streets are flooded and downtown buildings and hotels are ravaged. The windows of high rise hotels and office buildings have been blown in or sucked out, Katrina's tendrils reaching in to yank out hotel beds and office desks, which now litter the inundated streets of the central business district, mixed among the rubble of broken glass, shards of concrete, and the flotsam of garbage. At this point, it seems as if it will take weeks to clean up the wreckage and to repair all the damage.

But many areas, including the city's lucrative tourist spots, seem to have survived with mere bruises, and residents there are already cautiously emerging to inspect their drenched and damaged, but mostly intact, neighborhoods. Overall, the early assessments are that the damage could have been much worse.

There's just one problem. As Katrina turns her back on New Orleans, the floodwaters don't recede. In some areas, the water just sits there, stubborn and impassive, dark and oily and mean. In other areas, the water keeps rising. Downtown, in the Lower Ninth and Lakeview, in Chalmette and the rest of St. Bernard Parish, in Kenner and Metairie and other parts of Jefferson Parish, the water is rising. *Fast.*

6

A Liquid Funk

All through Monday, August 29, the Curtis family is largely oblivious, as is most of the world, to what exactly is happening along the 17th Street Canal, the Industrial Canal, the London Avenue Canal, oblivious to what *isn't* happening with the pumping stations of Jefferson Parish, now silent. They have no idea how high the flood waters have risen, how much of the city is now deluged, and that the waters continue to rise.

The many strands of the extended Curtis clan are holed up at their various evacuation spots: Baton Rouge, Birmingham, and beyond. J.T. and Lydia are in Houston, along with Johnny and Dawn, Joanna and Tommy, and their kids. They're all transfixed by the TV coverage. J.T.'s sisters, Kathy, Alicia, and Debbie, are part of a group of fourteen Curtises and seven dogs crammed into hotel rooms in Monroe, Louisiana.

Leon and his wife, Sue, had booked a room at a Holiday Inn in Memphis, but when they arrived they were told their reservation wasn't until Tuesday. Luckily, they found a room next door at the Marriott, but the manager could only promise them a night or two. At first, as they checked in and collapsed, that seemed like plenty of time.

Cell phone service is frustratingly spotty. The close-knit family hates to be out of touch. In normal circumstances, they talk to each other almost constantly, but now they're cut off. Leon and Sue lost touch with their sons, Matt, Steve, and Preston, yesterday afternoon. Not knowing where they are and whether they evacuated safely is unsettling.

Sue finally learns that her eldest, Preston, evacuated with his wife, Andrea, and their two kids. They're in Houston, where Andrea is trying to get through by phone to her mom, a nurse, who is back at West Jefferson Hospital on lockdown. Matt and Steve planned to stay behind at their homes in River Ridge, but promised Sue they'd evacuate if things got bad. She spends all morning trying to figure out how to send them cell phone text messages. She won't be able to confirm they've evacuated until late in the day.

Despite his promise to his mother, Matt was thinking he'd stay home no matter what, and figured that if the neighborhood flooded he'd go to the coaches' room, only a mile from his home. He ended up getting talked into leaving Sunday with friends heading to Baton Rouge. Steve and his fiancée, Ali, meanwhile, didn't leave town until Sunday afternoon, and might not have left at all if not for a phone call from Iraq.

Ali's cousin is stationed with the National Guard in Iraq. He was watching the storm on his laptop when an officer asked what he was doing. He said he was worried that his stubborn parents might not evacuate. "Would you like me to send someone to check on them?" the officer asked. Within thirty minutes, two soldiers were knocking on his parents' door in River Ridge, telling them their son in Iraq was worried. The couple then called Ali's parents, and everyone realized that if the National Guard was telling them to go, they should go. So, Steve and Ali decided to leave the city with her parents and after a seventeen-hour drive found a hotel room in Alabama, at four-thirty this morning.

While Sue tries getting through to her sons, Leon, who brought along sacks of combination locks for the new lockers he recently installed at the school, sits on the bed watching news coverage of the storm and silently checking the combinations of more than four hundred locks. He realizes that he forgot to pack the prescription for the steroid drops he has to regularly squirt into his eyes, due to a recent cornea transplant. The drops prevent his body from rejecting the transplanted corneas, but he is running low, and now worries that he won't be able to get a refill if he can't get back into the city soon.

Jeff and Toni and their kids made it safely out of town without needing the gun Jeff's neighbor gave him. They're in Eunice, Louisiana, at Toni's godfather's house. Like tens of thousands of other evacuees, after watching televised images of their battered city for hours, by late afternoon they are relieved that the worst appears to be over and anxious for the pumps to start drying up the city so they can go home.

In Houston, the Curtis men are so eager to get home that they're scheming to head back now. The women, Lydia, daughter Joanna, and daughter-in-law Dawn, make plans to shop at a nearby mall, and suggest that the men take the kids to an arcade or a movie. But J.T., Tommy, and Johnny suddenly announce they want to leave, maybe buy a trailer and roofing supplies at Home Depot, and get a jump on the return trip and the expected repairs back home. After a brief standoff and some shouting, the women relent and start packing. They'll head to Eunice today, to stay with Toni's godfather. In Eunice, they'll be two and a half hours from home, and figure that, by tomorrow morning, the city will be drained and they'll be able to get back to River Ridge. They're especially anxious to assess the damage to the school.

J.T. is thinking he'll have to cancel Tuesday's practice, but that he'll reopen school on Wednesday, and hold an intense practice that afternoon. Friday night's game against the Colts of Cottonwood High looms.

When they arrive in Eunice, though, they find Jeff and Toni sitting in shock before the television, and then finally learn about the severity of the levee breaks. The news hits them like a wallop to the gut. The first images from within the city are only now being broadcast. In stunned silence, the family watches the news trickling from CNN, FOX, and MSNBC: that the Industrial Canal levee has been breached in three spots; two sections of the London Avenue Canal have failed; the breach in the 17th Street Canal is widening. Clearly the dodged-a-bullet talk had been wildly premature.

News reports earlier in the day had been sketchy, and it was hard to keep track of what was happening. Each journalist's perspective was as narrow as his or her field of vision, which led to rumors being reported as news. Now, a fuller picture is emerging, and it's horrifying. So much water from Lake Pontchartrain, the Mississippi River, and their tributaries is spilling uncontrollably through the levee breaches that it is filling downtown New Orleans like a cesspool, and gushing unimpeded to the west into Jefferson Parish, and east into St. Bernard Parish.

The flood waters have become a toxic soup full of chemicals and fuels, filth and rot, and the seepage of human remains. Coffins are being unearthed from low-lying cemeteries, and some of Katrina's victims are floating face down in the streets.

Lydia feels as if she's watching a horror movie, and starts to imagine her home and the school swimming in Katrina's awful waters. "What are we going to do?" she cries in panic, looking around wildly at her family. "What are we going to do? *What are we going to do?*"

They stare at the shocking images, spellbound, a few of them in tears. No one has ever imagined this would really happen.

Realizing the city is going to be out of commission for many days, J.T. reluctantly calls the coach of Cottonwood High in Salt Lake City and tells him the obvious: Friday's game is canceled.

As the terrible day comes to a close, the diaspora of hurricane evacuees learns, in broken bits and pieces, about not only the levee breaches and the flooding, but about the rampant looting, the influx of terrified flood victims to the Superdome, and the hordes of people still stranded on their rooftops or on highway overpasses.

Any initial feelings of relief that the meat of the storm had hit east of the city now turn to horror. Near midnight, the *Times-Picayune* reports on its Web site that it will be unable to put out a newspaper for the foreseeable future and that employees have begun to evacuate the building, which is surrounded by water climbing higher by the minute.

"As night fell on a devastated region, the water was still rising in the city," the online report says, "and nobody was willing to predict when it would stop."

• • •

"The water continues to rise."

At dawn on Tuesday, August 30, that's the latest report from Jefferson Parish's emergency management director, Walter Maestri, speaking on WWL radio.

The breach in the 17th Street Canal continues to widen, and is nearing five hundred feet long. The three Industrial Canal breaches add up, cumulatively, to another five hundred feet. A huge barge has blasted through one of those breaches into a Lower Ninth Ward neighborhood. Water has poured through the various levee breaches all night.

This morning, beneath a bright blue sky, it has become clear that most of the region—80 percent of the city, by some estimates, and overall an area seven times larger than Manhattan—is under water, twenty feet deep in spots. Army Corps of Engineers helicopters are dropping three-thousand-pound sandbags into the levee breaches, trying to close them, but the huge sandbags just disappear, swallowed up.

Throughout the night, more and more people have escaped their flooded homes and waded to the Superdome. The Coast Guard is plucking people off rooftops by helicopter or rescuing them by boat, but there aren't enough boats, and city officials have issued a desperate plea to the owners of flat-bottomed boats to help with rescue efforts.

Meanwhile, even after they've been rescued, many people have no place to go. They're being dropped off on bridges and elevated sections of I-10, where the crowds of displaced people—exhausted, hungry, thirsty—are growing fast. Tourists are being asked to leave downtown hotels and head for the Superdome, where the restive crowd continues to grow.

The St. Claude Avenue bridge, which spans the Industrial Canal between the Lower Ninth Ward and the eastern edge of the Faubourg Marigny neighborhood, is packed with hundreds of evacuees who've been rescued from rooftops or floating debris. Among them is fifty-two-year-old Daniel Weber, who watched his wife drown, and spent fourteen hours floating in the polluted flood waters on a piece of driftwood. Sobbing, he tells a *Times-Picayune* reporter how he and his wife escaped from their home through a window. While trying to climb onto the roof, they slipped and fell into the water. His wife never resurfaced. "I'm not going to make it," he says, while waiting for a National Guard truck to take him to the Superdome. "I know I'm not."

Those who make it to the Superdome are confronted by chaos. All the toilets have backed up, people are being robbed by thugs wielding sticks and metal rods, and the National Guard and Red Cross have begun turning people away, telling them to head instead for the city's Convention Center.

As rescue efforts swing into high gear, Andrew Nierman is drawn into Katrina's mayhem. When he and his mom had arrived Sunday afternoon at Ochsner Hospital, in eastern Jefferson Parish, just a few blocks from the city line, the mood was so quiet and slow that Andrew managed to doze off on a hospital cot. By Monday night, he realized he would not be leaving any time soon. And today, any hopes of reading and studying for his ACT test are shattered by the chaotic influx of patients, who must be treated by an overworked, skeletal staff.

During the storm, the hospital's electricity was knocked out, and three backup generators were put into service. One of the generators then blew a circuit, and a second generator overheated. To ease the load of the last generator, the air conditioning has been turned off, and the hospital is now a sauna, with temperatures above 100 degrees in spots.

National Guard troops stop to tell hospital workers not to drink the water, which is no longer sanitary, and to advise them to start rationing their food and bottled water. Due to the concerns about limited power, Andrew can't even turn on the television and has no idea what's happening outside.

He is running around unloading and delivering supplies where they are needed, trying to stay away from the terrible things happening in the ER, where police and rescue workers have begun delivering the injured and the dead. Whenever he gets a break, he steals another visit to the chapel, the only place he feels relaxed, where he tells himself over and over that his life is now in God's hands.

Andrew is one of at least four Curtis students who have joined their mothers on lockdown shifts at area hospitals, many of which are now surrounded by water.

Patriots' wide receiver Scott Makepeace is at Memorial Hospital, just off Canal Street, along with his dog. Yesterday, someone stole the dog food he brought with him, so he and the dog have been eating bread and peanut butter. Today, his problems are much worse. The windows on the entire south side of the hospital shattered yesterday, and the basement and part of the first floor are flooded. This morning, he awoke to find the hospital surrounded by rising water.

People evacuating from other parts of the city are trying to enter the hospital, but the staff is trying to evacuate its 260 patients—workers are chasing away the newcomers. The power has been out since yesterday, and this morning's flooding has knocked out two backup generators. Scott learns that in the humid, 100-degee heat, some of the critically ill patients are dying. The sewage has backed up and there is no refrigeration for the corpses in the morgue. To keep the new arrivals from getting inside, hospital workers have boarded up the first-floor doors. Inside, the entire hospital is beginning to reek of putrefication.

Mitch and Luke Leshe, a senior and junior at John Curtis, are at East Jefferson General Hospital, where their mother works. The hospital borders the shores of Lake Pontchartrain. Last night, the brothers offered to help the overwhelmed nursing staff, and a supervisor didn't hesitate, asking them to move beds and mattresses, answer phones, and check on patients, many of whom are thirsty and complaining about the heat. This afternoon, the electricity and air conditioning are out, and floodwaters are beginning to surround the building. With no cable TV service, they can't watch the news, but a savvy patient has devised a makeshift antenna from a cell phone battery charger cable and a chain of paper clips. Mitch, his brother, and a group of patients have been watching fuzzy images of the bedlam happening all around them.

Then a group of National Guard troops arrives, carrying high-powered rifles. Mitch asks one of them what's going on, and is told that they're here "for your protection." A sniper is positioned on the roof. One of the soldiers tells Mitch's mom that there are reports of looters attacking the city's hospitals and raping and killing the nurses.

The raping and killing of nurses will turn out to be a rumor, one of many that have begun to circulate through the terrorized city. What *isn't* a rumor is that New Orleans is sliding toward havoc.

The police are stretched to their limit, some of them rescuing trapped residents and others evacuating thousands of inmates from the prisons. Police and rescue workers are so overwhelmed that "they're not even dealing with dead bodies," Mayor Nagin reports during a midday press conference. "They're just pushing them to the side."

Lawlessness begins to descend on the city. Looters have begun ransacking stores all over town. At the Wal-Mart on Tchoupitoulas Street, people are filling shopping carts with computers, televisions, and appliances. One man rolls a stack of vodka and whiskey cases out the door while another sits atop a jewelry case, yelling, "Free samples over here!" Among the looters are a few New Orleans police officers. One man tells a *Times-Picayune* reporter, "The police got all the best stuff. They're crookeder than us."

While attempting to arrest looters at a Chevron store, a city police officer is shot in the head. Drug addicts are looting pharmacies. "I'm telling you, it's like Sodom and Gomorrah," New Orleans City Council President Oliver Thomas tells the *Times-Picayune*.

Governor Blanco, after surveying the city in a police helicopter, says, "We have witnessed the most extraordinary devastation. The magnitude of the situation is unbelievable. It's just heartbreaking . . . This is catastrophic."

Late in the afternoon, Mayor Nagin issues an urgent bulletin through WWL-TV saying that efforts to stop the flow of water at the 17th Street Canal breach are failing. Pumps in the city can't handle the amount of water, and the floods are expected to rise even further. In his own bulletin, Jefferson Parish President Aaron Broussard announces that he's declared martial law, that schools have been closed indefinitely, and that no one is allowed back into the parish. He may allow residents to visit their homes for one day next week, but only so they can get enough clothes and supplies to survive for a month.

Evacuees all around the region sit terrified, again stuck to their TV screens all day, feeling absolutely helpless as the cameras zoom in on the corpses floating along the streets of Mardi Gras. No one knows yet how many have died, and won't for a long time. At the moment, rescue workers can only focus on the living. As a spokeswoman for the state Department of Wildlife and Fisheries, which is providing boats for rescue operations, puts it: "We're dealing only with live voices and heartbeats."

Kyle Collura, his parents, sister, and a cousin are at Kyle's great-aunt's house in McCall Creek, Mississippi, sitting around a battery-powered radio listening to the terrible updates. When Katrina hit, the house lost electricity, as did 1.1 million homes in Louisiana and Mississippi, and they've been unable to watch television. So, they've tuned in to WWL Radio, which has heroically managed to stay on the air throughout the crisis. Hearing the reports of the unfolding events on the radio is almost worse than seeing the scenes on television. They listen in disbelief to reporters' descriptions of mayhem at the Superdome, shoot-to-kill orders downtown, and the idled pumps in Kenner, where the Colluras live. Bizarre nuggets, like how red ants cluster into golf-ball-sized clumps to avoid drowning, and how those ants will swarm over any people they come in contact with, make a striking impression. WWL's Dave Cohen describes the flood-waters as "a horrific liquid funk that would harbor insects, disease, more death."

Kyle's mom, Melody, is a friend of Kenner's mayor, Phil Capitano, and keeps trying his cell. She finally gets through and he confirms that parts of Kenner are flooded. Just then, the line goes dead. The Colluras envision six feet of water in their living room.

Kyle tries to clear his head by walking his two dogs into the pasture behind the house, but one of the labradors gets too close to a water moccasin slithering beside a pond. The snake bites the dog on its scalp, and in no time the dog's head is swollen to the size of a melon. Now, on top of all the shocking news of the storm and the uncertainty of the state of his house, Kyle is worried that his pet is dying.

Mike Walker, his parents, and his sister are at their Dallas hotel, where Mike's dad finally gets through to the intensive-care unit at Kenner Regional Hospital to ask about his mother. They tell him they've been trying to reach him. They've got bad news: Her pneumonia has taken an unexpected turn for the worse. She's intubated and on life support. Kenner Regional isn't badly flooded, but it lost electricity and is now running on limited backup generator power. They've begun evacuating patients in critical condition. Mike's grandmother is number seven on the evacuation list, but they don't yet know exactly when she'll be evacuated, or to where. The hospital is waiting for the Red Cross to come through with an ambulance.

The doctor says he thinks Mike's grandmother is dying, and recommends the family say their final words to her. Then, he puts the call through to her room.

The hospitals of downtown, having realized that armies of military and police rescue workers are not coming, have begun trying to evacuate their remaining patients. But, as at Kenner Regional, ambulances are in short supply. Memorial Hospital has hired a private company to help remove patients by ambulance and MedEvac helicopter. At Charity Hospital, the situation is worse, with nurses using hand pumps to ventilate critically ill patients, because there's not enough electricity to power the oxygen machines. Patients are dying and the morgue is filled with water. At Ochsner, food and blood supplies are running out, and reports of shots fired by snipers are preventing the National Guard and Coast Guard from engaging in all-out evacuation efforts at the hospitals.

The Walkers decide they should try driving back to Louisiana, to get as close to the city as they can. As they're packing to leave, there's a knock on the door. It's their next-door neighbor from back home, who's staying at the same hotel and has been watching the news. He has a friend in Texas who's selling a house, and he wants to know if the Walkers want to go in on it fifty-fifty—at least they'll have a roof over their heads.

"What are you *talking* about?" Mike's mom says to the guy. This is when Mike realizes that Katrina is starting to drive people crazy.

Tank English and his mom, Althea, and their three elderly passengers arrived in Pineville, Louisiana at four in the morning on Monday, after a brutal eighteen-hour evacuation drive. Tank's grandfather's house in Alexandria was already too crowded with evacuees, so they went to Althea's cousin's home. Ten other relatives were already there.

All day Monday, they watched Katrina coverage. The family has many relatives whose homes are near the Industrial Canal and in New Orleans East, areas that they learned late that day have flooded so badly. Tank's uncle, who reluctantly evacuated with them, lives near Tremé in the Seventh Ward, now under four to eight feet of water. They know he would probably have drowned if he hadn't come with them. As they heard the news of the flooding, a few of Tank's relatives started crying and praying, realizing how many of their family and friends who stayed behind may have drowned, or at the very least have lost their homes.

Today they're all still mesmerized by the television, watching the horrible story unfold. Tank's mom has a friend who works at Kenner Regional and, on Tuesday, she calls Althea's to tell her that the Englishes' neighborhood is flooded. She's not sure about their house, but the neighborhood is now more or less a lake.

Tank usually loves watching television; it takes his mind off of schoolwork and the demands of football and relaxes him like nothing else. This is something entirely different. He pulls his eyes away from the screen, borrows a fishing rod, and walks out back to the pond behind the house. He sits on the shore, on top of an empty spackling bucket, and flings a hooked worm into the placid water.

Joe McKnight, meanwhile, is eating take-out food with the Tucker family at a nice hotel in Shreveport, hundreds of miles from New Orleans. His older sister, Johanna, is back at her college in Richmond, Virginia, having gotten out of New Orleans on a Friday night flight. But Joe still has no idea where his mom, brother, grandmother, aunts, and cousins are.

When the Tuckers left town Sunday morning, they tried to call Joe's mom, with no success. Nor could they get through to Joe's mom's cousin, with whom Joe had been staying. So, Mike Tucker decided Joe would come with them. During the eighteen-hour drive north to Shreveport, they tried repeatedly to reach Joe's mom on her cell. They couldn't get through to her yesterday or today, either.

Joe won't learn for another ten days that his mom, brother, grandmother, aunts, and cousins all evacuated together and are staying with relatives in Innis, a small town on the Mississippi River fifty miles northwest of Baton Rouge. The drive, which normally takes two hours, took twelve, because their three-car caravan got diverted off congested I-10 Sunday morning, and sent north into Mississippi. Along with many others, they had to drive an enormous loop, up to Jackson, Mississippi and around, to reach Innis.

Joe realizes, in a horrible sort of irony, that he doesn't have to worry about damage or flooding to his home, since he doesn't feel as if he's got a home of his own. He also realizes this might be the only time he's been happy about that fact.

He's not happy about what he and the Tuckers see on their hotel TV screen. It's as though they're looking at a war-ravaged city in some third-world country, or a sick Hollywood end-of-the-world flick. The television has become hypnotizing and horrifying. One Curtis student will later say the tube became "like a bad habit . . . like watching a bad train wreck over and over again." People simply can't tear themselves away.

Aerial footage of the city shows the entire downtown looking like a lake. In many neighborhoods, only the rooftops are visible. One video segment shows the two-hundred-foot cargo barge that was lifted up and through a breach in the Industrial Canal, surfing into the Lower Ninth Ward and smashing into the neighborhood where Kenny Dorsey lives. Some news reporters and others are speculating that the barge actually caused the breach.

A close-up shot of one end of the rusty barge reveals the yellow outline of a school bus roof, squashed beneath the barge. It is the bus that Kenny's mom drives, to offset the tuition payments for her son and daughter.

Kenny, his sister, and their parents are in Lake Charles at Kenny's aunt's house, which is filled with two dozen family members. Kenny is lost in a Nintendo game, trying to tune out the noise and the TV reports. When they hear about the Industrial Canal breach, they start flipping channels, trying to find a station to confirm exactly where the breach is. One of the stations shows the barge, but it's impossible to tell exactly where it has landed.

They decide to log onto Google Earth, a program that lets users access satellite imagery of the globe. By punching in an address, one can actually zoom in on a specific neighborhood. They type in the Dorseys' Jourdan Avenue address and wait as the site, starting with an outer-space shot of earth, zooms in closer and closer on America, then Louisiana, then New Orleans, then the Lower Ninth.

Finally, there it is . . . the fuzzy outline of the barge. As far as they can tell, it has come to rest across Jourdan Avenue from the levee, right near their home. In fact, it seems to be resting in the exact spot where their house should be. Without saying a word, they realize they no longer have a house. By viewing it from different angles, they can just make out the yellow roof of the school bus, whose nose appears to be stuck beneath the barge and whose roof is just below the water line. Sure enough, their house is nowhere to be found. They are homeless. The family breaks out into sobs.

Kenny walks off to be alone but, a short while later, he comes up to his dad. His eyes are red.

"Dad?" he practically whispers. "What are we gonna do?"

With the *Times-Picayune* and most local television stations out of commission, except for the *Picayune's* makeshift blog, the national news organizations dominate coverage of the storm's aftermath. Correspondents and experts predict that New Orleans will be closed for six weeks; some say three months; others six months.

Public officials can't predict how long the city will be closed. For the moment, they're still struggling to get people *out*. In an afternoon press conference, Governor Blanco says the New Orleans hospitals are slowly evacuating, but that it will take at least another day to find enough buses to start evacuating the Superdome. She describes her visit to the Dome, and calls the scene there "a very, very desperate situation."

"It's imperative that we get them out," she says.

Back at the Dome, officials are now shooing away newcomers, sending them to the Morial Convention Center, where the population of evacuees is growing fast and where terrible, unsanitary, dangerous conditions will soon rival those of the Superdome itself.

Far from the city, many evacuees, such as the Dorseys, have confirmed for themselves that they've lost their homes, that their entire neighborhood has been swamped. Many thousands of others can only imagine what their neighborhoods look like. The lack of specific information is maddening. So is the helplessness they are feeling.

Where are the police? It turns out that hundreds of officers evacuated and haven't returned to duty. Where is the military? While some National Guard troops are there, and more are on the way, their capacity is limited—the war in Iraq has stretched them too thin. Blanco has had a hard time getting through to President Bush, but when she finally reached him she implored him to send 40,000 military troops, "Whatever you've got."

And where is FEMA? In an interview with its director, Michael Brown, CNN's Larry King asks, "Where is the help?" Brown defends his agency, saying, "The help is there." He adds that there are fears for the safety of FEMA relief workers, so it may take another day or so for them to get into the city. The public will soon learn that Brown was fired from his previous job, as head of the International Arabian Horse Association, and that few of the top officials at FEMA had any prior experience with disaster relief. Reports will later reveal that, in an apparent effort to make Brown appear more aware of the severity of the situation, one of his handlers told him repeatedly to "Please roll up the sleeves of your shirt . . . on TV, you need to look more hardworking."

While a few agency workers have reached New Orleans, the biggest task for FEMA at the moment seems to be arguing with state officials over whose job it is to find buses to evacuate the Superdome. Promised supplies of food and water haven't arrived. And a request to FEMA by state Wildlife and Fisheries officials for a thousand rubber rafts, to reach people stranded by the floods, has been denied out of FEMA concern that the rafts might be punctured by sharp objects lurking in the water.

Although Bush will soon famously praise "Brownie" for doing a "heck of a job," it's clear to everyone else that Michael Brown and FEMA aren't even close to prepared for this disaster.

Just as Americans instantly understood the magnitude of the terrorist attacks of 9/11, they all know they're watching an historic event. It's staggering, a type of devastation they never expected to see on their own soil. All across the nation, they watch in lurid cinematic detail as one of America's most historic and beloved cities falls apart, imploding upon itself, transformed into a fetid swamp.

And the question so many are asking is: *How many have died?*

•   •   •

With the levee breaks and rising water, with the newscasters and public officials predicting that New Orleans will be out of commission and off limits for three months, if not twice that long, the real estate and rental market across southern Louisiana instantly spins into turmoil. Panicky displaced New Orleanians swarm into real estate offices, looking to buy houses in central Louisiana, East Texas, or southeastern Mississippi. Corporations start buying property, sight unseen, to house their employees. People grow desperate about where they are going to live.

One group of Curtises, including J.T.'s mother, Miss Merle; his three sisters; and their husbands and kids, are holed up at the Hampton Inn in Monroe, Louisiana, fourteen of them in all, plus seven dogs. The hotel lobby has become a meeting place of sorts, where hotel guests, all of them evacuees, share stories and console one another. J.T.'s sister, Kathy, is worried not only about the school and her home but about the students, and whether they've all evacuated safely. Everyone around her is nursing his or her own worries; as a counselor at the school, she can recognize the signs of depression setting in.

She and her sisters, Debbie and Alicia, have been unable to get through to their two brothers since Saturday. Their time will soon be up at the hotel; they have been told they will have to leave their four rooms tomorrow morning. They've never felt so vulnerable and uncertain about the future, and they're desperate to reach J.T. or Leon to see if they've got room for more, or have any ideas about where they can all stay.

Incredibly, while they're sitting in the lobby watching the news, a stranger walks up to Kathy and asks if she's a Curtis. The woman says her name is Trussell, and that her daughter attended LSU with Leon and Sue's sons and, in fact, had briefly dated Matt. The woman asks if the family needs any help, and Kathy explains their situation. Mrs. Trussell invites all fourteen of them, including the dogs, to come to her house that night for dinner and then move in with her the next day.

Mrs. Trussell's offer is a huge relief, but they know they can't stay with her long. They're going to need to find a place to *live*, maybe for several months, maybe longer.

Kathy finally gets an e-mail from Sue, who sends the number of the hotel in Memphis where she and Leon are staying. Kathy also gets a call from J.T. and learns that he and Lydia and their kids are still in Eunice. It seems everyone has the same question: Where do we go now?

After three days with no communication among them, it's a relief for the Curtises to finally be back in touch with one another. Still, none of them knows what kind of shape their school and homes are in, and no one knows when they'll be able to get back into the city to check. They have to consider that they might have to move out of the city permanently. J.T. talks to a real-estate woman about buying two houses for his extended family for $159,000 and $189,000. Leon has already looked into buying a Winnebago or two. Dawn starts surfing the Internet, looking for apartments *anywhere* in Louisiana.

It's terrifying and surreal how quickly and drastically their lives have been affected. Just four days ago, they were hosting orientation day and cheering the Patriots at the jamboree. Now, the school that's the center of their life is in jeopardy, as is the lifestyle they've all worked so hard to create. With limited cash reserves, they can't keep the school going for long without tuition payments coming in. And, even if they can reopen soon, if they lose too many students, they might not survive.

At least they've gotten out of the city with their lives and with one another. Now they just need to find someplace to hunker down and work things out. A solution presents itself unexpectedly.

Dawn gets a call on her cell from the wife of a John Curtis graduate. She has been looking for an apartment in Baton Rouge for herself, her husband, and her parents, and has just stumbled across a few newly vacant apartments at a sprawling complex near LSU. She's called Dawn to ask if she wants her to reserve an apartment or two. Dawn discusses it with Johnny and J.T. and they all decide to grab as many apartments as they can. Their plan is for the whole family to relocate to Baton Rouge, so that they can be with one another, and within a two-hour drive of the school. J.T. talks to the apartment manager and reserves the last four apartments in the entire complex. He offers to pay a year's rent up front, but the manager settles for three months.

The only problem, the manager warns, is that the apartments are a mess, which is why he hasn't rented them out yet. A group of college kids has just moved out. The carpets are beer-stained and the kitchen is filthy, and the manager's cleaning people haven't had the chance to get them ready for renters. "We don't care," J.T. says. "We'll fix them up ourselves."

The Curtises plan to move into the apartments that weekend.

When the fourteen Curtises and seven dogs descend on Mrs. Trussell's home Wednesday morning, they assure her that their intrusion will be brief. They explain to her about the apartments they've rented in Baton Rouge, which will be available in a few days. Not wanting to overwhelm her hospitality, five of the dogs are taken to the nearest kennel, and four of the Curtises find a hotel room.

What no one has dared to really discuss yet is that, although the apartments in Baton Rouge are a great safety net, they don't solve the larger problem. A few family members have already begun thinking about the need to find new jobs. Many of the second-generation coaches are just starting their families: Johnny and Dawn have two kids, with number three due soon; Jeff and Toni have two toddlers, and are thinking about a third child. If the school doesn't reopen soon, they'll need to find other work.

Wednesday night, Jeff entertains an actual job offer. He and Toni have driven from Eunice into Lafayette to have dinner with Toni's close friend and her husband, an ex-LSU quarterback whom Jeff knows. The meal is delicious, a break of serene normalcy after all the last days' trauma. After dinner, the husband offers Jeff a job with his company, which sells medical equipment. The guy also owns some real estate and Jeff and Toni and the kids can move into one of his houses, immediately. The couple even offers to hire Toni as a nanny for their kids until Toni is able to find a job. Jeff can start work right away, and the money will easily surpass what he makes at Curtis. Jeff tells him he'll think about it, but he's already thinking about it. It's too good an offer to ignore.

Then Jeff's cell phone rings, and the dinner is abruptly cut short. "*What?*" Jeff says. "When . . . ? *Now?* Okay, okay, I'll be there."

Jeff hangs up and tells Toni and their friends, "I've gotta go."

Dawn's father, Lenny, owns a company, called Service Master, that provides janitorial services for the huge New Orleans power company, Entergy, the city's lone Fortune 500 firm. Lenny's contract requires him to empty garbage and clean bathrooms at a number of Entergy buildings. An army of linesmen, pole workers, and electricians from all across the South is now descending on New Orleans to help restore electricity to the region, and Lenny has gotten calls from Entergy officials telling him those buildings need cleaning, *now*. But Lenny can't find his employees. In a panic, he called Johnny, who promised to round up a crew of Curtises.

Back at Toni's godfather's house, Jeff throws some clothes into a plastic garbage bag and says goodbye to his wife and kids, not knowing when he'll see them again. His father, brother, and brother-in-law arrive at the house at midnight to pick him up, and the crew—J.T., Johnny, Jeff, and Tommy, plus two family friends who volunteered to help—drive into Baton Rouge to sleep a few hours at a friend's house.

At dawn, they'll make their first drive back into a drastically deformed New Orleans.

7

War Zone

After a brief, restless sleep, the Curtis men awake before dawn on Thursday and begin their drive into New Orleans. With Entergy signs stuck magnetically on their car doors, and wearing Entergy and Service Master shirts, they ride in a caravan toward the city, following Interstate 10 east into La Place, where they're stopped by the security perimeter.

They aren't sure what to expect inside city limits and the drive is taut and quiet, as they reach the post where state troopers and National Guardsmen in fatigues are checking IDs and shooing away those unauthorized to enter. Jeff is especially nervous. The other men have brought along identification, but in his rush to get ready Jeff forgot his driver's license, and he's worried the gun-toting soldiers will yank him from the car and interrogate him.

Fortunately, one of the Guardsmen recognizes J.T. and waves the three cars through. In Kenner, where many John Curtis students live, the highways and neutral grounds are littered with uprooted trees, ruined cars, and displaced boats. No planes are taking off from Louis Armstrong International Airport. Instead, the air is filled with military helicopters.

The destruction grows more profound with every mile. Steel billboard supports, forty feet high and tree-trunk thick, have bent like pipe cleaners. House roofs lie in backyards, upside down, like helpless turtles. Walls of homes have been shorn off, exposing the shredded domestic innards. And scattered all about are tangles of trees, branches and shrubbery, street signs, trash, and assorted unrecognizable debris.

Past the security post and into Jefferson Parish, the only people they see are uniformed first responders, cops or firefighters or National Guardsmen. The streets are empty of regular citizens, and the neighborhoods are ghostly quiet except for the occasional chutter of the helicopters. Streets they've known their whole lives look as if they've been bombed. Later, when they report back to their families, they'll all use the same two words: *war zone.*

The men split up, with teams driving to three separate Entergy buildings. J.T., Jeff, and Tommy work at the Jefferson Highway building, which is closest to River Ridge. J.T. is already scheming to drive to his home and the school the first chance he gets. Johnny, meanwhile, heads off with his father-in-law to a building across the Mississippi.

The work is demoralizing: they have to empty garbage cans, mop floors, and clean toilets. The city's water pressure is low, so there's limited running water, which means there is not enough to properly flush the toilets. Electricity is still out in most of the city, and generators are powering the buildings' lights. With limited power, there's no air-conditioning and, in no time, the coaches of John Curtis are drenched in sweat, soiled by their toilet-cleaning duties, and smelling of chemical disinfectants and garbage.

At the end of their shift, J.T., Jeff, and Tommy get the hoped-for chance to slip away and check on their homes and the school. They decide they'll head straight for the school first, and check out their homes later.

J.T. fears the worst as he drives tentatively down Jefferson Highway, through the wreckage of Jefferson Parish. All three men silently pray as they roll slowly through the eerie, deserted streets.

As they get to River Ridge, they are enormously relieved to see that, because the town is slightly higher in elevation, much of it's been spared the terrible flooding. However, the hurricane's fierce winds and small tornadoes have shredded many homes and buildings. Billboard stanchions are twisted into strange angles, and massive highway signs and street-lamp posts are wrenched into drunken poses. The giant M of a McDonald's sign is contorted into the shape of a road-kill snake. Throughout all the yards and in the streets lie bashed-up cars, piles of wrecked lumber, mattresses, and appliances.

With electricity still out, traffic lights are dark at four-way intersections. J.T. drives slowly toward the school. No other cars are on the road, no pedestrians on the sidewalks. It's a ghost town. Fortunately, a bulldozer has plowed a one-lane path through the trash and debris. Except for the occasional exclamation, the men say little.

Approaching Manguno Street, J.T. feels his throat tighten until he can barely breathe. It is only three months since his father's death, and J.T. has just begun his first year as the school's new shepherd. Before he even heard the name *Katrina* he had been worried about filling his father's oversized shoes. He is so used to being second-in-command, guided in all matters except football by his father's strong hand. He can't believe that now, facing this grim crisis, his father is gone. The family is still grieving, many of them struggling not to cry when confronted with daily reminders of his passing. Some family members actually feel abandoned, vulnerable, and alone without the man who was such a dominant force in their lives.

Now, J.T. is wondering if the old man's school will be gone too, damaged beyond repair, like so many buildings shredded across Jefferson Parish.

John T. Curtis Sr. never set out to become an educator, let alone the founder of a school. His calling was to bring God's word to small, rural communities. Despite the hardships, he reveled in the life of a traveling preacher-man. His children will always look back with misty-eyed fondness on those ten-plus years of poverty and a vagabond's lifestyle. They were dirt poor, but they were close, and their lives felt like an adventure.

The family sometimes lived in the church building, with the congregation meeting on one side and the family's cramped living quarters on the other. The kids sometimes longed for some stability, and for more time with their father, who had to work side jobs to bring in extra money.

One year, Mr. Curtis was invited to preach at a church in Terre Haute, Indiana. As they pulled up, the kids were amazed that the building was made of brick, not one of the wooden shacks he so often preached in. It had stained glass windows, an organ, and actual pews. That evening, the church leaders offered him a full-time job, no ditch-digging required. There was even a cute little parsonage where the family could live. On the drive home J.T. elbowed Leon and gushed, "We're going to a big church, a *real church*."

The following week, Curtis was invited to preach for another congregation, in Wyanet, Illinois, a pinprick of a town two hours west of Chicago. The twenty or so congregants met in an abandoned movie theater. That night, these church leaders also invited Curtis to become their pastor. They'd pay him ten dollars to preach on Sunday and another ten dollars for a Wednesday service. He couldn't help himself. He knew his kids wanted the real church, but he also knew Wyanet needed him more than Terre Haute. J.T. and his siblings were heartsick, and wondered privately if their dad was maybe a little crazy.

It was in Wyanet that Curtis got his first taste of teaching. As he worked to build a church for his new congregation, the principal of the local high school offered him a part-time job teaching and coaching some football. "You'll reach more people teaching one year at this school than you will in five years preaching in the community," the principal told Curtis, and the words stuck with him. He also found that he loved working with kids.

When Curtis moved his family back home to New Orleans in 1956, he at first taught at Mid-City Baptist School and also coached some football there, taking J.T. and Leon to practices with him. At night, he worked toward a master's degree in administration and, in time, became the school's principal. But he quickly bristled against the school's dogmatic strictures, which emphasized religious doctrine above spiritual exploration. "Too much proselytizing," he would complain. So, in 1962, he announced his decision to leave Mid-City Baptist. His family was shocked.

He told them he might go back to preaching or maybe try evangelical work. *He really is crazy*, they thought. A short time later, his father picked J.T. up from high school and, as they were driving through the Uptown neighborhood, at the corner of Carrolton and Apple, his father suddenly swerved into the parking lot of Carrolton

Avenue Baptist Church, a run-down building that once housed government offices.

"Boy, that'd be a great place for a school," he said to J.T.

His dad knocked on the door and asked the janitor if he could look around. The third floor had been partitioned into cubbyhole offices, now vacant. Curtis walked around muttering "rip this out" and "tear that out." In subsequent weeks, he raised money from family and friends and spent fourteen-hour days gutting and rebuilding. The first student registered on August 3, 1962 and, by opening day, a month later, John Curtis Christian School had ninety-nine students from grades seven to twelve.

A year later, as enrollment grew, he moved the school to River Ridge, where he built a new campus on land that his father-in-law donated. J.T. and Leon helped him cut trees and clear the land, grading and seeding a rectangle for a football field and, at one point, got an awful case of poison ivy that kept the brothers in bed for a week. After their vagabond years, J.T. and his siblings learned to love the comforting pace and lifestyle of their dad's new school, and they put down deep roots in River Ridge.

Mr. Curtis had an uncanny ability to mix work and play, managing to find time not only for his new school but for his family. He had an unabashed love of the Miss America Pageant and, though he complained that the pageant was fixed, he would get his three daughters new hairdos each year before watching the big show on TV. When the girls, as teens, began borrowing and arguing about each other's clothes he'd take them shopping, and never got embarrassed asking salesclerks for nine pairs of panties, slips, and bras.

As much as he loved building things and improving his school, he also loved a good meal and a night on the town. The family never had much money, and never went on vacations. One thing Mr. Curtis insisted on was splurging for a night in New Orleans. He would announce in his booming voice, "Get dressed. We're going out tonight," and would put on a white suit and blue or pink shirt, with a silk tie and a white hat. He'd take the family into the French Quarter to dine at Antoine's or Arnaud's, where the maitre d's would greet him by name.

If food wasn't the night's goal, it was music. He'd take the kids to see Frank Sinatra at Municipal Stadium, to Preservation Hall, to the piano bars on Bourbon Street, or to the Blue Room at the Fairmont Hotel. He was a lousy singer but loved all kinds of music, gospel, jazz, blues, opera, or show tunes. In his later years, he'd often call some family member at ten o'clock on a Friday night, demanding that they drive him to the House of Blues to hear some great band he'd heard about.

When he took an interest in something, it often exploded into obsession. He couldn't have just one small tank of tropical fish, he had to have hundreds of fish in huge, two-hundred-gallon tanks throughout his house. His interest in art or antiques or porcelain figurines meant every inch of wall space in his home was eventually covered by artwork, and every shelf groaned beneath the weight of thousands of figurines, vases, hand-painted decoy ducks, or rare bells. The front yard became cluttered with sculptures and antique metalworks. He and Merle went to antique auctions every Saturday, and he built an addition to his house to accommodate his collections.

Mr. Curtis thrived on spontaneity and exploration, and never seemed to mind that his school and his house were constantly under construction. J.T. always admired his dad's exuberance, even if his own style is far more conservative. J.T. doesn't rush into anything. He diligently researches every angle, then makes his decision. It's one of many ways in which J.T. differs from his father, who once tried to buy flashy, star-covered red uniforms for the Patriots, a decision that J.T. overruled. Change doesn't come easy to J.T., who thrives on doing things the same way year after year after year.

Long before his father became ill, J.T. had known he would eventually take over, so he groomed himself to be more than just a football coach. Still, J.T. never really allowed himself to imagine the day would come when his father wasn't in charge. No one in the family truly believed that he would actually die; as Lydia said to J.T. one night during his father's illness, "He *can't* die." That's why, even before Katrina's arrival, the summer of 2005 was already fraught with uncertainty and unease.

Now, as he heads toward River Ridge, J.T. worries that the school Mr. Curtis built largely with his own hands may very well lie in ruins. Even if it's come through the storm, if too few students return, the school will quickly run short of funds. J.T. simply can't believe that his father isn't here to tell them all exactly what to do.

As he makes the right turn off Jefferson Highway onto Manguno, J.T.'s heart and head begin to pound. The white columns and the black-iron gates of the school are just ahead, and he prays silently, "Whatever it is, Lord, I'm gonna accept it."

Outside the front gate, he, Jeff, and Tommy get out and stand for a moment before the bronze sculpture of the sea nymph and fishes and coral, the edges worn and shiny from the touch of thousands of hands. They're relieved to see that, from the outside, the school looks intact. There are trees and branches strewn all over, but no roofs appear to have caved in; there's no obvious damage.

Jeff unlocks the front door of the main building and, as they walk down the hallways, they find the floors are dry and there's no light poking through holes in the ceiling. They continue walking nervously around the small compound, through the gym, across the football field, past the weight room and cafeteria, and J.T. suddenly chokes up.

Except for minor wind damage and some downed trees and scattered trash, the school is incredibly whole. The practice field, where he spends so much of his waking life, is completely untouched. J.T. gets into what he calls his "pentecostal mood," praising God, thanking his dad for watching over and protecting the school, weeping and laughing at the same time.

When they drive down the road to inspect the elementary school, they discover that the roof of one building has been ripped off, and a huge maple tree has fallen on another building, whose roof looks crushed beneath the massive limbs. The elementary school will be out of commission, but J.T. is already scheming, figuring that the younger kids can squeeze into the high school until their buildings are repaired.

As they leave the school, J.T. is feeling confident that, in no time, the school will be back in business—that is, as long as his students can make their way back to the city.

How many of them will be able to do so, though, is the next big question.

• • •

They head back to Entergy, but during another break after lunch, they drive back to River Ridge to check on their homes. Fortunately, none of their houses sustained any serious flooding or major damage, although Jeff's house got some water in his computer room and a tree has raked a hole in the roof of J.T. and Lydia's den.

There's a mandatory curfew in effect, so at the end of their Entergy shift, as the sky darkens toward dusk, they drive out of the battered, locked-down city, in search of the Fairway View Apartments in Baton Rouge. They decided earlier in the day to spend tonight at the newly rented apartments there rather than drive all the way back to Eunice. The lease won't start until tomorrow, but Dawn's friend said she'd pick up a set of keys from the manager and unlock one of the apartments for them. She also took it upon herself to put a fresh coat of paint on the walls. The men can't wait to collapse in sleep. They're due back on the job with Entergy again early tomorrow, for another day of toilets, trash, and wet mops.

On their way to Baton Rouge, along a disturbingly vacant Interstate 10, they witness still more dramatic evidence of Katrina's destruction, and feel grateful that their school is a remarkable exception. Along the highway sit the burned-out carcasses of cars that overheated and caught fire during the evacuation. At interchanges, gas stations are closed or out of gas, and even the fast-food restaurants are shut. On the car radio, they hear that President Bush flew over New Orleans this afternoon. Peering through the small oval window of Air Force One, he said it looked devastating from the air. "And it's got to be doubly devastating on the ground," he said.

Across the entire South, residents of the city who've endured five or six days away from their homes are frazzled by sleeplessness and the continued uncertainty and lack of information. Displaced residents know that the city remains largely under water. Beyond that, they are completely in the dark about what will happen next. They have no idea when they'll be able to return home. And like many Americans, they are baffled and angry about what seems to have been an unprecedented display of incompetence and inadequate planning and dereliction of duty on the part of public officials, from FEMA down to the mayor's office and police department.

Even Bush's flyover seemed to many to be an insufficient gesture, as if he didn't want to get his hands dirty or his feet wet by actually visiting the city, the way he visited New York soon after the 9/11 attacks. Indeed, the Superdome still hasn't been evacuated, and the restless crowds continue to grow larger at the Convention Center. People are still being rescued from their homes as the looting continues unabated. Mayor Nagin tells the Associated Press that "hundreds, perhaps thousands" are dead in New Orleans.

Mark Twain once said that "an American has not seen the United States until he has seen Mardi Gras in New Orleans." In the weeks to come, New Orleanians will learn that many of the warehouses that stored lavish Mardi Gras floats and costumes have been flooded or ruined by fire. Will Mardi Gras itself become one of Katrina's victims?

For many, just finding a place to sleep remains a frustrating adventure.

J.T., Jeff, and Tommy are the first to arrive at the apartment complex in Baton Rogue, but they're quickly stymied. Toni had told Jeff the apartment was number 142. It turns out there are thousands of apartments in dozens of three-story buildings spread throughout the enormous complex. They finally figure out the numbering system, and find the right building, and apartment number 142. When they try the doorknob, it's locked. Thinking the others must have gotten there first, Jeff starts pounding on the door.

"It's us," he yells. "Open up."

The door opens, and a confused looking man stands there, in a fully furnished apartment with a glowing TV set behind him. Jeff explains that he's looking for his brother and cousins, but the guy tells him he must have the wrong place.

"Either we got the wrong apartment," Jeff says, "or we've been taken."

They try calling their spouses and Johnny, but can't get through to anyone. After a quick, tasteless fast-food meal they decide to return to the maze of apartment buildings, and on a side road they spot a sign, PHASE II. Following the sign, they find another maze of apartment buildings and, finally, apartment number 142. The door is unlocked.

It's hardly a joyful homecoming, though. There are no mattresses or even towels. Dawn's friend had come earlier in the day and painted the walls, but the carpets are still dirty, giving off a faint whiff of stale beer that mixes with the sharp smell of paint. Jeff and Tommy are exhausted and a bit loopy. They joke about Johnny, who is still missing in action and, they assume, lost in the apartment maze. But J.T. doesn't think it's funny.

"Why're you laughing?" he barks. "He could be on the side of the road somewhere. Call your brother!"

"Dad," Jeff says. "I've called him a million times."

"Well, call him again."

Johnny, meanwhile, is knocking on the door of apartment number 142, in Phase I, shouting, "J.T.? Tommy? Jeff?" The same confused man opens the door, gives Johnny the same answer, and shuts the door in his face. Johnny stares at the door in disbelief. He's filthy from cleaning toilets all day. He's tired and hungry and hasn't eaten since the morning and can't reach anyone by cell phone. Finally, he gets through to Dawn, and starts screaming, in an absolute panic. Before she can tell him to look for PHASE II, the phone cuts out. She tries calling him back but can't get through.

He decides to go to the friend's house where he and the others had spent the previous night, but he gets lost. It's midnight, and as he drives along the dark streets of Baton Rouge, he sees evacuees sleeping in their cars at gas stations and in parking lots. In his exhausted state, he starts imagining terrible things, that he's going to get mugged. Maybe worse. He has never felt so scared and alone.

Finally he finds a pay phone and gets through to Dawn, who quickly tells him to find Phase II. Jeff and Tommy have just nodded off when they hear a knock on the door. Jeff opens it and there stands his grimy, scowling brother. Johnny looks into the apartment and sees that J.T. is curled up with the pillow and blanket he had brought with him but had left in J.T.'s truck. He just shakes his head, and Jeff and Tommy, overcome by the absurdity of it all, suddenly burst out laughing, waking up J.T.

"What are you laughing at?" he barks groggily. "Your brother could have been hurt."

Jeff and Tommy only laugh harder, and soon they're all laughing, feeling the pent-up tensions pouring out of them. Jeff tells them how twenty-four hours earlier he was on the verge of taking a job selling

MRI equipment. But now, it looks like the school might be able to reopen, so there's no way he's taking the job.

Father and sons finally drift off to sleep on the smelly carpet in their smelly Entergy uniforms. A few hours later, somewhere around three in the morning, J.T.'s cell phone trills, waking everyone up.

It's Kyle Collura. He's been trying to call the coaches for days, he says, but the cell service is so lousy the only time he can get more than a bar or two on his phone's service scale is after midnight. He's sorry to call in the middle of the night, and he knows tonight's game is probably canceled, but he didn't know what else to do, and he really needed to talk to someone.

J.T. emerges from the fog of sleep and tells Kyle to slow down.

"Hold on, hold on . . . Listen, it's going to be okay," he says, his voice phlegmy.

He quickly tells Kyle that they've just come from the school, that it's in good shape, and they should be able to reopen soon, though he can't tell him when for sure. He can tell Kyle is anxious to keep him on the line, that he's hungry for reassurance and a familiar voice, but J.T. is so exhausted he can barely keep his eyes open. He needs sleep, knowing he's got less than three hours left before another tough day as a janitor.

"Listen, I want to talk to you, but I'm too tired . . ." he tells Kyle. "But keep in shape, and keep in touch."

The next day is Friday. It should be the day of the Patriots' first regular season game of 2005, but they're flung far and wide, watching their hometown fall to ruin. From their various evacuation spots, they've all been trying to get through to J.T. or the other coaches by phone or e-mail. With the ongoing problems with cellular service and the coaches' lack of access to a computer, though, none of them except Kyle has had any luck.

They had all been dying to test their mettle against the big team coming in from Utah. They knew Cottonwood would be tough, but they had studied the films, had practiced and drilled. They were hardened and psyched for the game, physically and mentally prepared. With Greater New Orleans clearly out of commission and off limits for who knows how long, the Patriots have all by now figured out that tonight's game has been canceled. They are anxious for word that next week's game is still on. They can stand to miss one game, but two is unthinkable.

The rhythms and structure of football completely dominate their lives. They're conditioned to the tight schedules and well-worn routines football requires. For months, if not years, their coaches have told them exactly where to be and what to do and how to think and what to wear, day in and day out. Players have seen J.T. and the others nearly every day for six months. Being so out of touch feels irresponsible, and just plain out of whack. They need to get back to the practice field, the weight room, and the film room.

It's now been nearly a week since their last practice, which is unheard of in their world, especially at the beginning of a season. They also know well the dangers of missing a game, how important it is to gain real-time playing experience. It's one thing to work hard in practice, but it's another thing altogether to play in a game that matters, beneath the lights and in front of the fans, a game that counts toward a W or an L.

They're now beginning to realize, however, that when they said goodbye at the end of last Saturday's practice, it may have really been goodbye.

For a Louisiana high school football team, there's nothing normal about a Friday in September that isn't a prelude to a football game. It just feels wrong.

8

Crepe Myrtle

On Friday, September 2, the *Times-Picayune* publishes its first issue since the storm. The front-page headline reads, in bold block letters, HELP US, PLEASE. Beneath that is the photograph of a woman on her knees outside the Convention Center, screaming those words. The rest of the headline reads: AFTER THE DISASTER, CHAOS AND LAWLESS-NESS RULE THE STREETS.

For the students of John Curtis and their families, along with all of Greater New Orleans, the magnitude of the dislocation of their lives has begun to sink in.

It has been at least five days since they all endured the evacuation journeys that dispersed them across scores of southern cities. For the rest of their lives, they will all recall the details of their nightmarish escapes from the storm. Those who left on Saturday or before dawn on Sunday had an easier time of it, but those who waited until Sunday morning's mandatory evacuation endured hellish traffic jams and tense marathon drives. As the contraflow became overwhelmed and cars idled for hours, baking in the sun, some of them overheated and burst into flames. Evacuees scrummed for dwindling supplies of gas, picked clean the shelves of convenience marts, and battled to get, and then keep, their hotel rooms.

Patriots' running back David Seeman felt like he practically walked to Houston, since he spent most of the eighteen-hour trek trotting with his dog beside the car while his mom drove. He worried constantly about his dad, who lives in Slidell, not far from where the

Patriots played their jamboree game last Friday, and who decided to stay behind with his dogs and his trucks. David and his mom and sister are now at an aunt's house in Houston, where they have learned that Slidell flooded to twelve feet in some areas, and the water has yet to recede. They have been unable to reach David's dad.

Some students have ended up in places they never could have imagined. Marc Macaluso, a junior and a Patriots' linebacker, has been staying at a hotel in Arkansas that looks like the set of a horror flick. When his family first pulled up, the proprietor, an old woman, was sitting out front spitting tobacco juice into a can, and he thought to himself, "These are going to be the most awful days of my life."

Senior Ashley Funck had spent the Saturday before Katrina at her aunt and uncle's house, and ended up evacuating with them, while her parents evacuated to Texas. Now, Ashley and her cousins are sleeping in tents at a state park in Zwolle, Louisiana. She misses her parents and is worried about her boyfriend, Michael Floyd, a volunteer firefighter who stayed behind during Katrina. She's hoping her parents can come get her soon. In the meantime, she's been "freaking out" and getting angry at all the journalists referring to her and the other displaced New Orleanians as *refugees*.

For junior Brittany Rodrigue, her car has become her new home. Brittany had recently moved out of her mother's house in Raceland, southeast of New Orleans, and moved in with an aunt, who had bought a new house in Metairie. Brittany had just enrolled at John Curtis and was looking forward to the first day of school, and the start of a new life. After only a few nights in her new bedroom, she evacuated to her great-grandmother's house forty miles west of New Orleans. The house is now crowded with evacuee relatives. The power has been knocked out, so there's no air conditioning, and it is suffocating. She has spent the last four nights sleeping in her car, calling it "a major low in my life."

Those who stayed behind endured their own lows. Seventh-grader Terry Johnson and his family had stocked up on candles, batteries, and flashlights, with brave plans for a hurricane party. When Katrina slammed into their Kenner neighborhood like a freight train Monday morning, the storm shook the house and peeled off part of the roof. Terry was awakened by water streaming onto his face. The family stood looking out the front windows as the storm uprooted trees and juggled huge limbs through the air. When the winds died, the water rose quickly to waist height. Terry and his family waded through the neighborhood, past a convenience store filled with looters—"like ants running around," Terry thought. His family helped themselves to a couple bags of potato chips. Later, he watched neighbors break into pawn shops, walking off with TVs and guns.

Colby Arceneaux, whose family rode out the storm on his dad's supply ships, has finally reunited with his uncle and grandfather, who had stayed at their home in Chalmette, and were stranded outside on their roof for two days. The two men eventually swam and waded to some elevated train tracks and followed the tracks out of Chalmette. They broke into a damaged seafood shack in a desperate search for food. As they trekked away from New Orleans, occasionally hiding behind bushes to avoid roving groups of gun-toting looters, they met up with an older couple who had also lost their home. They finally got through to Colby's dad, who drove to pick them all up. More than two dozen evacuees are now living on Colby's dad's boat.

At least Colby's uncle and grandfather made it out of the city alive. Far too many did not.

Later, when the Curtis family cobbles together their students' evacuation stories, they will learn that no student died and no one lost any immediate family members. However, one student's aunt, who was terminally ill with cancer, stayed in her Kenner home during the storm. When the electricity knocked out her air conditioning, the elderly woman died. Days later, the family has still been unable to find someone to remove her body. Similarly, a neighbor of Coach Jerry's stayed behind with their terminally ill son. He died a day after the storm and, unable to find someone to assist with his body, they had to bury him in the backyard. It will take weeks for the coroner to remove the body.

Katrina has carved apart many families, some of whom can't reach their loved ones because landlines and cell service are still out.

Lindsey Grimes's parents were in Las Vegas and couldn't get a flight home. Her grandparents refused to evacuate, so the twelfth-grader fled with a neighbor, driving twenty hours to Texas. When she finally got through to her parents, she learned they had rented a car and were driving toward home. Lindsey managed to get a ride back to an aunt's house in Ponchatoula, Louisiana, where she is waiting for her parents. Electricity is out at the house, but they've kept a generator running. On the day of Lindsey's arrival, her aunt's next-door neighbor was overcome by fumes from the generator he'd kept running in his garage, and was killed.

Scores of John Curtis students have been separated from one or both parents for nearly a week. Michael Floyd, whose father is a Jefferson Parish firefighter, decided to stay with his father and work at the firehouse while his mother evacuated to Houston. Bryan Munch, a hulking Patriots' lineman whose father is chief of police in the west bank town of Westwego, evacuated with his mom to Lake Charles while his dad stayed behind. Bryan still hasn't been able to reach his dad, and he's been a nervous wreck. "The not knowing is the worst feeling I've ever had," he'll say later.

Jasmine Smith, a Curtis sophomore, decided to stay in Kenner with her sick grandfather while her parents evacuated west to La Place. Her grandfather's house is still surrounded by water and the streets filled with trees, power lines, and trash. They're running low on food and water, but her parents now can't get back into Kenner to help.

Linebacker Lincston Jones hasn't seen his mom for a week, and doesn't know when he'll see her again. He had said goodbye to her the morning before last Saturday's practice. She then went to her job at a home for the mentally handicapped. That afternoon, her supervisors decided to evacuate all the residents to a location north of New Orleans. Lincston and his dad evacuated to his uncle's house, two hours west of the city.

Linebacker John Ruttley's dad stayed behind while his mom evacuated. John went his own way. He picked up his classmate, Chuck Mataya, and they drove to Panama City, but couldn't find a hotel and slept in the car. On Monday, Chuck convinced a hotel clerk that he was twenty-one and they were able to get a room. For one night, they lived the high life, eating fast food and watching television with the air conditioning on high. By Tuesday, John was worried that he hadn't been able to reach either of his parents. He and Chuck started to drive home but forgot to fill up on gas. Somewhere in Alabama, with the tank on empty, they pulled over, expecting to spend another night in the car. Out of nowhere a woman drove up who had spare tanks of gas and gave them two gallons. To John it was a gift from God.

Children of divorced parents are living with the tough decision they made last week: whether to leave town with mom or dad. Gloria, a Curtis student, evacuated with her mother, who dropped her off at her dad's house in Mississippi. Her mom then left with her boyfriend to find another place to stay, and now Gloria can't reach her. As Gloria was lying outside, tanning in the sun one afternoon, her dad called her into the house. Inside, he started to cry, and her stepmother had to explain what's happened. Gloria's stepfather lost his job at the Convention Center and was being transferred to Florida. Her mom was going with him, immediately. Gloria ran outside, screaming, "No, no, no, no, no . . ."

Brandi Godwin's dad stayed behind at his home in Chalmette while she evacuated with her mom. On Wednesday, the senior volleyball player got a call from her dad. He had borrowed a stranger's phone to tell his daughter he was on a school bus headed to Lake Charles. She and her mom drove to a horrible-smelling tent shelter there and, after asking around, finally found him curled up on an air mattress, filthy and asleep.

Families who evacuated intact at least have each other to lean on. But, after five days crammed into hotel rooms or relatives' spare bedrooms, nerves are frayed and tensions are high. Hotel rooms are feeling smaller and relatives' couches feeling less comfortable by the day. Kids can't get through to their friends or boyfriends or girlfriends by phone or online. They're bored, lonely, and scared. Many evacuees are also worried about pets left behind, because no one expected to be gone more than a day or two. Nothing feels normal, and no one seems to be able to say when anything *will* be normal.

Worst of all is the uncertainty about what the coming days will bring. Some families are beginning to get vague reports about the extent of the damage or flooding to their neighborhoods, but word about the status of their own homes remains elusive. Most students have no clue what kind of shape their houses are in, and don't even know when they'll be able to get back to inspect their homes. Are they homeless? If so, for how long? Jefferson Parish, it seems, will be off limits until at least next week.

Officials are worried about letting residents back into the parish while looters continue ransacking stores. In response, some residents who stayed have taken matters into their own hands, patrolling their front porches with shotguns and posting signs outside their homes that read, YOU LOOT, I SHOOT. Between the looting and the vigilantism, Jefferson Parish President Aaron Broussard announces during a radio interview that his parish is now a dictatorship to be called Jeffertania, and that he's the dictator. He warns that parish police officers will stop looting by any means.

John Curtis students come from all corners of Greater New Orleans. For those who live in the harder-hit neighborhoods—Kenner, Lakeview, and eastern New Orleans—the news remains very bad, even five days after Katrina. Most of those neighborhoods are still under water and, while the Army Corps of Engineers has closed one of the breaches in the 17th Street Canal levee, they've been unable to repair the other levees, let alone begin draining the city. Governor Blanco has now asked President Bush to send no less than forty thousand troops to help her beleaguered state.

Mayor Nagin ventures that there may be as many as ten thousand bodies to recover once the flood waters ebb, and Mississippi Governor Haley Barbour frets on national television that "there are a lot of dead people down there." Homeland Security Secretary Michael Chertoff tells Reuters that when the city finally dries out, "We're going to uncover people who died hiding in houses . . . It is going to be about as ugly a scene as you can imagine."

Already, dozens of corpses are being found throughout sections of Lakeview, and television newscasts have zoomed in close on the bodies floating elsewhere or left to rot on the streets. Not only have many victims drowned, but others have been electrocuted and some killed by carbon monoxide poisoning, including four people in one house in Marrero.

Most of the media attention remains rightly focused on the Ninth Ward and parts of St. Bernard Parish, but Jefferson Parish was not spared its share of tragedy. With the coroner's office in adjacent Orleans Parish under water, and so many dead in New Orleans proper, the corpses in Jefferson Parish must wait; in many cases, they'll still be waiting two weeks later.

For the displaced evacuees, among the few distractions is television, but that's filled with constant reminders of why they're in need of distraction. Aerial shots of the region show floodwaters still at or above the rooftops of many thousands of homes. WWL-TV has begun broadcasting heartbreaking footage of the increasingly frustrated, desperate, and hungry crowds at the Superdome and Convention Center. More National Guard troops have finally arrived and buses have begun evacuating people from the Superdome to Houston's Astrodome. But there aren't yet enough buses to evacuate the Convention Center crowds, now more than twenty thousand strong and simmering on the verge of a riot. The *Times-Picayune*, in Friday morning's edition, described a city teetering on the brink of anarchy and "a complete collapse of public order."

Looters have set fire to the Oakwood mall, across the river in Jefferson Parish, burning it to the ground. An explosion ripped through a propane storage tank facility, and numerous other fires are raging unchecked. The air is filled with Coast Guard rescue helicopters and Blackhawk choppers ferrying in more National Guard troops. The sound of gunfire is everywhere, shots fired by looters who have broken into pawn shops, and shots fired by the cops in response. Hundreds of other city police officers, meanwhile, are abandoning their posts. For some, the widespread looting, the senseless deaths and abandoned corpses, and the destruction of the city is just too much. At least two city officers have used their weapons to commit suicide.

With all the bedlam and the obvious breakdown in emergency response, most Americans are shocked when President Bush calls Katrina's devastation a "temporary disruption," and, on Friday, commends FEMA's Michael Brown for doing a "heck of a job." The president's mother, Barbara, visiting some of the fifteen thousand evacuees who've reached Houston's Astrodome, says that many of

Katrina's victims are "underprivileged anyway, so this is working very well for them."

Such comments lead some observers to claim that the federal government's response to Katrina wouldn't have been so sloppy if New Orleans wasn't a largely African-American city. "For those who were alone in the water, alone on the roof, you might ask 'What did we do to deserve this?' " Rev. Lowell Case asks his congregation at St. Francis Xavier Church in Baton Rouge. "A lot of us think being black may have had something to do with it, being poor and black in New Orleans."

Elsewhere, people have begun to say some hurtful things. One radio host, Chris Beck, complains that the media is focusing too little on Mississippi and Alabama and too much on the "scumbags" of New Orleans. In Washington, House Speaker Dennis Hastert suggests that a lot of the damaged city neighborhoods could simply be bulldozed, and Louisiana Congressman Richard Baker claims that Katrina has "finally cleaned up public housing in New Orleans. We couldn't do it, but God did it." Other theories posit that Katrina was God's way of punishing New Orleans for its decadent lifestyle.

Even the rational speakers are predicting that parts of the city and its suburbs will be ghost towns for as many as nine months, and that some residents may remain homeless for up to two years. Not only do the levees have to be repaired and the floodwaters drained, but the homes, businesses, and infrastructure of a region that's been soaking in chemical-filled waters for nearly a week will require many months to dry out. In the meantime, mold is growing like a fuzzy cancer throughout the saturated homes.

On Sunday morning, September 4, those tuned to NBC's *Meet the Press* witness an especially unnerving interview with Broussard, who tells Tim Russert that New Orleans has been "abandoned by our own country." He claims that FEMA has botched the rescue operations, has turned back trucks trying to deliver water to his parish, has stolen his parish's diesel fuel, and that FEMA cut his emergency communication lines.

"Hurricane Katrina will go down as one of the worst abandonments of Americans on American soil ever in U.S. history," he says. "It's not just Katrina that caused all these deaths in New Orleans here. Bureaucracy has committed murder here in the greater New Orleans area and bureaucracy has to stand trial."

Broussard continues by telling Russert about one of his emergency management employees, whose mother was trapped in a St. Bernard Parish nursing home. "She called him and said, 'Are you coming, son? Is somebody coming?' And he said, 'Yeah, Mama, somebody's coming to get you.' Somebody's coming to get you on Tuesday. Somebody's coming to get you on Wednesday. Somebody's coming to get you on Thursday. Somebody's coming to get you on Friday . . . and she drowned Friday night. She drowned Friday night!" Broussard begins sobbing uncontrollably, as Russert tries to calm him.

"Nobody's coming to get us! Nobody's coming to get us!" Broussard pushes on, wracked with sobs. "Everybody's promised. They've had press conferences. I'm *sick* of the press conferences. For God sakes, shut up and send us somebody!"

Before anyone can even get in to begin fixing the city, many people are still trying to find their way *out*. Frustrated with the lack of emergency busing, they're desperate to flee, but the escape routes are few and, in one case, a few thousand evacuees are turned back into the flooded city at gunpoint. The group includes out-of-town guests who were kicked out of their hotel rooms and turned away from the Superdome and Convention Center and now have no place to stay. Armed officers in the Jefferson Parish town of Gretna refuse to let them cross the Crescent City Connection, a bridge across the Mississippi. The police fire warning shots at the group, chasing them back. The Gretna Bridge Incident, as it is soon known, incites more claims of racial injustice, since most of the thousands of refugees on the bridge are African American.

Elsewhere in New Orleans, walking across a bridge turns out to be a deadly exercise. On September 4, New Orleans police open fire on suspected looters who were crossing a bridge in Lakeview and, as New Orleans police superintendent Steven Nichols tells Reuters news service, "Exchanged gunfire with police." Two of the men are killed. Later, it turns out they weren't looters but members of two families and a few others who swam away from their flooded homes and were trying to get out of the city. One of the victims died in front of his wife, who lost an arm, and his son, who was seriously wounded. Seven officers will later be charged with murder or attempted murder.

As the news that so much of the city will be shut down for so long hits Curtis parents, they begin to worry about what will happen to their jobs. Even if they can get back into their homes, so many businesses in and around New Orleans have been damaged that many thousands of jobs will be in jeopardy. Some employers have begun tracking down employees and making plans for them to start working shifts at temporary offices, in some cases far from home.

Some parents now have to deal with the stress of being transferred to new towns. Linebacker Preston Numa's mother, Shirelle Wiltz, has gotten a call from her employer, the Internal Revenue Service, telling her to report next week to the Baton Rouge office. She can't believe she has to contend with that when she's worried about relatives who stayed behind in their homes, in Gentilly and New Orleans East, to whom she still hasn't gotten through. And she's still desperately concerned about her own home, which is a mile from the London Avenue Canal breach. But what choice does she have? She's planning to find an apartment in Baton Rouge, and has already begun talking with Preston about going to school there.

Preston doesn't want to start all over at a new school, again. He had only started attending Curtis two years ago, as a freshman, after years of being home schooled. And now, at the start of his junior year, he's finally begun to feel at home. Preston's whole life revolves around Curtis and the Patriots. He hasn't seen his father in years and has no siblings at home. He considers his coaches, teachers, and classmates his family. No way does he want to suddenly start from scratch again at some alien school where nobody knows him, where he'd have to make friends all over again. And he simply can't believe that he might not be playing football this season. *Again.* When he broke his jaw last year, and it had to be wired shut for weeks, he still attended every practice, film session, and game. He had been so frustrated standing on the sidelines that he once threatened to take a pair of wire cutters and snip the wires off himself.

This season was supposed to be his big year. Like his teammates, he's been calling J.T. and the other coaches almost constantly for days, with no luck. He just wants to hear that somehow the team will be playing again soon, that J.T. has figured out some way to get them all together.

Preston is hardly the only one facing the dreaded prospect of enrolling in a new school. Officials are already suggesting that displaced students enroll for the time being in a school near the town to which they've evacuated, at least until New Orleans and the suburban parishes reopen, whenever that may be. Uprooted and scattered teachers are also being told to find new jobs if they can.

In New Orleans and Orleans Parish alone, dozens of public schools have been destroyed, as have many parochial schools, home to 40 percent of the 65,000 students in the city and parish. Other schools across southern Louisiana are also seriously, if not fatally, damaged or are waiting for electricity to be restored, and are unlikely to reopen any time soon. Jefferson Parish officials have said some of their schools may not open until January.

J.T. and his family are stunned by the advisories, and the realization sinks in that, even though their school is unharmed, they may not be able to keep it running. They may lose too many students to enrollment elsewhere. The stress is so intense that Lydia is suffering from panic attacks.

John Curtis has never been a cash cow. They've always kept the tuition low, so low that it just covers the expense of running the place, with very little to spare for improvements or emergencies. Enrollment this year was already fifty students lower than last year, and they don't have large cash reserves.

Text messages and e-mails start trickling in to J.T. and the others from students asking, "What should we do?" With a new urgency, the Curtises realize they have to act fast. Johnny, who has been able to receive calls more consistently on his cell phone, tells his students to follow the instructions of public officials but to stay in touch, that they're going to try to reopen soon. He comes to believe that the school's ability to survive rides on the outcome of the coming days, and tells his father, "We've got to be proactive."

• • •

On Saturday, September 3, after a distraught week of separation in their various evacuation posts, the Curtises reunite. Three dozen family members converge on the four Baton Rouge apartments they've rented and fling themselves into turning the apartments into makeshift homes.

The adults are so unaccustomed to the idleness they've endured in the last few days that they're relieved to have some work to do, and they jump into action. One group braves Baton Rouge's evacuee-choked streets to buy card tables and camp chairs, paper plates and plastic cups from Wal-Mart. J.T. and a few of the coaches, meanwhile, use their Entergy passes to get back into River Ridge. They revisit their houses to empty rotting food from refrigerators and freezers, which have been without electricity for nearly a week.

J.T.'s sister, Alicia, and her husband, Mark, also manage to get past the security perimeter and into Jefferson Parish. At the school, they tackle the putrescent task of emptying the freezers. Only days before Katrina, in advance of a new school year, the cafeteria had been stocked with six thousand dollars' worth of pizzas, burritos, chicken patties, and burgers, all of it now a decomposing mess. When Mark opens the first of the freezer doors he's overwhelmed by the stench. He turns away and begins throwing up. He and Alicia wrap T-shirts around their faces as they empty eight more freezers.

After emptying the ruined food from their homes and cleaning up the yards, J.T., Leon, and the others meet at the high school to pick up the cube truck they use to haul football equipment. They drive Mike Neeley's War Wagon to a few houses and pick up twenty mattresses, pots and pans, some extra clothes, and other items they'll need to make the apartments their temporary homes. Then they head back to the Baton Rouge apartments.

Everyone is grateful that Johnny thought to evacuate with his new fifty-two-inch television, which they prop in the corner of one apartment. There's no cable hookup, but Johnny manages to create an antenna of sorts with aluminum foil, and the television quickly becomes the family hearth. They all gather around, watching the ceaselessly disturbing news coverage.

The next day, the family convenes for an official John Curtis Christian School business meeting. They come up with an aggressive plan to track down students and become the first school in New Orleans to reopen, so that their students won't have to enroll elsewhere—at least those who still have homes. For those whose homes have been damaged, FEMA trailers are said to be on the way.

They know the school will give kids a comforting daytime sanctuary, even if their homes are in ruins. As longtime educators, the Curtises know how traumatic it can be for a kid to switch schools in midstream, they see it all the time when apprehensive new kids transfer to Curtis, leaving behind networks of friends and the comforting familiarity of their old school.

They're also worried about their teachers, many of whom are surely concerned about the status of their jobs, and the Curtises agree to get the word out quickly that they'll honor all teacher contracts, actually verbal contracts, which was the way Mr. Curtis handled such things. They plan to mail or even hand deliver the next paychecks in the coming days, even before the school reopens, as a sign of the school's commitment to them.

The Curtises also decide to set up an information hotline right away. In another effort to spread the word, one group goes to Kinko's and prints up thousands of flyers that say PLEASE CALL US and NOW ACCEPTING NEW STUDENTS. They'll post those flyers on telephone poles and hand them out to local businesses and, when they're able to get back, will start to distribute them throughout Jefferson Parish. Another group starts working on a Web site on which they'll post updates and reopening information. They also start compiling an e-mail list, and will begin sending e-mails to students and parents. Thanks to a football connection, they're able to use a computer at LSU's weight room. Yet another group goes to Wal-Mart to buy supplies to create a large sign they'll put on the interstate to catch the eye of kids and their families traveling in or out of Baton Rouge.

Additionally, they begin trying to contact students and parents by phone, finding that, while cellular service is mostly out of commission, they can still send text messages. That requires terse, abbreviated notes such as "jccs reopening soon, call us." They can't provide a specific date because there's still no word on when the lockdown will be lifted. At least they can assure kids and parents that the school is okay. Some of them have never sent a text message before; Leon has never even used a cell phone. The younger Curtises teach them the system.

Despite these efforts, many John Curtis parents decide to follow the advisories and begin to look for schools for their children to attend in Texas, Mississippi, Alabama, Arkansas, and in northern Louisiana. It's been announced that parish residents will be allowed back for a one-day visit on Monday September 5, to grab some clothes, check on their homes, then leave by dusk. The Curtises hope that parents will then see for themselves that they don't need to transfer their kids.

Still, it will likely be a while before students living in New Orleans proper get to see their homes, and it's now up to public officials to determine when the city will reopen. In the meantime, all the Curtises can do is rush to get the school into shape.

J.T. and Leon, Jeff and Johnny and a few of the other coaches descend on the school for a massive cleanup. The men decide to clean up all the tree limbs and garbage first, and tackle the huge maple tree last.

They dive into the tangles of wood with chain saws and axes, dragging the debris to the curb, alongside the garbage bags of rotting food that had been cleaned out of the freezers. Other residents have piled bags of spoiled food beside the street and the entire neighborhood reeks.

The neighborhood also smells of danger. Some residents have posted warning signs—YOU COME IN AND I'LL KILL YOU—and, on the way to their homes and the school, the Curtises see a number of people patrolling their property, standing guard on their front porches with handguns or shotguns. J.T. and Johnny get a menacing taste of the danger while trying to siphon some gas from one of the buses parked behind the school. With so many stations closed, gas has become a precious commodity. Suddenly, two military helicopters start circling overhead, then drop lower, then lower, until they are aiming their side-mounted machine guns right at them. "Let's go," J.T. says, and they all raise their hands and back slowly away from the buses.

J.T.'s brother-in-law, Mark, manages to get stacks of MREs from a nearby National Guard post and, as the men take a break from the cleanup and dine on MREs in their ruined, putrid neighborhood, the war in Iraq doesn't seem so far away.

Finally, late in the day, they decide to tackle the huge maple tree that has fallen on the elementary school. Leon climbs onto the roof and starts chainsawing off some of the outer limbs and tossing them down to the others. At one point, a CNN camera crew arrives and films the Curtises. Leon, mistakenly thinking the video photographer is his brother-in-law, Bob, who works for a local TV station, starts clowning around. With his pants riding low, he bends over and practically moons the CNN crew, yelling down, "Hey Bob, get a shot of this." J.T. tries to ignore him, and tells the CNN reporter, "New Orleans is gonna come back." When the crew leaves, J.T. yells up to his brother, "Leon, what the heck were you doing?" Leon replies, "What? It's just Bob." Given all the stress they've been under, the comic relief is much appreciated, and they all burst out laughing.

After more cutting, Leon thinks he's getting close to the section of the tree trunk that's leaning against the building. He warns the others, "Get outa the way! It's gonna crash," then attacks another thick limb, thinking the trunk might be ready to shift position or fall. He cuts clear through the limb and jumps out of the way, but as the severed limb falls to the ground, the tree still doesn't budge. He keeps cutting, and tossing off more limbs, expecting any minute to see where the tree has crunched the thin tin roof. Each hacked-off branch reveals more of the roof, and yet the more he cuts the more baffled Leon becomes.

"I can't see any hole," he finally calls down to the others.

It doesn't seem possible. The tree is enormous. There's no way it wouldn't have punctured the flimsy metal roof. After removing a few more limbs, they discover why the roof has been spared.

Mr. Curtis loved trees and plants, and he believed they taught life lessons through their growth and beauty. In the early 1970s, he planted a row of crepe myrtle trees beside the elementary school, and he told anyone who'd listen that some of those trees sprouted flowers early in the spring, some bloomed later, but by summer they were all in full, beautiful bloom, just like kids. He loved those crepe myrtles, babied them, fertilized them, and raved about them. Over the years they had matured into thick, strong specimens. The huge maple had fallen against one of those crepe myrtles, and the myrtle sustained the brunt of the fall.

To the Curtis men it seems a sign that the old man is watching over them still. They are filthy, exhausted, sleep-deprived, and anxiety-ridden about the future of their school, their livelihoods, and their city.

They've all been harboring fears that if the school can't reopen, their family will be torn apart. In just one week, everything they've devoted their lives to has been jeopardized.

With their emotions on a knife edge, the sight of that little crepe myrtle shielding the school's roof hits them hard and a few turn away to hide tears.

J. T. Curtis's record at the start of the 2005 season—417–47–6—made him the second most winning high school football coach in America. Across thirty-five years, he had won the Louisiana state championship nineteen times. (Courtesy of Romaguera Photographers)

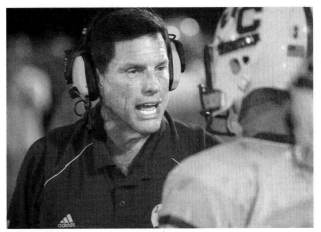

John T. Curtis Sr., whom everyone called "Mr. Curtis," sitting in his chair on the sideline of a game during the 2004 season. (Courtesy of Chris Medley)

The Curtis family, circa 1955: (*rear, left to right*) Leon, Miss Merle, J.T., and Mr. Curtis; (*front, left to right*) Alicia, Debbie, and Kathy. All five of his children would come to work at his school. (Courtesy of the Curtis family)

Leon Curtis, J.T.'s brother. He oversees the defense and has been J.T.'s right-hand man and alter ego for more than thirty years. (Courtesy of Chris Medley)

J.T. and his two sons, Johnny (arms folded) and Jeff (to Johnny's left), on the sidelines. At the start of the 2005 season, nine of J.T.'s twelve assistant coaches were Curtis family members. (Courtesy of *The Shreveport Times*)

Tommy Fabacher (*left*) on the sidelines with Johnny (*right*). Tommy had attended John Curtis, played for J.T. in high school, married his daughter Joanna, and now coaches the Patriots' defensive backs. (Courtesy of Chris Medley)

John Curtis has never been able to afford its own stadium, but J.T. babies his practice field as if it were a prized Turkish rug. "Ninety percent of a game is won on the practice field," J.T. likes to tell his players.   (Chris Granger, ESPN.com)

To spruce up the otherwise drab buildings of concrete block and tin roofs, Mr. Curtis filled his school with sometimes eccentric works of art. This sea nymph sculpture has greeted generations of students at the school's front doors.   (Photo by Neal Thompson)

An enormous breach in the Industrial Canal causes devastating flooding in the Lower Ninth Ward. A barge surfs through (or has possibly contributed to) the breach, and will come to rest atop the home of two John Curtis students. (Courtesy of FEMA)

When the floodwaters recede, the barge lands on and crushes the nose of the bus that Kenny and Jané Dorsey's mom drove to help pay for their tuition at John Curtis. (Courtesy of Marc Naccari)

Mike Walker and Tank English are among the many Curtis students whose houses are badly flooded and uninhabitable. Mike's family lives in a FEMA trailer while Mike and his dad gut their home. Tank moves in with J.T., as does Joe McKnight.   (Chris Granger, ESPN.com)

J.T.'s wife, Lydia, sings the national anthem at the team's rare "home" games, which are played at a borrowed stadium. (Courtesy of Chris Medley)

Mr. Curtis's chair, unveiled at the season-opening jamboree, becomes a memorial of sorts and reminds the players and coaches of his absence. Some players and coaches would walk past the chair, touch it, and cross themselves. (Courtesy of Chris Medley)

Since John Curtis is a small school, its fans are often outnumbered. They compensate by shaking homemade noisemakers: plastic milkjugs filled with coins or dried beans. (Courtesy of Chris Medley)

J.T. leading his team in prayer. He often implores them to "play like Christian gentlemen," and reminds them that it's more than just a game. (Courtesy of Chris Medley)

Even before Katrina, the 2005 season was going to be a challenge for the Patriots' young and inexperienced quarterback, Kyle Collura, who had broken his collarbone in a spring scrimmage. (Courtesy of Chris Medley)

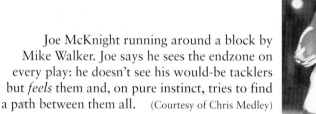

Joe McKnight running around a block by Mike Walker. Joe says he sees the endzone on every play: he doesn't see his would-be tacklers but *feels* them and, on pure instinct, tries to find a path between them all. (Courtesy of Chris Medley)

Offensive lineman Andrew Nierman spent nearly a week on lockdown at Ochsner Medical Center with his mother, an emergency room nurse. He'd later say of the experience, "Katrina will forever burn a hole in my heart." (Courtesy of Chris Medley)

The coaches at first weren't sure what to expect of their easy-going running back David Seeman. Across the season, he would grow to become a surprisingly tenacious ball carrier.
(Courtesy of Chris Medley)

9

For the Love of the Game

On Friday, September 2, all across the country, the high-school football season is about to commence. In many thousands of stadiums, from coast to coast, teenaged boys are suiting up for the season's first game, their thunderous friends and anxious families in the grandstands.

Instead of suiting up for the Battle on the Bayou against the Cottonwood Colts, Patriots' running back David Seeman is in Humble, Texas, sitting in the nosebleed seats of a high-school stadium that feels large enough to hold an NFL crowd. He has motored here on a golf cart from his aunt and uncle's house, where his family is now living. He'd always heard about Texas football, and he's awed by the biggest high-school stadium he's ever seen. But it feels absurd being a spectator on a Friday night in September.

It's not always easy for a high-school boy to pinpoint just what it is he loves about his chosen sport. The appeal varies from kid to kid. For some, it's all about the victory, about confronting an adrenalized opponent and beating them to a pulp. For others, it's the glory, the thrill of having thousands of fans and beautiful cheerleaders calling *your* name as you dance or dive into the endzone. Others could choose from a long list of football's more obvious attributes: pride, teamwork, brotherhood, tradition, achievement.

Some boys just like hitting people. There's something pure and raw about the sheer, physical brutality of the game, the satisfaction many players get from going head to head in the trenches against a noble peer and then outrunning, outblocking, or outwitting him, dragging him down. It may be a cliché, but it's true: a football game is a war without guns or death.

Some kids, like Kenny Dorsey, actually love the practice sessions as much as the games themselves. In practice, the endless repetitions and drills hone players' skills, developing in them a supreme confidence in their ability to throw the perfect block and make the perfect tackle.

Which gets to the meat of the game: As Chicago Bears Hall of Famer Red Grange said, football comes down to two things, "blocking and tackling." Likewise, legendary college coach Pop Warner, who helped create the nation's Pop Warner youth leagues, long insisted that there's no substitute for knocking the other guy down.

"When you hit, hit hard," he always told his players.

As Warner learned during a career that spanned American football's first half-century, high-schoolers are still just boys, but they're playing a man's game. Coached properly, the game can teach them more about themselves and their abilities than many classroom lessons ever could. Coached poorly, they learn darker lessons: that the slower, weaker guys get cut; that pain should be ignored; that winning is the only thing.

Because it's hardly a solitary game, each lesson, each success and failure, occurs before parents, grandparents, siblings, friends, girlfriends, and a few thousand strangers. Washington Redskins quarterback Sonny Jurgensen once likened football games to group therapy for fifty thousand people a week. His coach, the most legendary of all, Vince Lombardi, always stressed that execution and fundamentals were the key, just as J.T. does. But Lombardi's players always knew that winning was the real goal—"the *only* thing," in Lombardi's word—and that anything less than first place was, as Lombardi put it, just "hinky-dink."

There's a fine line between pushing teen boys too hard and not hard enough. J.T. is among those who strive to walk that tightrope, to expose kids to more physical discomfort than they'd ever imagined, then show them how overcoming that discomfort means they can achieve things they once thought impossible. It's not just a football lesson, but one they can take with them to college, to the military, to Wall Street, to forever.

From J.T. and his assistants, the Patriots have learned plenty about the thrill of victory and the payoff of perseverance. They've come to realize that Curtis football is teaching them about respect, dignity, poise, patience, trust, and the value of hard work, about life. J.T. always reminds players that he's not only coaching them to win on Friday nights, but to win every day. Yet the lessons of the game vary wildly from school to school. At many schools, coaches model themselves after stone-faced drill sergeants and pound on their impressionable young players, calling them insulting names and instilling in them that football is all about inflicting pain, being macho, being a *man*.

High school football has, after all, become big business. MTV has launched a reality show, *Two-a-Days*, featuring Alabama's Hoover High and its pugnacious coach. Hoover's games will be watched by a million viewers. Their stadium holds 15,000 and the school spends $450,000 a year on its football program, nearly twice John Curtis's entire athletic budget.

In many football-rabid communities, coaches spend huge amounts of time raising funds to pay for their twenty-thousand-seat stadiums. College recruiters now start visiting promising players as early as eighth grade, and the recruitment game has become a spectator sport in itself, played on Web sites such as Scout.com, Rivals.com, MaxPreps.com, and the magazine *Rise*. *USA Today* and *Sports Illustrated* are also expending more and more ink on high-school football and the recruitment game. These days, when a top high-school player signs with a top college, ESPN is there.

All of which gives players a taste of the big leagues and stokes their wildest fantasies of fame and fortune. Potential stars like Joe McKnight have been lured toward a college career since their first days of high school. Younger kids are already asking Joe for his autograph. J.T. cautions his team that only a small number of high-school players have the talent to earn a football scholarship, and only one in many thousands has a shot at a professional career. He tells them constantly that the odds are long and hopes are often dashed. Instead of thinking ahead to the NFL, they should focus on enjoying every last minute of high-school football, he says, and perform as if each game is their last.

Some players recognize that they're not NFL material, and are mature enough to enjoy the camaraderie of the sport, being part of a unique club that's one of the few places where race and economic status mean nothing. Football is a great leveler. This year's Patriots include the son of a preacher who owns his own corporate jet alongside the sons of fast-food workers. Their disparate backgrounds are irrelevant on the field. The satisfaction of pulling off a perfectly choreographed play is sublime, and the nights when everyone is doing his job, playing in synch like a well-oiled, efficient machine, and the scoreboard shows it . . . they'll remember those nights 'til the day they die.

J.T.'s lessons go against the grain of an increasingly zealous football culture that emphasizes the razzle-dazzle and showboating of the individual more than the team. He is wary of this trend, but tries to impress on his kids that being part of a successful team can be its own victory. As Cowboys running back Emmitt Smith, the NFL's all-time rushing leader, once said: "For me, winning isn't something that happens on the field when the whistle blows and the crowds roar. Winning is something that builds physically and mentally every day that you train and every night that you dream."

Every high-school football player dreams of making the big play under the Friday night lights, hurling the fifty-yard touchdown bomb or running an interception or kickoff return the whole length of the field for a triumphant score. Among the Patriots, every last one of them also dreams of winning a championship. It's what's expected of them as a Patriot. And they'll give everything they've got to make that dream come true.

That's why it's so horribly painful, on the first Friday night of September, to be relegated to the sidelines.

Across the rest of the country, young men are charging onto their fields of battle tonight. At the bigger schools with the deeper pockets, players are greeted by pyrotechnics, elaborate set pieces, and choreographed explosions or fireworks, mimicking a Super Bowl halftime show. They blast through giant archways that are replicas of their team mascot, streaming onto the field through the mouth of a bulldog or an alligator. Some teams emerge dramatically from a fog-machine-generated cloud of smoke.

In southern Louisiana, and along the Gulf Coast of Mississippi and Alabama, though, the season is in absolute shambles. Hundreds of opening-day games have been canceled, and no one knows when players might be able to get back on the field. Some coaches are looking at the prospect of having no season at all.

Just ten days ago, the Patriots had been in peak condition, and fired up for what many of them believed would be the biggest, toughest game of the year. They'd heard that the Cottonwood Colts had raised more than one hundred thousand dollars to travel all the way from Utah, so they knew their opponent was fired up, too. They couldn't wait to prove that a little 2A school could beat a big 5A school through sheer determination and smarts.

The spotty performance in the jamboree game certainly exposed some of the Patriots' weaknesses. But what better way for Kyle and the others to make a statement at the start of the 2005 season than to beat Cottonwood?

As Preston Numa said in anticipation of the game, "I can *taste* it." Instead, they're out of commission, and it's killing them.

Tank English has been sitting atop his spackling bucket and fishing without success for nearly a week. He's still at his mom's cousin's house in Alexandria, two hundred miles from home. He and his mom have been sleeping on air mattresses on the floor in a den with fifteen other family members and friends, including his mother's elderly friends who evacuated with them on Sunday.

His mother has been calling J.T. practically every hour, but keeps getting the same error message. Occasionally she reaches his voice mail and leaves a message, but she and Tank both know J.T. doesn't do voice-mail, just as he doesn't do e-mail. They keep hoping that maybe he'll answer, or that he or one of the other coaches will call them, giving Tank some reassuring marching orders.

Tank is by nature relentlessly cheery and optimistic. His mom has never seen him so miserable, so somber and quiet.

He's always struggled to keep his weight down, ever since childhood, when he was too heavy for the playground football leagues. Ever since coming to John Curtis in the fourth grade, the coaches have helped him stay active and control his weight. Now, without the regular workouts, and with nothing to do but fish and eat, he's already put on ten pounds. He feels he had played well in the jamboree game, but now worries that all the hard work over the summer is just slipping away. "I just want some *normalcy* back in my life," he tells his mom.

She knows how important football is to him, and she's desperate to help him get back to what he loves most. The pain of losing his father during his freshman-year football season is still raw, and football is what got him through mourning. Now, his dream of becoming the leader of the mighty Curtis defensive line, of catching the eyes of the college scouts and earning a scholarship and making his father proud, is imperiled.

Althea is also worried about how she's going to support them. For twenty-three years, she worked to make her day care business, the Little Professor Development Center, a success. But the center is in the Uptown section of New Orleans, most of which remains under water. Even if the waters drained tomorrow, she's sure the building will have suffered long-term damage. And even if by some miracle she's able to reopen quickly, will her clients return? She caters to inner-city families and their children, and she's deeply concerned about how they have weathered Katrina.

She's equally concerned about her own home in Kenner, but it's been impossible to get any details about her little house on Tulane Drive. She has suggested to Jonathan—she never calls him Tank— that they temporarily enroll him in a school in Alexandria, where he can get back to playing some football, at least until New Orleans and John Curtis are reopened. He won't even talk about it. When he finally manages to get through to his friend Preston Numa one day, he learns that Preston is leaving his Texas motel and will immediately move into an apartment with his mom in Baton Rouge, and, incredibly, he's already planning to enroll at Woodlawn High there.

Preston tells Tank that he's not crazy about the idea. But, like Tank and Althea, Preston and his mom are a team, with no siblings and no father in the house. Preston's mom has a good job with the IRS and can't take a chance on turning down her employer's request that she transfer. Preston really has no choice, he tells Tank.

Along with Mike Walker, Tank and Preston were planning to be the rock-solid core of the Patriots' defense this year. Preston is a born and bred New Orleanian and a lifelong Saints fan (on his MySpace page, he lists football as his occupation and describes himself as a "7th ward hardhead") and the thought of moving to Baton Rouge is killing him. He asks Tank to come to Woodlawn High with him, but Tank says no thanks.

Tank's conversation with Preston only firms his resolve . . . there's no way he's going to start fresh with a strange new school or team.

"It's the law," his mother says to him at one point. "You have to go back to school."

A few of the relatives chime in, too. But Tank is adamant. He's not going to school anywhere except John Curtis, and he's not playing football for some other team. He plans to keep fishing until he gets his life and his friends back.

Kenny Dorsey has already learned that his home and his entire Lower Ninth Ward neighborhood have been destroyed. In recent days, the huge barge that landed on his house has become a national symbol of how disproportionately Katrina terrorized the Lower Ninth. Now, Kenny is wondering if his school is gone, too. His family has spent six tense days in the crowded home of his great-aunt in Lake Charles. Kenny is normally a quiet, impassive kid, so his dad can't tell just what's going on inside his head. He's mostly been playing Nintendo games with his sister and cousins. Occasionally, he walks off by himself and, when he returns, his dad has noticed more than once that his eyes are moist and red.

The TV news repeatedly shows aerial shots of the steel-hulled cargo barge called ING 4727, which had recently delivered a load of cement to New Orleans via the Mister Go waterway and came loose from its moorings during the storm. Already, a group of Lower Ninth homeowners are preparing to sue the barge owners, but the Dorseys don't hold out much hope that they'll see any financial recompense.

The barge, which will soon become a morbid tourist attraction, visited by Prince Charles and the Rev. Jesse Jackson, is a constant reminder to the Dorseys that there's nothing left for them in New Orleans. They're planning to move into an apartment in Lake Charles. Kenny's parents are figuring they'll hunker down there while they decide what to do next, and whether to return to New Orleans at all. Kenny is desperate to return to John Curtis but, in the meantime, he and his sister will enroll at LaGrange High School, where Kenny will talk to the coach about joining the team. Kenny's dad is even thinking of bending the family's religious rules and allowing Kenny to play football on Fridays and Saturdays, to give his son an escape from his ravaged new life.

Kyle Collura has been at his aunt's house in McCall Creek, Mississippi, a rural patch more than a hundred miles north of New Orleans. His aunt owns a large piece of farmland, and Katrina's winds shredded trees and fences that have littered the property. Kyle and one of his cousins have been busy cleaning up. He's actually relieved to have work to do. It's a good workout, and will help him stay in shape, and it keeps his mind off the sadness and confusion. With the power out at his aunt's house, he and his family went days without seeing any of the televised images of Katrina's destruction. A cousin has since brought a generator, and they've been able to hook up the television. Like Tank, Kyle keeps trying to find ways to stay away from the screen.

Kyle typically handles life's ups the same as the downs, with a laconic shrug and a mellow self-confidence, a belief that everything will work itself out. Now he's worried about everything: his house, his school, and his football season, which seems to be over before he's even had a chance to throw his first completion in a real game. He was hugely relieved to get through to J.T. late last night. Yet, while J.T. assured him that the school was fine and they'll reopen in a week or two, it just doesn't seem possible. Catching bits of TV news, it's hard to imagine he'll be back home any time soon. Still, J.T. told Kyle he was looking for games, and if there's even a chance they'll be playing again, Kyle will keep chopping wood and hauling brush, maintaining his body as best he can.

Kyle's mom is counting on J.T.'s assurances that John Curtis will reopen soon, and has decided not to enroll Kyle at another school— not yet. His father, a carpenter, has spoken with his boss and plans to head back into Jefferson Parish this weekend to start tackling demolition and cleanup work, and Kyle is hoping his dad will get some better information on the status of their house in Kenner.

Mike Walker has been calling J.T. and e-mailing the other coaches constantly but hasn't had any luck getting through to any of them. His dad has been frantically trying to get word on his hospitalized mother. On Thursday afternoon, three days after Katrina, he finally reached a Red Cross worker who said that Mike's grandmother had been safely evacuated from the hospital in Kenner. She was loaded onto the back of a pickup truck and taken to nearby Louis Armstrong Airport, where she was transferred by plane to a South Carolina hospital. She's still in critical condition, but has stabilized, and it looks like she's out of danger and going to pull through. Mike's father has flown to be with her. Meanwhile, Mike and his mom and sister checked out of their Dallas hotel and drove to Lafayette, Louisiana, where, incredibly, they've found an available hotel room, mainly because there's a messy hole in the ceiling.

The Walkers live in the Jefferson Parish town of Metairie, just west of downtown New Orleans, and they're terrified that the flooding has spread into their neighborhood. Mike's dad, a manager at a Folger's coffee plant in the city, and his mom, who works as a legal secretary, are also both worried about the status of their jobs, though they've learned that the huge Folger's manufacturing plant wasn't too badly damaged.

Mike keeps punching the buttons of his cell phone's tiny keypad, sending text messages to friends, such as "where u at?" and "how u doing?" or just "sup?" If he hears from any of them, his first follow-up question is, "u playing football?"

On Friday, he finally has a real conversation with his teammate, Jacob Dufrene, who is back at his home in Cut-Off, which is south of New Orleans and, despite some storm damage, at least habitable. Jacob is thinking about enrolling in a new school near his home, and invites Mike to come live with him for awhile and attend the new school. Mike isn't ready for that yet. Like Tank, he can't imagine starting over at a new school.

That same afternoon, Mike's mom, Donna, finally reaches Coach Johnny. Donna says she's thinking of sending Mike to live with the Dufrene family, where he and Jacob could go to school together until John Curtis reopens. Johnny tells her it'd be okay for Mike to enroll elsewhere, but that he should think twice before playing football there: According to the state's high school athletics rules, if Mike plays for another team, he'll jeopardize his eligibility to play for Curtis later in the season.

Mike is usually the family joker and loves to make his parents or sister crack up, but he has been oddly quiet the past few days. On Friday night, with his dad still in South Carolina, and with the offer to live with the Dufrenes weighing on his mind, his mom and sister decide to take him out to eat at his favorite restaurant, Outback Steakhouse. On the way home, Mike sees some lights up ahead and bolts upright in his seat, shouting to his startled mom, "Look! Lights! *Football* lights!" He begs his mom to go watch the game. As they pull into the parking lot, the familiar blare of marching bands and the cheerleaders and the crowds gives him the chills. They get some popcorn and sit in their car in the parking lot, looking out on the field as two unknown teams go at it. At first, Mike is loving it, feeling that familiar adrenaline rush. Then he starts to think about how he should be out on the field right now, slamming into Cottonwood's offense.

Mike knows his main weakness as a linebacker is a lack of speed, and he was determined to make up for it by playing smart this year, reading the offense well and being a factor on every play. He did just that in the jamboree game, and knows J.T. was impressed. Suddenly, the game seems far away, and his enthusiasm wanes.

At halftime, he turns to his mother and says, "Okay, we can go now."

The hotel in Lafayette has a pool and a small exercise room, and Mike decides to start swimming laps, lifting weights, and taking long runs on the treadmill. He's not ready to transfer to another school, and he's not going to let himself get out of shape.

Though a few John Curtis graduates have made it to the NFL—an impressive feat for a school with fewer than 500 students—and many have played at top colleges, the truth is that few Patriots have a real shot at top Division I-A colleges, much less the NFL. High school, as J.T. often tells them, may be the high-water mark of their sports careers. Yet, if there's even a slim chance of making it to

LSU or Ole Miss, the time is now, this season. A player simply has to be seen by the scouts or captured on film, making great plays.

College recruiters have been watching Joe McKnight since he was a freshman, and were eager to see how he'd perform this year. Joe knew they'd be watching and spent every day this summer working out in the weight room and running laps at Lincoln Playground while wearing a weighted vest. He knows he's good, but also knows there are others better than him, and he intends to keep working harder than all the rest.

J.T. has already been prepping Joe on how to speak to college coaches. J.T. will call a coach, because NCAA rules prohibit them from calling Joe, and then hand the phone to Joe, who speaks quietly, twirling the cord in his hand. "Yes, sir . . . Yeah, I know a lot about Michigan," he says. "No, sir, I don't have any questions . . . Yeah, I'll try to come up and see you soon."

Football has always loomed as Joe's ticket out of Kenner, and now the season is starting without him. Joe is still living with his friends, the Tuckers, in Shreveport. After a few days at a Holiday Inn, they've all moved into an apartment in town, owned by a relative of the Tuckers. Joe has finally spoken with his mom, Jennifer, and learned that she and his little brother, Jonathan, safely evacuated and are staying with relatives in Innis, fifty miles northwest of Baton Rouge.

Mike Tucker has enrolled his son and daughter at nearby Evangel Christian Academy, a well-known private school in Shreveport that's taking in hurricane evacuees and, in many cases, waiving tuition. Joe is thinking about signing up at Evangel, too.

Evangel is similar in many ways to John Curtis: a small school that's turned itself into a football powerhouse with a string of football championships behind it. The school's most recent star, John David Booty, is now at the University of Southern California as backup quarterback, poised to take over when the starting quarterback, Matt Leinart, graduates. Leinart will go on to win the 2005 Heisman Trophy, bound for the NFL.

As at Curtis, the Evangel coaches have been accused of running a football factory. When other Louisiana schools complain about the dominance of a few of the state's football programs, Evangel and John Curtis are always mentioned in the same sentence. And when the LHSAA last year changed its rules and stopped allowing smaller schools to play up against larger schools, Evangel was bumped all the way back from the state's highest division, 5A, to the lowest, 1A.

That's fine with Joe, who just wants to play. Ever since third grade, when he started at John Curtis, Joe has felt most at home on the football field. It's the place where he feels in control of his life, where everything else just disappears.

He still remembers his first touchdown.

The first time he touched the ball on offense, he fumbled, and continued to fumble the rest of his third-grade season. Coach Corey believed in Joe and kept calling the same plays and kept giving Joe the ball. In the season's last game, the Patriots were losing 6–0, and Joe just kept fumbling. Then, late in the game, on a run up the middle, he broke through a hole and sprinted fifty yards for his first touchdown, which tied the game. Corey went for a two-point conversion, calling the exact same play. Joe was stopped at the goal line, but managed to spin around his tacklers to score, giving the Patriots the victory and teaching him a lesson he'd never forget. He had recently recounted that very story for a *Times-Picayune* reporter, and the lesson he said he learned was this: "Don't look back."

With his return to John Curtis now in question, Joe has decided not to look back. Evangel's season has been unscathed by Katrina. The team, the Eagles, is known for its fast-paced, air-attack offense and—if Joe plays for them—he might be able to rack up more points than he would have at Curtis. And maybe, like John David Booty before him, he'll get scooped up by USC and be on his way to the NFL. In the short term, he'll be able to create a new life for himself, a fresh start. If the Tuckers stay in Shreveport, maybe he can keep living with them. There'd at least be food in the house. Maybe he'd even have a bed.

He hasn't mentioned these plans to Mike Tucker yet. Nor to his mom.

Joe has always been afraid of moving out of his mom's house for good. Whenever he stays with friends or cousins or the Tuckers, the understanding is always that it's just a temporary thing. To make a permanent move would be like giving up on his mom. Katrina may be providing Joe the perfect excuse to make a definitive move without hurting her. He tries not to think about how J.T. and the other assistants and his teammates at Curtis will react to his transfer.

The Curtis coaches have been so good to him, but he can't help it. The idea of playing for Evangel is too alluring: *a new beginning, new people, and a new place.*

He finally visits with the coaches at Evangel. One of them, Ronnie Alexander, knows all about Joe McKnight: "One of the best athletes to ever walk on this campus," he'll later say, and encourages Joe to enroll. The coaches even offer to let Joe play running back and wide receiver. He'll be their new star.

J.T. knows he's got to act fast to keep his team together and rebuild the season.

He starts calling coaches all around the state, even teams in Florida and other southern states, trying to land games. "Our responsibility is to make our kids realize we all have to pick ourselves up, that we all have to move forward," he tells his sons. "We can't allow ourselves to get down. And we're going to have to do a good job as the adults to make sure we keep them busy, keep them moving toward the future."

He quickly learns that the four schools in his new Class 2A district, all of them roughly an hour west of New Orleans, have not sustained any significant hurricane damage and will be able to play their regularly scheduled games. For this season, anyway, the move to the distant district has ironically worked in their favor. Those district games won't begin until late October, however, so J.T. needs to find opponents willing to play sooner. He keeps calling every coach and every school he can think of.

When he finally manages to land a game against Ferriday High, a big school north of New Orleans across the Mississippi from Natchez, the other coaches, thrilled at the prospect of salvaging their season, begin frantically calling their players.

Each coach is responsible for a dozen or so players, whose cellphone numbers and e-mail addresses they'd collected at the Saturday practice before Katrina. They send an e-mail, then try the cell phone. If they manage to get through to a player by cell, they quickly tell the kid that the school is fine and that the football season will happen. They then tell the kid to call, e-mail, or text message other players, and to spread the word that John Curtis is reopening soon. If they can't get through by cell they send a text message that reads "we are opening" or "we're coming back" or "everything is fine."

Johnny, whose Nextel cell phone has worked better than the others for making and receiving calls, is among the few coaches who's communicated with numerous players, mostly via short text message saying "heard school's not opening" and "heard school washed away" and "what do we do?" Those he's been able to talk to have sounded near tears asking him what they should do, telling him their parents are pressuring them to enroll at other schools. He reassures them that the school is coming back, but the parents still find it hard to believe that John Curtis can reopen soon. They're still hearing so much bad news about how long New Orleans area schools will be closed.

Complicating the situation further is an emergency ruling by the LHSAA to suspend its normal eligibility rules and allow displaced student athletes from storm-affected parishes to play for any school they choose, essentially making them free agents. The prohibition against returning to play for Curtis later, which Johnny had just warned Mike Walker's mother about, has been lifted. Kids are being lured to schools with appealing recruitment offers. Larry Favre, the coach at Fontainebleau, which John Curtis played in the jamboree game, is interviewed on ESPN and accuses another school of looting four of his players. The head of the LHSAA, Tommy Henry, acknowledges to a *Times-Picayune* reporter that he's heard about coaches volunteering at shelters as a way to recruit new players.

Johnny receives calls from players saying that schools are pressuring them, telling them John Curtis is underwater or fell down. Some private schools are offering free tuition or assuring kids spots on the varsity team. For the seniors, the offers are enticing; they're worried about not playing at all in their last year of high school.

Johnny finds himself practically shouting at kids or their parents, trying to convince them that John Curtis and the surrounding River Ridge neighborhood is not underwater. "I'm tellin' ya, I'm standing on the field right now," he tells one player. He even offers to drive by families' houses to assure them it's still standing and not flooded.

"I'm in front of your house," he'll tell them. "It's *fine*."

The John Curtis coaches learn that one of the first post-Katrina football games in Greater New Orleans will be played Friday, September 9, when the St. James Wildcats host the Terrebonne Tigers. "We know it's not the most important thing," St. James's coach Rick Gaille tells the *Times-Picayune*. "But it does give some sign that normalcy for everybody could be right around the corner."

Tommy, Johnny, and a few of the assistant coaches decide to drive down. The Patriots are scheduled to face St. James later in the season, so tonight is a great chance to scout them. With so many schools still closed, coaches and players converge on St. James and sit in the stands alongside rival coaches and players from all across southern Louisiana. The game is like a reunion of sorts, and the talk revolves around which schools are open and which aren't, about whose season is dead and whose is still alive.

At one point, a coach from a rival school leans over to Leon's son, Steve, and says, "I heard John Curtis fell down." Another coach adds, "Yeah, and I heard Joe McKnight ain't coming back." In no time, others chime in, having fun with it, "John Curtis is not going to be the same," one taunts, "you all are going to lose McKnight."

What was supposed to be a nice break from the sweaty chores at the school and the increasingly tense confines of the Baton Rouge apartments has suddenly become a bust, an infuriating reminder that life for the John Curtis Christian School and its Patriots is still up in the air. On the drive home, Tommy expresses the dread the others are feeling.

"I don't like this," he says. "It doesn't feel right." He can't stop thinking about kids he's worked with for years—*his* kids—suiting up to play football for a rival coach, and asks the others, "Do I really want other coaches to coach *my* players?"

Back in the apartments, Jeff has more bad news.

While watching the sports report on Johnny's television, he saw a brief clip about the Evangel Eagles, who lost 45–10 to the Texas High Tigers of Texarkana.

The only bright spot for the Eagles was the opening kickoff. On that play, Joe McKnight, the Eagles' new all-purpose kick returner, punt returner, running back, and wide receiver, caught the kickoff at the Eagles' ten-yard line, blasted past the first few defenders, spun, and sprinted down the sideline. As soon as he hit the open field, he opened his stride, looking effortless as he passed midfield. A defender approached from the side, and Joe reached out with one arm and swatted the guy down like he was a mosquito. Joe seemed headed for a touchdown, but was finally pushed out of bounds inside the fifteen-yard line, having taken the ball back seventy-five yards. He twisted his ankle at the end of the play, limped off the field, and did not return again all night.

"I don't like this at all," Tommy says, and shuts the door to the small bedroom where his wife and two children are sleeping.

10

Reentry

During the school year, the Curtis family works side by side all day in a pressure-cooker environment of constantly flaring crises. Phones usually start ringing at dawn: a bus broke down and ten kids need a ride; two teachers called in sick; a couple of baseball players broke the team curfew.

After a day of teaching, feeding, disciplining, and coaching hundreds of children and teens, you'd think the Curtises would want nothing more than a night of peace, maybe even a few drinks, but few of them drink liquor. "I just don't like the taste," J.T. says. Instead of solitude, they thrive on being together. Once a week, the family converges on J.T. and Lydia's house for a weekly family dinner. On weekends, piles of them get together for church, barbecues, and sporting events. They enter each others' homes without invitation, without even knocking. They even vacation together, the bulk of the clan heading each August to a cluster of adjacent beach houses in Florida. Cousins grow up together, as close as brothers and sisters.

But no one ever wanted to be this close. Like so many of Katrina's evacuees, they're dealing with the stresses of cramped quarters and the mounting anxiety of an uncertain future.

Three dozen Curtises are crammed together in their four small apartments. If anyone wakes up at night to go to the bathroom, *everyone* wakes up. The young kids are having trouble sleeping and are missing their own beds and bedrooms, their toys and games. The grownups take turns keeping the younger ones busy, working on

167

spelling and math quizzes or taking them outside to kick a soccer ball around. The meager playground keeps the little ones occupied for an hour or so, but the nearby garbage bins are overflowing and the grounds are filthy and smelly. The apartment complex has a swimming pool, but it's closed.

Two full weeks after the storm, hundreds of thousands are still displaced in hotel rooms, racking up credit-card debt or cutting deeply into their savings. They are sleeping on couches or air mattresses in the homes of friends and relatives, whose nerves have been frayed by the onslaught of so many unexpected visitors.

It's difficult to drive around Baton Rouge, because so many people are in the same boat, tens of thousands of refugees in an unknown city. One day, a large group of Curtises decides to brave the traffic and visit a nearby shopping mall, where they shuffle around zombielike, unable to muster any enthusiasm for the Gap or the food court. Restaurants are a spotty endeavor, crowded and unappetizing. Even the local Wendy's hamburger joint has run out of beef.

At least for a few days, the Curtis men kept busy heading into River Ridge to clean freezers and chainsaw trees and branches, but they've done all that. Leon's son Preston once said that working at John Curtis—especially when Mr. Curtis was alive—felt like a football game every day of the week. There was always a chore to complete or a class to teach or a disciplinary issue to address or a crisis to solve. They had to be on their toes every moment.

They've never had so little to do in their lives, and the Fairway View Apartments have begun to feel like prison cells.

Johnny's wife, Dawn, is six months pregnant and has been throwing up every other day. She's unsure if it's the pregnancy, the stress, or both. She incessantly calls her home in River Ridge to see if the answering machine clicks on, a sign that the electricity is back. As coach of the John Curtis girls' volleyball team, she is also text messaging her players, sending the same messages the football coaches send their players.

One day, after a shopping trip at Wal-Mart, Dawn begins experiencing painful cramps, which feel like contractions, and she's worried she's having stress-induced premature labor. She calls Johnny, who is helping a friend clean up his church. He rushes back to the apartment and is ready to take her to the hospital, but the cramps subside and they spend the night watching a college football game on television, rattled by the scare.

Johnny had been on edge since well before the storm. Back in March, he was mowing a baseball field when the mower jammed. When he turned off the machine and reached underneath to unclog the grass, the blades shot forward and tore into his hands, nearly severing both thumbs. Surgeons reattached his thumbs, but to prevent infection inserted a pick line in a vein that pumped antibiotics to his heart. He began having anxiety attacks and insomnia and had to see a therapist. The attacks flared up when his grandfather died. And now, he and his pregnant wife are stuck in an apartment in Baton Rouge, and he's worried the attacks and insomnia will return.

For others, everyday problems have become magnified by the forced separation from home. Leon had worried about being able to renew his prescription for the eye drops he takes to prevent his body from rejecting his transplanted corneas. Now, he is running seriously low, but can't reach his doctor and get the prescription refilled. J.T., meanwhile, is limping due to an ankle injury he was supposed to get fixed. He put off the surgery, but now has to wear open-heeled shoes, so he doesn't rub the wounded Achilles tendon and make it worse.

Preston's wife, Andrea, who gave birth to their second child two months ago, is suffering from postpartum depression. Despite her antianxiety medication, she's angry and lashes out at anyone who comes near. Andrea works at The Blood Center in New Orleans, and learns that some of her coworkers who stayed behind had to be rescued from the roof of the flooded building. Her mother-in-law, Leon's wife, Sue, keeps trying to help by taking care of Andrea's two children but one day, Andrea snaps, crying, "Stop trying to take over my family!" She later apologizes, explaining, "I just want to be left alone to cry and be mad and sad."

One night, the family tried to have some fun by throwing a birthday party for Jeff's wife, Toni. For days, Toni had been unable to reach her parents, and was getting increasingly frantic about their safety. The others felt that Toni, and all of them, needed a party. In one of the apartments, they lifted the beds and leaned them against the wall, then whipped together a meal of red beans and rice. Without telling Toni in advance, her parents arrived to surprise her with a huge cake and she burst into tears when they arrived, collapsing into their arms.

Irritations keep mounting. Toni's eye has begun twitching uncontrollably, and Jeff has been taking steroid shots for a horrible case of poison ivy he got clearing brush at the school. It seems as if everyone is sleep-deprived, edgy, hurting. "I have never felt more alone with so many people around me," Toni will later say about this period in limbo.

Leon and Sue's son Steve has been obsessively calling everyone he knows, just hoping to hear a friendly voice. He keeps finding himself suddenly wanting to cry, and when he feels the tears, he dials another number. On the rare occasion that he actually gets through, he tries to keep perfectly still, fearful of losing the cellular signal. Too often, though, the voices are overcome by static and abruptly disappear.

Grumpiest of all is Tommy, who thinks he's going crazy. He doesn't know what to do with himself. He tries watching television, but regularly storms off and sits on the small balcony, staring vacantly, occasionally barking at anyone who comes near. He's been stalking around the apartment, growling, "I've gotta get *out* of here."

It took years for Tommy to get used to the lifestyle he married into, dominated by the demands of John Curtis Christian School. But those cycles and routines have become his life, and now he can't sit still. "I can't do this anymore!" he screams one afternoon, telling Joanna he needs to be in his own environment. He starts packing, but Joanna yells back, telling him he can't split up the family. He knows she's right and stomps back out to the balcony to stare out at the sprawl of apartment buildings.

Even more fragile than the others is Lydia, who frequently breaks into wracking sobs. Her nerves are completely shot. She's terrified that if they can't reopen the school her kids will leave to find jobs elsewhere, and the family will be torn apart. She can't help herself from asking J.T. repeatedly how many students he thinks will return.

"What do you think?" she says. "Will we get a third of the kids back? Half?"

"Lydia, I honestly don't know," J.T. tells her. "I have no idea."

• • •

By Monday, September 12, as the displacement of Greater New Orleans enters its third week, students who have been cut off from the comforting routines of their lives at school begin finding creative ways to communicate with each other. The Internet, e-mail, and text messaging are already compulsive distractions in every teenager's life, but now they've become vital lifelines. That is, when they're working, and when the students can steal a few minutes of computer time.

At libraries or on borrowed laptops, they furiously send e-mails, update their blogs, or send messages to friends via MySpace and Facebook. They view uploaded digital photos of friends, images that remind them of better days. One student, Jasmine Thomas, is already attending a new school in Texas; her father works for the New Orleans Saints, and the team has made San Antonio a temporary home. Jasmine decided she has no interest in the city. "Oh, man. I'm ready to go home," she writes in an e-mail to a friend. "I don't like living in this lame environment. I'm really missing New Orleans food."

Girlfriends post "I love you" messages to boyfriends' My Space pages, and friends fire off "where u at big dawg" and "sup my nigga" messages. One such MySpace profile now reads, "Ima Katrina Survivor who rode out the storm not 2 far away from New Orleans . . . talk about some scary $#!+." Another student, whose father is buried in a low-lying cemetery in an area of heavy flooding, posts this message on her MySpace blog: "August 27, 2005 was the last day of my old life . . . Katrina took my life. She ruined it."

Over the past week, more federal troops have arrived to take control of the city's lawless streets and to evacuate those remaining stranded. More than two hundred thousand evacuees have now been transported to Texas, which is struggling to keep up with the influx. Officials have begun to create makeshift morgues to finally collect the bodies floating throughout New Orleans. No one yet knows how many have died, but Governor Blanco has said she expects the death toll to reach thousands.

The Army Corps of Engineers has made progress sealing the breached levees, but Corps officials have said it will take months for the city to fully drain and dry. President Bush, acknowledging that people "are angry and desperate," has signed a $10.5 billion federal assistance package, and promised that more federal billions are on the way. "The tasks before us are enormous," he says in a speech, "but so is the heart of America. In America, we do not abandon our fellow citizens in our hour of need."

But across the Internet pipeline and the blogosphere—which have become conduits for a giant group therapy session—there is skepticism, doubt, and a deep, shared sorrow. On blogspot.com, a writer named Bobby Schroeder, in his "Bobby's World" blog, tries to capture the collective feelings of anger and despair:

> Every professional journalist I see on tv, read on the paper or the internet, or hear on the radio, is having trouble trying to find the words to say. So how am I, just an amateur blogger, supposed to have a prayer? I wish I could tell what the storm did to my neighborhood, but since it is under maybe 15 feet of water, water that is up to the second-story level in a one-story place of living, I can't . . . I don't know what's going to happen next. We are homeless, unemployed, along with about a million other people. We have about three to four pairs of clothes, some shoes, our end-of-August paychecks, and the few irreplaceable things we were able to cram into our cars. And compared to some people we know, we have a lot. At some point, we will be allowed back in to survey the damage and see if anything is salvagable. We will collect our insurance checks. We will purchase the things we need to . . . basically start over. We have our loved ones and our families and friends. We can start over. We know we will. We just don't know how, or when, or where that will be.

On Tuesday, September 13, Mayor Nagin finally announces that parts of the city will begin reopening to citizens next week. That same afternoon, commercial flights resume at Louis Armstrong International Airport. And two days later, Jefferson Parish officials unveil a staggered re-entry plan, allowing residents to return in stages to different sections of the parish, beginning on Saturday, September 17.

The Curtises immediately decide to reopen the school on Monday, September 19. When they mention their plan to parish officials, they're told that it's too soon. With electricity still out in half the parish and much of the sewage system out of commission, the area is still dangerous and unsanitary, which is why it's been announced that the earliest any public schools will reopen is October 3. The Curtises insist that they're able to reopen sooner than that, and parish officials finally grant them permission to reopen on Monday, September 26.

No way, though, is J.T. going to wait that long to get his team back on the practice field.

He decides to hold a Patriots practice on September 19. Through all of his frantic calling, he's managed to schedule a game for that Friday, the twenty-third, and he's determined to get his kids prepared.

After three weeks of displacement, and with all they've seen and been through, they'll be out of shape, physically *and* mentally. The hardened muscle of late August will have softened. Missing three weeks of almost daily practice and weight-lifting sessions—at the start of the season, no less—is like Lance Armstrong deciding to give up his bike a month before the Tour de France. His players will have lost their focus, the edge that a summer of two-a-day and three-a-day practices develop, and he's worried there may not be enough time in the weird, short season he's putting together for them to regain that intensity.

By cell phone, text message, and e-mail, the coaching staff begins spreading the word. Leon has become a text-messaging whiz. His son, Preston, stays up until two and three calling kids, because that's when he seems to get the best cellular reception.

Occasionally there's an actual conversation between coach and player, and the coaches realize just how right they were to get their kids back as soon as possible. When Johnny gets through to defensive back Kelby Wuertz, he can hear the emotion in Kelby's voice. Kelby has been on the verge of tears in recent days worrying about having to transfer to a new school. He tells Johnny, "This is the first time in three years I've been happy to hear from you."

J.T. often tells his players, "God has a plan for you." Oscar Ponce de Leon, a massive, six-foot-three, 290-pound defensive lineman who lives in Kenner, has been thinking about that and what a lousy plan it turns out God had in store. Oscar evacuated to Baton Rouge and then San Antonio, where he watched the Saints play at their temporary camp. Every day he's been feeling more distressed that his dreams of playing college ball are over. He's a senior, and if he doesn't play this season, he may never play again.

Just as he is beginning to resign himself to going to another high school, he gets a call from J.T. The school is opening, the season is on, and there's a practice at two o'clock, next Monday, J.T. tells him. Oscar is stunned and speechless.

Maybe there was a plan after all.

Residents have been told they can now visit their homes between the hours of six in the morning and six in the evening. They must leave before dark because the city is still so dangerous.

Thus begins a period of reckoning, taking stock of what was lost and what was spared. Many thousands of evacuees are now finally able to see for themselves what has happened to their homes. As with the stages of grief, for many the initial shock of the storm will be replaced by a deeper, more mournful ache.

Jesse Danna, a gangly sophomore Patriots wide receiver with tightly curled red hair, lives beside the 17th Street Canal in Lakeview. He and his parents knew, when they first heard about the break in the 17th Street levees, that their home was in jeopardy. But because their house was nearly a mile from the breach, they held out a sliver of hope that somehow it wasn't too badly flooded. Jesse and his parents decide to venture into the city and have a look. Their neighborhood is still under six to ten feet of water, but they've borrowed a boat from Jesse's uncle, determined to see at last just how bad the damage to their home is. They drive into New Orleans as far as they can, until they are stopped by roadblocks at the edge of the Lakeview flooding.

The National Guard helps them launch the boat from the corner of Veterans Highway and Fleur de Lis, the main street through Lakeview. As they motor down the street, the three of them fall silent beneath the motor's *put-a-put-a-put-a*.

They zigzag between fallen trees and upside-down cars, past a house with a car punched through the front window and another with a refrigerator hanging off the roof. The houses all display the ominous spray-painted symbols of the search and rescue teams. Jesse and his parents can't recall if 1 and 2 means people were found dead or alive. Minnows skitter through the water, and it's creepy to think about what lies beneath them.

Jesse is quiet the whole way, and they're all silently praying. Then they turn the corner and see it. Their house is a duplex that sits atop a high foundation, with steps leading up to the front door. They rent out the top floor and live downstairs, which now bears an unmistakable water mark, almost as high as the second story. The water is still almost six feet deep in the yard and about three feet above the first floor. They float *over* the Toyota they'd left behind in their driveway and then up to the front door. They can see through the broken windows that the home is still a flooded mess. Jesse uses a hammer and crowbar to break through the door, which is swollen shut.

He crawls inside and calls out to his parents, "It looks like a blender went through here." The ceilings have caved in and the furniture is in pieces. Antiques that had been handed down over the decades are shattered. Everything is covered in a slimy sludge. He wades through his living room, like he's searching through an archeological dig, looking for anything at all to salvage.

Finally, he makes his way to his bedroom. The door is blocked by a foosball table and won't open, so Jesse punches a hole in the wall and crawls through. He's hoping to find his new baseball bat, his trophies, his favorite shirt, and the shotgun his grandfather made for him. When he finds the shotgun, he sees that the wooden stock, which his grandpa had carved by hand, is waterlogged and distorted, and the metal barrel is rusted. Holding the ruined gun, he begins to cry, then starts tearing apart his waterlogged dresser, in search of his favorite shirt. His parents, bobbing outside the window, peer in and see their son, normally so stoic and strong, slumped on his mold-caked bed, sobbing. The reality of all they've lost hits them, and they break down, too.

A few days later, Jesse runs into Coach Rob at a grocery store in Many, Louisiana, near where Jesse's family has been staying, and Coach Rob tells him that the school is okay. Jesse's folks had been thinking they were going to have to enroll Jesse at a nearby school, but they'd been stalling, and now Jesse is hugely relieved. A day later, he receives a follow-up text message from Coach Jeff with the news that there's a football practice scheduled for September 19, at two o'clock. He has no idea where he'll be living, but Jesse knows he'll be at that practice.

Many students and parents receiving calls or e-mails from the Curtises are still incredulous that the school can really be reopening any time soon. Reports say there will be no electricity in the city for three months or more. Much of Jefferson Parish is still without water, power, or sewerage. The word from the Curtises is the only good news they've had since the storm hit, but it just sounds too good to be true. For Patriot players, though, the news is a lifeline.

Kyle Collura has by now visited his home and it was hardly a joyful homecoming. After speaking with J.T. by phone in the middle of the night two weeks earlier, and learning that the school was unharmed, Kyle and his parents drove into New Orleans last week from their Mississippi evacuation post to take a look at their home. Driving nervously along debris-choked streets, they felt like the only people in Kenner. The damage was random: Some houses were intact, but the Rite Aid Pharmacy was just gone, apparently hit by one of the tornadoes that had swirled inside Katrina, and the roofs of some houses were torn off or battered.

When they turned on to their street, they could tell immediately that it had flooded. At their house, the fence was gone, and though the big magnolia out front had survived, other trees had fallen all over the yard. The floodwaters had risen halfway up the Lincoln Town Car that Kyle's grandfather had given him, and the car seemed beyond repair. They walked up the front steps, had to kick in their front door, and were immediately overcome by swarms of flies and the stench of rotten food. The water had risen at least eight inches, and the walls were covered with the creepy green-black fur of mold and mildew.

Kyle and his dad, Steve, started tearing out sodden carpeting and moldy drywall, while his mom, Melody, waited for three hours in a shopping center parking lot to get water, ice, and MREs from National Guard troops. They realized they can't move into their home any time soon, and at dusk they left Kenner and drove back toward Mississippi.

No matter. Kyle is determined to be at Monday's practice, and will stay that night at his grandfather's house in Metairie. His parents are still trying to figure out where they'll all end up living, hoping they won't need one of the FEMA trailers.

Many of his teammates are finding their homes trashed, too.

After two weeks of fishing, hour after hour, day after day, Tank English has caught just two fish. He's never been so bored in all his life, and when he learns from Coach Johnny about the practice on the nineteenth, he tells Johnny it's the best call he'd ever gotten in his life, and then tells his mom that nothing is going to keep him from being there.

On Thursday, September 15, Tank and his mom drive into Kenner toward their house. All through their neighborhood roofs are missing and trees have slammed into homes. When they pull up to their house, the roof is thankfully intact. But when Tank shoves open the front door and steps inside, there's a heart-breaking *squish*.

The water had risen to three feet inside the house and, after sitting there for more than a week, baked by the sun, the house has become a giant Petri dish, with fuzzy mold crawling up the walls and across the furniture, blooming in closets and drawers. Everything is ruined—clothing, shoes, electronics. Tank counts ten wrecked pairs of tennis shoes, but finds one pair on top of the water heater that survived. All of his sports trophies are ruined, as is the All-Star jacket he loved. He tells himself, "You can always buy new clothes."

Before evacuating, Tank's mom had taken pictures off the walls and collected photo albums and put them atop the refrigerator. However, when the water poured inside, it lifted the buoyant fridge and toppled it. Two pictures smashed atop the stove and were saved, but everything else landed in the water, including Althea's wedding album, which held some of the best and only photographs of her now deceased husband.

Althea has learned that her day-care center also flooded, as she had feared, and the building sustained serious structural damage. She will not be able to reopen soon, if ever. Like countless others returning to New Orleans, she and her son are confronting two stark, unthinkable facts: no home, and no job.

As they drive back out of Kenner, Althea frets about the overwhelming difficulties ahead, wishing desperately her husband were still alive. Who will fix their home? Who will pay for it? Where will she work? Where will they live?

The next day, she calls J.T. to talk about her situation, and he offers a suggestion.

"Why not let Jonathan stay with us?"

J.T. and Lydia are planning to move back into their house in a few days. J.T. tells Althea that Tank would have his own room and could walk the few blocks from the house to and from school and football practice. That would allow her to take care of her urgent problems, like the displaced elderly relatives now relying on her help.

When she mentions the idea to Tank, he tells her he's been so bored he wants to move in with Coach J.T. immediately. The idea of giving her son his own bed, not to mention something of a father figure, is enormously comforting to her, and she agrees to drive him into River Ridge that Saturday, September 17.

The coaches have no idea how many of their kids received their messages and how many will show for Monday's practice. J.T. has decided that even if only a quarter of his one hundred Patriots show up, they're playing. They need a season, and he's going to give it to them. It may end up being the ugliest Patriots season since his first, in 1969, when J.T. struggled to a 0–10 finish with just twenty-five players. But J.T. figures that even a losing season would be better than none at all.

Unfortunately, one player he's learned won't be coming on Monday is Joe McKnight.

He heard about Joe's first game at Evangel, how he ran the opening kickoff back seventy-five yards and almost scored. He hates to lose Joe, but J.T. has never been one to beg. If a player wants to leave, he lets them. That's what he did when Johnnie Thiel took off. His message is . . . *you need us more than we need you.*

He has to give Joe credit, though. Football is his great gift, his ticket to a new life, and Joe isn't taking any chances. As always, he's doing what he needs to do to survive. And at Evangel, he might just become the touchdown-scoring machine that the John Curtis program doesn't make concessions to. Still, it's a harsh blow, and J.T.

hates the thought of missing the chance to coach Joe for two more years.

The truth is, as much as J.T. likes to maintain his you-need-us-more-than-we-need-you attitude toward players, Joe is different. He's like family to the Curtises, who know bits and pieces of the story of Joe's childhood and have helped him, his brother, and his sister, whenever they can, with car rides, a meal, a couple of bucks. The entire team is familial with and protective of Joe. Losing him will devastate them. Out of the thousands of Patriots J.T. has coached over the years, Joe may be the best of them all.

J.T. is also deeply worried that Joe has switched to Evangel to get away from the troubles of his life, and he's afraid that the coaches there won't give him the same level of steady support he got at Curtis, even though he's sure they'll make him feel like a star.

Sure enough, at Evangel, the coaches have greeted Joe like he's special—and it feels good. He is quickly becoming a school celebrity and, with the twisted ankle he sustained in last week's game now healed, he can't wait for this Friday's game.

Two days before that game, J.T. finally gets a chance for a long telephone conversation with Joe. J.T. is hunkered down in his Baton Rouge apartment, along with Tommy, who has spent so much time with Joe. He tries to convince Joe that Curtis is still the right place for him, that it's his home and his family, as it has been for years. J.T. repeats the offer he's made time and again to let Joe stay at his house. He tells Joe that he won't be alone because Tank is going to be moving into his house, too. And he reminds Joe that he'd have his own room and bed. But Joe says, "No, thanks." He's staying at Evangel.

J.T. wants to say more, to convey to Joe how much he means to him and his family, but he can't quite bring himself to get the right words out.

"Here," J.T. says, holding the phone up for Tommy. "You talk to him."

Tommy shakes his head, but J.T. waves the phone until Tommy takes it.

Tommy has spent untold hours in the weight room with Joe and has always been able to talk to him, even when—maybe especially when—Joe loses his temper and has one of his fits, berating himself,

"I'm nothin' but a *thug.*" Tommy probably knows Joe better than any of the other coaches, but is reluctant to talk to him now because of what he is about to say. He takes the phone into another room and shuts the door.

"Listen, Joe," Tommy says. "I'm gonna tell you something nobody else is gonna tell you. If you need to stay at Evangel to get away from your life and to start over, I understand that, and I'm not gonna tell you you're making a wrong decision.

"But if you stay at Evangel because you're running away from your life, and if you think by running it's all gonna go away, then you're making the wrong decision."

Tommy reminds Joe that J.T. cares about him, even if he doesn't always know how to show it, and that the other coaches and players care about him, too. He also assures him that their disrupted season is going to get pieced back together, that there's plenty of football left to play this fall. But, Tommy says, whatever he decides, he should make sure it's what's best for Joe McKnight in the long run.

"I love you," he says. "And I won't hold it against you if it's what you need to do."

Two days later, Joe is dressed in the red-white-and-blue uniform of the Evangel Eagles, for a game against the powerful Lobos of Longview High, Texas.

Most of the football games in the southern half of Louisiana are still canceled, but way up north in Shreveport, the Eagles are into their third game. They've lost their first two, one of the worst starts in recent school history, but the coaches, parents, students, and alumni are all counting on their new star to get them back into contention.

Playing an hour west of Shreveport, in the Lobos' huge stadium in East Texas, the Evangel Eagles are stifled on their first possession and forced to punt. Three plays later, the Lobos score, taking a 7–0 lead. Joe is back to receive the kickoff, along with his speedy new friend, Ramon Broadway, but the kick flies to Ramon's side of the field. Helped by a fierce block from Joe, Ramon runs the kick back eighty-two yards for a touchdown.

The Lobos score on their next possession, and Joe and Ramon are again back to receive the kickoff. This time, the ball comes to Joe, who catches it cleanly and then, as he's been so rigorously taught, takes a half-step backwards, waiting for his blockers to line up in front of him.

Joe has often been asked what he sees when he has a football in his hands, and he always gives the same answer: the end zone. He doesn't even see his would-be tacklers, and instead *feels* them and, on pure instinct, tries to find a path between them all. When the Lobos' kickoff lands in Joe's gut, he cradles the ball with both hands, bullies his way over and through a few defenders, and, as soon as he reaches the open field, he switches the ball to his right hand and starts pumping, finding what J.T. calls his second gear.

In a trademark Joe McKnight run, he opens up his stride and streaks eighty-one eloquent yards into the end zone, ten yards ahead of the nearest defender.

The Eagles will not score again, and go on to lose the game by the demoralizing score of 52–14. But Joe leads his team in rushing for the night. He catches three passes and earns a total of 138 yards on five kick returns, scoring half the team's fourteen points.

The next day, Tank arrives at J.T.'s house, carrying a duffel bag that contains just about all his worldly possessions: a couple of changes of clothes and two pairs of tennis shoes. As Tank settles into his new home, he is sickened to learn that Joe, who has been his good friend for most of his life, is no longer a Patriot. The team had so much riding on Joe, especially this newly reshuffled, botched-up season, and now he's gone.

Practice is just two days away, and the question that now haunts every player and coach is, how many Patriots will still be Patriots come next week?

11

I'm Not Gonna Cancel the Game!

After two weeks of more than thirty Curtises living practically on top of each other, the family begins returning home to River Ridge the weekend of September 16. Some leave Baton Rouge on Friday and others on Saturday, bringing to an end the longest period most of them have ever been away from John Curtis Christian School. They were hugely relieved and grateful to have secured the apartments there, but now they can't wait to leave.

Friday is J.T. and Lydia's thirty-seventh wedding anniversary. When they got married in 1968, they both knew that the start of football season was a terrible time for a football coach's wedding, and J.T. usually forgets their anniversary. This year, they have both forgotten.

J.T. and Lydia arrive in Jefferson Parish that afternoon. It's the first time Lydia has been back since the hurricane, and she's a nervous wreck as they exit Interstate 10 and head south to River Ridge. She grows quiet and tense as they stop at a security post, where soldiers check their drivers' licenses before waving them through. Though she's seen much of it on television, the devastation of the region is a piercing shock. At the house, she is relieved to see for herself that the big family room that's become the central hub of her family's life really hasn't been harmed. But J.T. forgot to warn her about the fallen tree that punched a hole in the ceiling above her den. Although the ceiling caved in and smashed her desk and chair, other homes in the neighborhood have sustained far more damage, and the floodwaters didn't come anywhere near her house. Lydia is deeply grateful to find her home still standing and largely spared. She dives into cleaning up the mess in the den and unpacking, and then starts preparing Jeff and Johnny's old room for Tank.

Late that afternoon, she drives to the grocery store, which is mobbed with returning residents trying to restock their fridges. The shelves are eerily bare, and the store is entirely sold out of milk and meat. The shopping trip takes two hours and she's only able to get a fraction of the things on her list. She'll have to try again tomorrow.

Leon and Sue stay an extra night in Baton Rouge, so that Leon can scout a nearby football team, Donaldsonville High, who the Patriots will face in late October. They drive home the next day. It's Sue's first time back into the city, too, and just as Lydia had experienced, the magnitude of the destruction hits her hard. None of the TV coverage prepared her for seeing the damage with her own eyes. As they reach Jefferson Parish and turn onto Jefferson Highway, the neutral ground is incongruously filled with colorful, hopeful John Curtis signs. Driving past the school, she begins to sob. This is the first time she's cried since the evacuation, and everything she's kept bottled up comes pouring out. As they pull into their driveway she's crying so hard she can barely see. But there, waiting in an expectant huddle, are her three sons, her daughter-in-law, her son's fiancée, and her two grandchildren. She's never been so happy to see people in her whole life.

There's not much time for family catchup, though. Sue and Leon also have to get ready for houseguests. Tonight, one student's family, whose house is full of mold, will move into Leon and Sue's spare bedroom and, later this week, they'll take on two other students whose parents have been unable to get back to the city. Other Curtises, including J.T. mother, Miss Merle, whose house was not damaged, are also opening their homes.

On Sunday, Sue and a few of the other Curtis women help serve spaghetti to people at their church, Riverside Baptist, which has become a makeshift relief center. Volunteers distribute water and serve thousands of meals a day to hungry residents returning to ruined homes and empty grocery shelves.

Johnny, Jeff, and Tommy have wasted no time throwing themselves back into football, along with Leon. They all arrived home Friday afternoon and began to unpack. Joanna planned to host a family dinner at her house but then the phones started to ring, and the men decided to meet Leon and scout the Donaldsonville High game with him. Jeff was about to leave when the electricity went out in his house, a common affliction around the city. The neighborhood still feels like a war zone. The next day, Dawn is outside her house, watching her two sons play in the front yard, when a convoy of ten military trucks rumbles past. In a panic, she screams at her children, "Get inside! Get inside!"

They're all relieved to be back home, but life is far from normal.

On Monday, the coaches arrive early to prepare the field for the day's two o'clock practice. They clear the last bits of brush, leaves, and twigs from the field, then Leon chugs proudly around on his mower. The grass had grown long and straggly, and he hadn't wanted to chop it down all at once. So, he trimmed a bit over the weekend, and today is shaving it down to a half-inch, until the field looks as smooth and green as a golf-course fairway. His sons then paint bright new white yardage marks on the field, and other coaches begin setting out equipment, bags of footballs, orange cones, and blocking dummies. Laying down the lines and lining up the equipment is a deeply therapeutic exercise, almost a religious experience.

J.T. has told his staff that if at least twenty-five players show up today, they'll have enough for a team. Less than that, well, they'll just have to wait and see.

With the field now in perfect shape, an almost surreal patch of pristine normalcy amidst all the Katrina ruin, the coaches head up to their offices to start preparing for a season that's filling up with teams they've never played before. J.T. has so far managed to firm up a half-dozen games, beginning with a three-hour trip north this Friday to face Ferriday High, a well-regarded 3A team near Natchez, Mississippi. The coaches haven't been able to get their hands on any video footage and will be going into Friday's game blind. Although, with Joe McKnight at Evangel, Preston Numa at Woodlawn, and

185

other Patriots playing at other schools, they're still not sure they'll even have enough players to field a team.

That morning of the nineteenth sees a steady, somber parade of evacuees returning from their far-off refugee posts, a sort of anti–Mardi Gras of frazzled families driving slowly along traffic-jammed highways into greater New Orleans, terrified of what they'll find when they pull up to their front door.

Mike Walker and his parents are part of that procession, nervously crawling toward their Metairie home. They can barely squeeze down the streets, weaving beneath canopies of fallen trees and around downed telephone poles and wrecked cars. They stop at Mike's grandmother's house first, expecting to find two dead dogs. She had been rushed to the hospital just before the storm, and Mike's family didn't have time to get the dogs before evacuating. They've brought garbage bags and shovels, expecting to bury them. His grandmother's house is undamaged and, incredibly, the dogs are still alive, though scared and emaciated. Mike and his dad quickly break open boxes of crackers and canned vegetables to feed them.

At Mike's house, they're greeted by the sight of two trees that have fallen on the roof. As they step inside, they hear the terrible *squish* that's greeting so many returnees, and see the high-water mark about a foot up the walls. The smell is revolting. Mike and his dad dig a pit in the backyard and bury the rotten food in a spot that will later become a stunning sunflower garden. They plan to start cutting out the soaked carpeting and padding later that night.

Mike figures that tearing off all the mold-caked sheetrock and rebuilding the interior walls will take a few weeks, but his parents realize they won't be able to live in their house for some time. They decide they should head to the nearest FEMA office right away to apply for a trailer. Mike thinks it's a waste because they'll be back in their house soon enough.

He's anxious to get to practice early to catch up with friends, so, on their way to the FEMA office, just past one o'clock, his parents drop him off at the school.

When he arrives, the school looks deserted, and he heads right to the locker room. There he finds defensive lineman Mike Klein, whose fishing camp was destroyed. Turns out he's been there for hours. He knew practice started at two o'clock, but couldn't wait to get there. He and his parents returned to their Metairie home yesterday and, after finding there was no storm damage, he borrowed his dad's truck and drove to visit the school. He drove back today before noon, walked onto the field, and looked around, wondering *Where is everyone?* Then he went to the locker room, just happy to be inside that dank cave with the musty blue carpet and the wimpy air conditioner.

Soon, Mike Walker's friend, offensive lineman Jeff Middleton, shows up, followed by defensive back Kelby Wuertz. Tentatively, the boys talk a bit about their experiences, and one by one a few more early birds arrive, including Kyle Collura, Andrew Nierman, and Tank English, who's walked over from J.T.'s house.

As the clock ticks closer to two, the dozen boys who've arrived early leave the cool locker room. The coaches are gathered quietly at midfield, and they come over to greet the kids. The silence of the neighborhood is deafening, and the coaches and players are all nervous about why more Patriots haven't shown up. J.T. feels like he's standing inside an empty house, waiting anxiously for the occupants to return home.

Then, just before two, a car pulls up. It's followed shortly by another, and in no time a stream of cars is pulling up, and players begin trickling onto the field. Some of them, after spending weeks in hotel rooms or squeezed into relatives' homes in Texas and Alabama, Florida and Arkansas, have driven hundreds of miles and came straight here, even before going home.

Players march across the field and the coaches greet them with hugs, backslaps, or handshakes. At least two dozen kids have now shown up, and more cars keep arriving. The players mingle awkwardly, and Tank feels like it's the first day of kindergarten, like they're starting all over again getting to know one another. Slowly, they begin to share bits of information. Oscar Ponce de Leon is still in San Antonio and Brandon Scott is in Galveston. Kenny Dorsey is in Lake Charles. His house was destroyed. Preston Numa is playing for Woodlawn. His house is ruined, too. J.T. had invited him to come live at his house, along with Tank, but Preston didn't want to leave his mom. "It's just her and me," he told J.T. Most of the players have information on one or another teammate, but there are more questions than answers. Where's Darryl Brister? Jerico Nelson? Randell Legette? Those who haven't already heard the bad news learn that Joe McKnight is playing for Evangel. What are they gonna do without him?

As the last car pulls away, J.T. figures he's got nearly fifty players back. He's missing some key starters, and over half his team, but they've got a season.

He has decided that he'll get right back to business and throw the kids into drills and routines. His coaching has always been about consistency and repetition, and the last thing his players need now is for him to go soft on them; he's not about to let them down with the indignity of low expectations.

One of J.T.'s well-worn football sayings is, "Those who fail to plan, plan to fail," which he uses to explain to players that they always need a contingency plan. "Without one, you have no chance," he says. It's all about execution, and J.T. often tells players never to let a botched play or missed tackle stop them from executing. "If you get knocked down, get up, and chase the ball," he often says. "You can't ever let what happened in the past affect what you do in the future."

His goal now for this cobbled-together season is to use the rigor of his football preparations to get these kids back to normal and help them bury Katrina in the past. The season will be unlike any he's ever coached, a season as much about recovery as it is about victory. And it may not be pretty. But he has faith that his players will regroup.

J.T. has always prided himself on his stoicism and businesslike approach to the game, and he intends to start today's practice with just a low-key meeting in the gym. "This is gonna be just like any other day," he's told the assistant coaches.

He calls all the players there, to the exact spot where they'd said goodbye nearly a month ago. "We're glad we're back together, and we're glad you're safe," he begins. "We missed you."

Then he tells them about Friday's game against Ferriday High and the next few games he has lined up. He goes over the game plan for the day's practice, a regular Monday routine, just shoulder pads and helmets. Then he stops.

He looks around at his players standing awkwardly before him, many of them skittish and wide-eyed. "You know," he says. "With all this stuff going on and trying to get everything back to normal, I forgot to tell you guys . . . I love each and every one of you."

He walks to the nearest player and throws his arms around the startled kid. Then he turns to the next player and swallows him in a bear hug, too. One by one, J.T. goes around the room giving each player an enormous embrace. He asks the kids how they're making out, how their family is, gathering information for his mental checklist. By the time he's gotten halfway around the circle, the kids begin turning to hug the guys next to them, a few of them in tears.

After the last big bear hug, J.T. steps out in front of his team and says, "Now, it's time to start moving forward . . ."

He calls them together for a prayer, and they all put their hands on each other's shoulders and bow their heads. "Lord, we're thankful for the ones who're here and we pray for those who aren't. Please guide us through the rest of the season, and help us play like Christian gentlemen." J.T. then lifts his head and again looks around at his team.

"And listen, listen up," he says. "This has nothing to do with winning or losing. Because this is not just a football team, not just a school—it's a family. We're a *family*, and we are able to help each other. Remember that *every day* of the season.

"Now," he says matter-of-factly, "let's go to *work*."

As the players take the field, everything around them is eerily quiet. The last time they'd met on this field, dragonflies dive-bombed them, cicadas chirped and buzzed, and the neighborhood was noisy with the hammering and sawing of hurricane preparations. Today, there are no bugs flying or buzzing, no neighbors walking dogs toward PJ's Coffee, which is closed. Scant few cars and trucks are grumbling along nearby roads, and even the main drag, Jefferson

Highway, is mostly vacant. The players dutifully work through their stretching routine and then split up into their position groups, but they're oddly tentative, and the coaches think they actually look a little scared.

On the far end of the field, Coach Rob shouts at the offensive linemen, leading them in a drill against the five-man blocking sled, while Coach Jerry, playing things like normal, starts screaming to a defensive lineman about his stance, "You don't play football with your feet that wide!" Near one end zone, Tommy barks out, "Quick steps, quick steps" to his defensive backs, and, at midfield, Jeff leads the quarterbacks, receivers, and running backs in passing drills. Kyle Collura's arm looks good as he connects to David Seeman and Jesse Danna.

But most of them are sluggish, and the coaches feel their earlier excitement wane as the practice begins to feel morbid. "They're like zombies," is how Leon puts it.

Johnny's working on explode-and-release drills with the linebackers, but they seem worlds away, and he mutters, "Y'all are acting like somebody *died*." As practice winds down, J.T. feels uneasy and tense. Something just doesn't seem right, and he can tell they're all feeling it. He shouts "Everybody *up*!" signaling the end of practice, and the players sprint to midfield. There, he sees a strange look in his players' eyes, as if they've all done something wrong and are afraid of getting caught. He knows it's been good to get the first practice behind them, but he can sense their uneasiness, and assumes it's because so many of their friends and teammates aren't there.

"Every day will be a new day," he assures them. "A better day."

They shuffle into the locker room, many of them lingering for more than an hour before heading back toward home—or, in many cases, to a friend's home or a relative's place or back out of the city to a hotel room. Usually, the end of football practice is a giddy time, with players making plans to meet later for sushi, po'boys, Chinese food, or a trip to the mall. But most of the restaurants are still closed, as are the malls.

Kyle heads back to his house to tear out more smelly, soggy carpeting with his dad; later, he'll stay at an aunt's house. Mike Walker will also tear out carpeting with his dad before spending the night at

Jacob Dufrene's house. Robby Green's dad is waiting for him after practice. They are headed straight to visit their house, for the first time since the storm.

They live in the Algiers section of New Orleans, not far from the Mississippi River bridge where refugees were stopped at gunpoint from entering Jefferson Parish two weeks earlier. Robby's mother and his eight-year-old brother are living in Dallas, where Robby's mom's employer has transferred her. His father, who works for Cox Cable, has also been transferred, to Baton Rouge. With school scheduled to begin next Monday, Robby plans to start living with a classmate's family.

Robby's dad was afraid to take his son with him to see their house, and tried to talk him out of it—a curfew is still in effect for Algiers, and National Guard troops still patrol the streets. But Robby insisted, reminding his father that he'd told him on the eve of Katrina to "be a man." So, the two men ride together toward home that afternoon.

They're relieved to find no flooding, although the exterior was raked and scratched by wind damage and they have no power or water. By the time they finish cleaning up the yard and emptying the rotten food from the fridge, it's dark, and they're afraid to drive through the city after curfew. So, they spend the night, falling asleep on the living-room floor.

The next day, Robby's dad drops him off again at the football field for practice, before heading back to Baton Rouge.

A dozen more kids show for Tuesday's practice, bringing the team above fifty. The morbid mood lifts a bit, and the players seem looser, more relaxed, and less awkward and shell-shocked. J.T. and his assistants feel the group is enough, maybe not for a great team, but one that can play.

There is a another sign of renewal as well. During practice, J.T. notices a tall, wiry African-American kid leaning against the chain-link fence outside the practice field. He starts walking toward the kid, who enters a side gate and lopes across the field toward J.T.

"Can I help you, son?" J.T. asks.

The kid introduces himself as P. J. Smith, a sophomore at Archbishop Rummel High, a Catholic prep school for boys in eastern Jefferson Parish, the school whose coaches cut Mike Walker from their team. P.J. explains that his school is scheduled to reopen in a few days, but he's worried about the football season. Finally, he asks, "Can I play for you?"

P.J. grew up in Kenner, playing football in the same playground leagues as Kyle, Joe, Tank, and Mike. He later moved to Metairie, and started playing football last year as a freshman.

After Katrina, P.J. and his family spent three and a half weeks with aunts, uncles, cousins, and grandparents in Mississippi, twenty-nine family members crammed in a small, three-bedroom house. When they returned home to Metairie, they were relieved to discover that their house wasn't too badly damaged. His school is okay, too, and will be reopening soon. Not only will it be reopening, but Rummel has decided to create the state's first "transition school," taking on fifteen hundred students from closed schools by creating a second school day. The prior thirteen hundred students will attend class from six fifty in the morning to twelve thirty in the afternoon, then the displaced students—mostly girls, and most from Catholic schools in New Orleans—will meet from one thirty to six ten. It will be the first time in Rummel's history that classes are coed.

While P.J. likes the coed idea, he explains to J.T. that he's concerned about football. The Rummel Raiders play in the Catholic league, and many of that league's teams lost their schools, so P.J.'s coach isn't sure they'll have a season at all. That's why P.J. rode his bike all the way over here. He's always heard great things about the John Curtis program and he decided to come see the legendary J. T. Curtis for himself. Watching practice, he was immediately impressed.

J.T. has a good feeling about the kid. He gives him a playful slap on the cheek and says, "Don't worry, son, we'll take care of you."

Bringing P.J. onto the field, he introduces him to the coaches, and after practice finds him pads and a uniform. P.J. had only intended to watch today's practice and learn a bit about the team. When he gets home, he tells his dad, "I'm a Patriot."

P. J. Smith is only the first in a string of students displaced from their own schools or teams, players who will make John Curtis their new home.

On Wednesday afternoon, September 21, the John Curtis coaches and players are happily caught up in the preparations for Friday night's game against the Bulldogs of Ferriday High. Getting a first game under their belt will be a crucial step in getting back on track, and the players can't wait. But now, incredibly, nature is threatening to strike once again. Weather forecasters have begun warning about a second deadly hurricane fast approaching.

Tropical storm Rita has been traveling west from her birthplace in the Caribbean, slicing between Cuba and Florida and headed for the warm, open waters of the Gulf. Forecasters started to eye the slow-building storm Sunday and, early this morning, she was upgraded to a Category 3 hurricane. Twelve hours later, the National Hurricane Center announced that Rita had gathered unprecedented strength, skipping Category 4 entirely; by six, she has intensified into a full-fledged Category 5. It's the only time two Category 5 hurricanes have stalked the United States just weeks apart, and one of the few times meteorologists need an R name, as hurricane seasons rarely get past the letter M. *US News & World Report* calls Rita "Katrina's evil twin."

By Wednesday night, Rita is carving a path eerily similar to Katrina's, and has reached an even more vicious intensity. She's racing through the Gulf with sustained winds of 180 miles an hour and gusts well above two hundred. Already, she's begun tearing apart oil rigs in the Gulf. The barometric pressure inside the storm, measured by reconnaissance aircraft, is 895 milibars, one of the lowest readings ever recorded. A meteorologist tells the Weather Channel that Rita is "the strongest storm that I've ever been in."

On Thursday, New Orleans Mayor Nagin tells residents who are in the process of returning home to do an about-face. And Governor Blanco instructs all those living south of I-10, including residents of Jefferson Parish, who've only been back in their homes for a week or so, to evacuate. She urges citizens to write their name and Social Security Number on their arms in permanent ink. No one needs her to spell out the reason why. All across southern Louisiana, the collective groan is, *not again!*

Then, instead of turning north when she hits the middle of the Gulf, as Katrina did, Rita stays on a northwesterly course. By late Thursday she seems aimed at southeastern Texas, targeting Galveston, which ninety-seven years earlier was undone by a hurricane that killed thousands, and Houston. Major evacuations of those cities begin.

In a horrible twist of fate, many families who have been displaced from New Orleans are now living temporarily in eastern Texas or southwestern Louisiana. They are directly in the path of this new killer. Among them are Kenny Dorsey and his family, who've already lost their home in the Lower Ninth Ward. They're still living in the apartment complex in Lake Charles, an oil-refining town near the Texas border. They cannot believe they have to flee once again but, along with millions along the coasts of Texas and Louisiana, they begin preparing to evacuate. They, like many Rita evacuees, feel chased by some unrelenting evil force.

J.T. is infuriated that Rita is threatening to interfere with Friday's game against the Bulldogs. The Patriots are traveling three hours north to Ferriday for the game, which is on the Louisiana–Mississippi border, and he figures that since Rita is supposed to pass well south and west of Ferriday, if New Orleans is ordered to evacuate, he'll just take the whole team up to Ferriday for the night. They'll stay there overnight in a hotel if they have to. He is not going to tell his players this game is off.

Meanwhile, Thursday afternoon, just after practice, J.T. is in the coaches' room when he gets a call from his sister, Debbie, the principal of the elementary school.

"Part of the roof fell in," she says. "You better come over."

School is scheduled to reopen on Monday, so they're going to have to do something fast. J.T. and a few of the assistant coaches drive over and examine the roof, which had been pounded and crumpled by Katrina's winds. While cleaning up the school grounds in the days after Katrina, the Curtis boys had covered the roof with a blue tarp, but hadn't noticed that one of the support beams was loose. That beam has since shifted, and there's now a big dip in the roof, which seems on the verge of caving in.

They stabilize the beam but are worried about the roof surviving another hurricane. So, they call a friend whose kids went to the school and who makes metal roof panels. The guy agrees to supply the roofing panels, but won't be able to install them. The Curtises will have to do that themselves.

So, late Thursday, J.T. calls his sons and nephews and tells them to meet at the school at five the next morning. It's a big job and they'll need to get it done well before loading the buses for Ferriday.

Friday morning, the entire coaching staff arrives with power tools and tool belts. Even Leon's son Preston, who has some kind of stomach virus and is throwing up, is there. It's still dark, so they park in a semicircle around the building and turn on their headlights. The roofing guy has delivered all the panels and shows the crew how to interlock them and screw them down.

The work starts slowly as the men get used to the awkward, wobbly panels. Then, Rita's winds start reaching into Jefferson Parish, and the job devolves quickly from merely awkward to dangerous. At seven, Lydia stops by to give J.T. a weather report. Rita has altered her path yet again, this time turning slightly north, away from a direct hit on Galveston and Houston. Now, she's aimed at western Louisiana. If she continues on this path, she'll pass through Lake Charles and veer up the middle part of the state, barreling right past Ferriday High School. J.T. and the others can't believe the news. In fact, they refuse to believe it.

"I'm not gonna cancel the game," J.T. declares emphatically.

By ten, most of the panels are installed, but it begins to rain, making it difficult to keep their footing. J.T. repeats, more urgently, almost angrily, "I'm *not* gonna cancel the game." As the winds keep picking up, he repeats like a mantra, again and again, "We're going! We're gonna play!" Preston stops every once in a while to vomit over the side of the building. The crew can't help themselves; they start laughing at the absurdity of the situation and the intensity of J.T.'s furor. Then ever-stronger gusts of wind start plucking at the panels, and the men are nearly whisked, kitelike, off the roof. At one point Jeff has to grab onto his brother's belt as he wrestles with a panel and quickly screws it down. The laughing stops.

A state trooper who lives nearby stops by and tells J.T. that Rita is looking bad. The levees south and east of New Orleans are already filling up again. Most of tonight's football games across the state have been canceled already. Even if they manage to get up to Ferriday, he says, how are they going to get home or book a hotel with the storm raging?

Grudgingly, J.T. realizes he needs to call Ferriday's principal to at least discuss whether or not they can still play. At eleven o'clock, he gives her a call.

"Coach," she says. "We think we're going to get high, high winds and tornadoes. I'm just not comfortable playing."

J.T. suggests rescheduling the game for Saturday, but that's when Rita is scheduled to make landfall, she reminds him. Sunday is no good either, she patiently explains.

"I understand," J.T. finally relents.

After packing up their tools, they retreat to the coaches' room and call their players with the bad news, telling them to be back for practice Monday afternoon. Then they head home, some of them to pack for their second evacuation in three weeks.

J.T. trudges home, thinking, *How much more are these kids supposed to take?*

Rita makes landfall at three Saturday morning, September 24, slamming into the Gulf Coast and dumping an eight-foot surge of water along the Texas–Louisiana border. She has declined from a Category 5 to a Category 3, but is still throwing 120-mile-per-hour winds at the coast, and pushing and pulling huge walls of water ashore.

Bayou towns throughout the parishes south and west of New Orleans are taken by surprise by Rita's storm surge. Hundreds of residents are suddenly stranded on rooftops. Streets have again become raging rivers and neighborhoods have become lakes. Electricity is knocked out all across southern Louisiana and eastern Texas.

Parts of Orleans Parish flood again, a foot or two deep in Lakeview and Gentilly, which had just begun to dry out from Katrina. In St. Bernard Parish, parts of Chalmette fill with eight feet of water.

South of New Orleans, levees are also breached in Plaquemines Parish and in southern Jefferson Parish, where the storm pushes the waters of Bayou Barataria inland, chasing residents who've refused to evacuate onto their roofs and damaging or swamping some homes that had been spared by Katrina, including the homes of a few other John Curtis students.

It's almost unfathomable when the Lower Ninth Ward again fills with water. Another section of the weakened Industrial Canal levee collapses, and the murky waters quickly rise back up, reaching twelve feet in some sections, and refloating the barge that had landed on Kenny Dorsey's house. The barge begins smashing into what's left of other nearby homes. (When the waters later recede, they'll find the barge and the John Curtis school bus have come to rest beside a street sign that reads, No Dumping. $500 Fine.)

Kenny Dorsey and his family have moved to a hotel in Birmingham, Alabama, following a nineteen-hour drive away from their apartment in Lake Charles. Kenny and his sister, Jané, are now enrolled at LaGrange High School in Lake Charles. Their parents had realized that they couldn't move back to the Lower Ninth Ward and probably will never be able to rebuild their house. So, the family decided to go ahead and rent an apartment in Lake Charles until the insurance claims can be settled and they can buy a new house. Kenny has even started playing football.

After losing his home and transferring schools and being stuck in a house with two dozen other evacuees for a week, Kenny's parents decided they should bend their church's rules about the Sabbath and allow Kenny to play on Friday nights. But Rita's approach forced last night's game to be cancelled.

While in their Birmingham hotel watching coverage of the storm, the Dorseys learn that Lake Charles has been severely hit. The city is under six feet of water in places and off limits to residents. Electricity is out. There's no water or sewage. Looters are roaming the streets, and the state police and National Guard have been called in to restore order. Boats and barges slammed into an I-10 bridge near downtown, shutting down the interstate. Residents are being told not to return home for at least ten days.

Then the news gets worse.

Late in the day, they learn that Rita has flattened the apartment complex where they had recently moved. The entire building, and their meager belongings, are gone.

Kenny and his family are homeless once more.

In the aftermath of Rita, public officials struggle to tally the damage of the two hurricanes, and to assess the unstable future of the entire region.

Hundreds of thousands of homes have been destroyed or seriously damaged, and repairing that damage will take many, many months. The next phase will soon begin, a painstaking and disillusioning period during which affected residents will file insurance claims and seek financial assistance from the federal government and try to hire building contractors to fix their homes. The economy of southern Louisiana is in tatters. Oil rigs and refineries have been smashed. Rice pastures and sugar-cane fields have been ruined by salt water. Bayou towns sustained by shrimping and crawfishing have been scratched off the earth. Even little-known industries like alligator farming, which supplies farm-raised gator skins for luggage and handbags, have been decimated.

Mayor Nagin is already talking about a new New Orleans with half the population it had just a few weeks ago, and is worried about losing the city's multiracial culture. Nagin will soon famously declare that New Orleans needs to lure back African-Americans, who comprise the bulk of the city's population, so that New Orleans can remain "a chocolate city." He knows that many of the missing are those too poor to rebuild and start again, and many of those are African-American.

J.T. and his family are also deeply worried about who will return, who won't, and about what effect the hurricanes will have on the delicately balanced mixed-race culture of their school's student body, not to mention the school's financial stability.

Rita thankfully did little damage to Jefferson Parish, and hasn't threatened the school's reopening, scheduled for Monday, September 26. The Curtis men managed to finish fixing the elementary school's roof before Rita's winds became too fierce.

Now, the day the Curtises worried might never come is just a day away.

They've posted notices on the Web about the reopening. They've printed and distributed thousands of flyers and put the big, hand-painted JOHN CURTIS REOPENING sign up along Interstate 10. They've also had a desk out in front of the school for several days, displaying a sign, ACCEPTING NEW APPLICANTS, and a few families have come by to fill out registration forms. Ever since returning to their homes over a week ago, they've left all the school lights on each night, to let all passersby know that the school is ready to go.

John Curtis will be among just a handful of schools in Greater New Orleans to welcome students back on Monday. Most other schools throughout the region won't reopen until October 3 or October 10, at the earliest.

The first day of school is always a tense and exciting one for educators, but tomorrow's kickoff will surely be the oddest schoolday the Curtises have faced.

At a quiet Sunday night dinner, Lydia and J.T. talk about what to expect tomorrow, nervous about how many kids will show. Before Katrina, the school's total enrollment for all grades was 648. The big question is how many of them will be able to make it back, not only for Monday, but *ever*. Will it be only the kids from the upper and middle-class families? Only the *white* families? Katrina was initially indiscriminate, forcing every student—black or white, rich or poor—to evacuate. The flooding, however, *did* discriminate, dealing a far harsher blow to lower-income, predominantly African-American, neighborhoods. Many of the school's African-American students lived in those neighborhoods, and the Curtises are worried they won't make it back.

"Do you think we'll get a third of them back?" Lydia asks J.T. "*Half?*"

"Lydia, I just don't know," J.T. says. He tries to remind himself that God has a plan. Silently, however, he's thinking they'll be lucky to get half their students back.

12

Gunning for Johnnie

The procession begins at eight on the morning of Monday, September 26, a steady stream of cars turning off Jefferson Highway and onto Manguno Street to offload kids at the front gates of John Curtis Christian School. Students bustle past the sea-nymph statue in the school's front courtyard, tromp through the halls, and steer magnetically to their favorite spots to wait for first period: the picnic tables beside the outdoor lockers; the air conditioning and padded floor of the weight room; the metal bleachers beside the football field.

J.T. stands outside his office in the front hallway. This is his first official schoolday as acting headmaster, and the only time in school history that his dad hasn't been on hand to welcome back the flock. J.T.'s voice booms above all others, echoing up and down the hall as he welcomes the girls with a hug and a "Hello, sweetheart" or "darlin' " and the boys with a slap on the back and a friendly insult about their haircut or clothes.

Instead of the patriotic color scheme of John Curtis clothes the kids normally wear to school, many are wearing a mish-mash of donated hand-me-downs. The school's dress code is already a loose one, requiring only that kids wear red, white, or blue Curtis T-shirts or sweatshirts with slacks or jeans and brown or black shoes—no sneakers. So many kids lost all their clothes in the storm that the Curtises have decided to let them wear whatever they want for the time being. They've also decided to let them use cell phones. With parents living or working in new towns, the logistics of getting kids to and from school will be nightmarish, and cell phones will be important.

The Curtises are also scrambling to get school supplies to kids who lost their backpacks, notebooks, pens, and pencils in the flooding. A few schools and local companies have donated some supplies, which they pile on a table in the hallway, and tell kids to help themselves

J.T. closely observes the kids as they walk past, and he worries about how they're holding up. Many walk tentatively, with a distant, puzzled look on their faces, as if they're trying to remember something. Others seem fretful and bug-eyed. They're clearly struggling to keep up with laundry and regular showers. The air is soon filled with a redolent mix of smells, predominantly body odor and dirty socks, feebly covered up by deodorant and Febreze.

Of forty-seven teachers employed at the combined schools, only three have been unable to return. It's a huge relief for the Curtises to have so many teachers back in the halls for this first day. So much will be expected of the staff this semester. For one thing, to make up the days lost to Katrina, the school day will start twenty minutes earlier and stretch an extra ten minutes later each afternoon. Teachers will have to help students catch up academically and also act as counselors.

Of great concern is the fragile psyche of the students. Larry Manguno, the school's principal and Mr. Curtis's brother-in-law, asked his daughter, an Episcopal minister and psychologist, to conduct a two-hour seminar last week to prepare teachers for what they might face. She spoke with them about recognizing and handling the signs of posttraumatic stress disorder (PTSD), not only in the kids, but in themselves.

Many New Orleans residents are still in shock at both the physical destruction of their city and the utterly botched recovery efforts. Feelings of hopelessness and abandonment are rampant and, in the coming weeks, the city will see a sharp increase in suicides and suicide attempts, as will cities hosting large numbers of evacuees, such as Houston. At a Bourbon Street nightclub, a man recently drew a gun and shot himself in the head as dancers performed on stage. Alcohol and drug abuse are on the rise, as are insomnia and anxiety attacks. Across the region, families have lost painfully irreplaceable items, baby pictures and wedding albums and old letters and heirlooms; artists and filmmakers have lost their life's work; musicians have lost their instruments; doctors and lawyers have lost all their files. Police are still finding distraught homeowners weeping inconsolably in their ruined houses, and federal and state mental-health experts and psychiatrists are calling the aftermath an unprecedented mental-health disaster.

One New Orleans psychotherapist tells the *New York Times* that "there are a lot of people walking around with an endemic low-grade depression," and another psychiatrist reports meeting with kids as young as five talking about wanting to die. Normal support networks have been fractured, with families scattered and separated. John Curtis and other schools will soon learn that many students are now living alone or with elderly relatives, because their parents have been transferred to far-off cities.

J.T.'s sisters, Alicia and Kathy, have distributed handouts to teachers with tips on PTSD and suggestions on handling their emotionally fragile students. Mainly, the goal is to let kids know they're safe and they have someone to talk to if needed. They've scheduled counseling sessions in the library next week for students. In the meantime, they've asked teachers to keep an eye out for kids who seem excessively distracted or sad, and they've posted a notice in the school bulletin saying, "If you need to talk about anything related to Katrina, come see us."

The counseling experts have told the Curtis teachers not to expect many discipline problems in the first weeks. Kids will be shell-shocked at first, and still processing the upheaval of their lives. In a few months, however, their emotions will start catching up with them and the kids will likely start acting out. Kathy worries that the deeper emotions won't emerge until later, especially if kids are still not able to get back into their homes by Thanksgiving or, God forbid, Christmas.

Manguno understands why, after getting so much bad news day after day, his kids simply can't talk about it yet. His plan is to try to just give them the reliable daily structure of classes and homework that will help them to get back into the rhythm of their prior lives. Many students are living with relatives or neighbors. Coach Jerry has taken a freshman into his house. Some are in hotel rooms or apartment buildings, sleeping on air mattresses and using suitcases for furniture. A handful are still sleeping in Red Cross shelters or tents or rented RVs. One family is sleeping in the school gym. Tank's mom and two aunts are scheduled to move in with Leon and Sue next week.

Many Curtis families are beginning to accept delivery of the government subsidized trailers that will become their eight-by-twenty-eight-foot homes, 224 square feet of living space in all. In the weeks to come, FEMA will provide more than one hundred thousand of the white rectangles, and as *FEMA trailer* enters the New Orleans lexicon, the thirty-foot models, with sixteen extra square feet, will become highly sought-after commodities.

Mike Walker's parents are on the waiting list for a trailer, although, for the life of him, Mike still can't understand why. He told his dad the trailer was a huge mistake, and that they'd have the sheet rock torn out of their house and replaced in just a few weeks, by Thanksgiving at the very latest. As for so many New Orleans residents, the reality of what it takes to restore a flooded house hasn't yet sunk in. Until the trailer comes, Mike's parents have agreed to let him stay in River Ridge with his teammate, Jacob Dufrene, in the apartment Jacob's parents rent for him near the school. Meanwhile, Mike's dad's boss at the Folger's coffee plant has transferred him to an office ninety minutes away, and Mike's mom is working temporarily in Baton Rouge, also ninety minutes from home.

Though the Curtises know that this school year is going to be a formidable challenge, the good news is how many of their kids are back. Despite fears of losing half their 648 students, at the end of the first day, when class attendance sheets are tallied, they discover that enrollment is over four hundred, and in the coming weeks it will climb above five hundred. Also of great relief is the number of faces of color this morning. Ultimately, the African-American contingent of students will rise to 15 percent for the year, and the overall minority population will again reach above 20 percent.

For the Patriot players, the most encouraging thing about this first week back is that there will be a football game Friday night. At last. A return to one true, normal thing.

• • •

Amidst the flurry of calls J.T. has been making to line up games, he connected with Larry Dauterive, head coach of the East St. John High Wildcats, located an hour west of New Orleans—the team Johnnie Thiel had defected to.

J.T. has known Dauterive, who everyone calls Coach Doe, for years. In fact, Dauterive's daughter attended Curtis and was homecoming queen and *Miss Patriot* before graduating in 1987. It was his daughter who saw a John Curtis Web site that mentioned that the Patriots were looking for games, prompting Dauterive to call J.T. Even though East St. John was unscathed by Katrina, all ten of the school's games have been canceled because of the damage to opponents' schools. Just like J.T., Coach Doe has spent many hours on the phone trying to scare up a game, desperate to get his kids back into a football season. "I would have lined up in a Wal-Mart parking lot to play the New Orleans Saints to get the kids a game," Dauterive will later tell *USA Today.*

J.T. actually might have preferred to play the Saints rather than the Wildcats, a big team with a strong, storied football program of their own. Just before Katrina, they were ranked second in Louisiana's 5A division. But it's not East St. John's ranking that's bothering him. John Curtis is used to playing larger schools. What the Patriots are not used to is playing against exteammates. And with their ranks depleted and their players out of shape, facing their talented exquarterback in their first game is not how J.T. wanted to open the season. His team needs a game, though, and he feels he has no choice.

"Well, I'm ready to commit to play if you want to," he said when he and Coach Doe connected. Doe said he was tired of waiting, and the two men agreed to play September 30, seven o'clock, under the lights at East St. John. As they finalized the details of the game, neither coach mentioned Johnnie Thiel's name. They didn't need to.

When the Patriots learned they'd be playing their first game against Johnnie, the muttering was instantaneous, with lots of tough talk of showing him up, knocking him out of the game. J.T. and his staff have told their players to focus on the basics and forget about John-nie, that the game isn't going to be a grudge match against him. It's just another football game against a good team called East St. John. Out of the coaches' earshot, though, the Patriots keep venting their thoughts, *He knows all our plays. He thought he was too good for us.* They want to make Johnnie pay the price for leaving them.

What's troubling, though, is that they're going to have to face Johnnie without Joe McKnight. They have no idea how their offense is going to perform without him, and they know Johnnie isn't going to make it easy for them.

It's been difficult for the Patriots to accept that Joe has decamped to Evangel. They all know that football is Joe's ticket to a new life, and that he had good reason to latch onto a school that would help him escape his less than ideal family situation. But losing Joe feels like they've lost a favorite older brother, not to mention their best player.

The Patriots have all heard about Joe becoming Evangel's newest star, but they held out hope that, when John Curtis reopened, he'd come back. Coach Corey, who nurtured Joe from third through eighth grade, wasn't about to let another school take him away without a fight, and he made one last try to get him to come back to John Curtis.

Last Sunday, he drove the six hours up to Shreveport to meet with Joe face to face. He assured Joe that J.T. was fast reassembling the Patriots' season, that the team wanted him back, and that J.T. was sincere about letting Joe live with him for awhile. And he reminded him that Tank had moved in with the Curtises, so he wouldn't be alone.

Corey also told Joe about going up against the East St. John Wildcats, hoping to motivate him to come back to face his old friend. But Joe said he was going to stay put.

Shortly after Corey's visit, though, Joe talks things over with Mike Tucker. He tells Mike he feels awkward about moving in with J.T. He's worried about getting heat from his African-American friends, and can hear them asking, "*What's a black football player doing living with his white coach?*" He's also afraid that moving in with J.T. will be symbolically shutting a door on his mother. They've had their problems over the years, but he still loves her and doesn't want to hurt her. Sleeping at a friend's house or with his cousins or his grandmother was one thing. Moving in with J.T. and Lydia would be different, like making a commitment to a whole different kind of life.

There's one other issue that's nagging at him, he says. Is J.T. bending over backwards to bring him back solely because of football? Just because he's a star?

Mike tells Joe that, sure, moving in with J.T. will be a hard pill to swallow, but it might be the best thing for him right now. He explains that he had already spoken with J.T. about all this, and that it's clear to him that J.T. is more concerned with Joe's day-to-day life than his football career. Of course Joe's a vital player, and of course J.T. wants to see him play for Curtis, but that doesn't mean he's not concerned for Joe's future. After all, J.T. will take some heat too, Mike says, about inviting his best player to live with him. J.T. has known Joe since he was a little kid, and Mike is convinced that he really cares about helping Joe get onto a better track in life.

"J.T.'s offering up his home, his life, and his children to help you succeed," he says. "You have to realize it's not just about football. Ain't that much football in the world." Joe tells Mike he'll think it over.

Then, on Tuesday night, Joe calls J.T. and tells him, "I think I should come back and give it a try, coach."

Mike Tucker drives him down from Shreveport the next afternoon, and pulls up at the small brick rancher on Wagner Street, where Joe will have his own bedroom for the first time in his life.

It's a Wednesday night, which means family dinner night. All the siblings, cousins, nieces, nephews, and in-laws are back by now, so this week's dinner is a busy one. When Joe and Mike Tucker enter the house, J.T.'s grandkids are running around, yelling. Jeff, Johnny, Tommy, and their spouses are loudly discussing the first three days of school and J.T. and Lydia are busy cooking. The kitchen is steamy with red beans and rice.

In no time, the little ones are on the attack, milling around Joe and begging for attention. "Joe, will you chase me? Tickle me Joe, tickle me. Here, Joe—catch." Tank is settled comfortably on a couch, watching the large-screen television in the corner of the family room. He's been here almost two weeks, so this is his second family dinner. He's starting to get used to the kids and the noise. Joe looks downright scared. He's never seen anything like it, and he gives Mike Tucker a disconcerted look that says, "Maybe I don't belong here."

After a brief catch up with J.T. and a plate of red beans and rice, Joe goes to his new room and stays there the rest of the night. For the first time in his life, he has his own room, and relishing his own inner sanctum, he locks the door.

Ever since childhood, Johnnie Thiel had known he was special. His coaches at Curtis were typically stingy with praise, but others told him year after year, *you're going to be a star*. A stallion on the basketball court as well as the football field, he'd make bets that he could sink a shot from half court, backward. In football, he displayed enviable natural abilities. He wasn't always the fastest guy on the field, but he was elusive and his moves were wonderful to watch. John Curtis had never been much of a passing team, but with Johnnie's ability to drop back and juke around in the pocket without getting sacked, the coaches had decided to work a few more passing plays into the Patriots' offense.

Winning a Curtis championship and being named MVP of the 2004 championship game had been special for Johnnie, but he wanted to play someplace where he could stand out and become some team's secret weapon. "At Curtis, we only threw the ball two or three times per game," he explained after transferring to East St. John. "I wanted to throw the ball more. J.T. just didn't want to change his style."

When Johnnie transferred, J.T. expressed no hard feelings, believing Johnnie did what he felt he needed to do. Without emotion, he told the *Times-Picayune*, "I hope he has a nice career." But, privately, J.T. thought if Johnnie didn't wholeheartedly want to be a team player, it was probably best for everyone that he move on. Other students and coaches weren't as diplomatic. It was complicated, losing someone like Johnnie, and a few called him "traitor" and "thug."

Oddly, even after his transfer, Johnnie couldn't stay away, and tried to maintain his friendship with Joe and others at Curtis. He'd stop by Curtis during spring training and hang out in the parking lot, watching his former team practice. Once, Joe got frustrated and stepped out of the huddle and yelled, "Hey Johnnie! You wanna play? We'll play you any time."

Johnnie just laughed and slapped his knee. But Joe wasn't laughing. "You wanna play Wednesday? Or how about Saturday? Or Friday? C'mon, Johnnie. Let's *play*."

Before Katrina, there had been little chance Johnnie and Joe would face each other, with East St. John in division 5A and Curtis now relegated to 2A. But Katrina has made it happen.

At Thursday afternoon's practice, the talk is all about Johnnie Thiel. In his first practice back, Joe makes no bones about it, admitting, "I want to hurt him."

Making the matchup even more challenging, East St. John is now an ever tougher team than it was before Katrina. In addition to Johnnie, they've taken on a slew of new players from other schools.

East St. John wasn't hurt by either Katrina or Rita and, as one of the few unscathed schools in the area, became a repository for displaced students, taking in hundreds. Coach Doe has taken on so many new players that he's struggled to find enough pads and uniforms for a team that has grown to 140 young men. With less than a hundred jersey numbers, dozens of players must wear the same number. Some must wear XXL pants because the school ran out of smaller sizes. Kids in oversized pants plead with Coach Doe, who just says, "Tighten your belt up!"

On Friday, September 30, a story in the *Times-Picayune* sports pages declares that high-school football has returned to New Orleans, with more games scheduled for the night than on any Friday since Katrina and Rita. "Normal," the story begins. "Everyone is trying to get back there. We have power, we have water, we even have cable. And we have football."

John Curtis has never placed much emphasis on rowdy pregame pep rallies, though most games are preceded by a modest rally in the gym. Today, however, even though the student body could desperately use a lift, there's just not enough time or psychic energy to arrange for a rally. Life at the school has been hectic enough.

After school, J.T. goes home for his pregame ritual: a nap, followed by a bowl of soup, arriving back at the coaches' room ten minutes before departure time. Instead of three school buses, only two are now needed for the team.

During the hourlong bus ride west, the players are perfectly quiet, as J.T. insists they be. Joe sits in the front seat, across the aisle from J.T., listening to Al Pacino's *Any Given Sunday* speech: "Either we heal as a team or we are going to crumble. Inch by inch, play by play, 'til we're finished. We are in hell right now, gentlemen, believe me. And we can stay here and get the shit kicked out of us or we can fight our way, back into the light. We can climb out of hell. One inch, at a time."

J.T. has told his players not to expect many fans on their side of the field. Many parents still haven't moved back home or have just gotten back and will probably be working on their houses. He even offered to let Coach Doe keep 60 percent of the ticket sales, instead of the typical 50-50 split, because he expected such a limited Patriots' turnout. But, as the players unload, they see that there's an impressive contingent of red, white, and blue waiting for them, both in the visitors' stands and in the parking lot.

A giddy crowd of Curtis parents, teachers, students, and alumni are tailgating. They've brought pots of jambalaya and gumbo. Mike Walker's parents have handed out their popcorn balls and are hanging out with the Niermans and the Dufrenes. Tank's mom is in the stands, sitting not far from Kyle's parents and Joe's mom, Jennifer, who has driven two hours down from Innis, where she and Joe's brother are still staying. Not all of the parents have been able to come, however: Robby Green's mom, for one, is still in Dallas, though his dad has come from Baton Rouge.

J.T. is surprised to see a number of alumni, people he hasn't seen in years. As he watches old friends shake hands and embrace, he realizes that this game means more to the John Curtis community than he realized. By game time, the visitors' stands are teeming. The home team's stands are even more packed, and the total attendance is close to three thousand.

The Patriots' cheerleaders hold up a ten-foot-tall, hand-painted sign in the end zone, which reads, WE'RE BACK!!!! The players crash through it onto the field, tearing the sign to shreds, pumping their fists, exhorting their fans to make some noise. All too recently, it seemed as if they'd never be playing football again, and some players haven't let themselves believe it was real until this very moment. On the sideline for the first time in weeks, the adrenaline is pumping, their muscles are twitching, itching to get onto the field and make contact. As a female East St. John student belts out the national anthem, it's almost too much to bear, and the Patriot players are bouncing up and down, clenching their fists, punching, shoving, head-butting, and shouting at each other.

As the Wildcats take the field, their black pants, black jerseys, and black helmets stand in sharp contrast to the Patriots' white pants, white jerseys, and white helmets.

East St. John lost its season opener, but won its next game by a landslide, after Johnnie Thiel threw three touchdown passes and rushed for two more. Having played twice already, with a bigger, better-seasoned team, the Wildcats enjoy a distinct advantage. The *Times-Picayune* has predicted that East St. John will spank John Curtis, 35–20.

J.T. attributes his team's long-term success primarily to running the same plays year after year, until they've become pounded into the players' beings and into the team's institutional memory. It's that consistency that's allowed him to start this season with 417 career victories, nearly as many as Bear Bryant (323) and Knute Rockne (105) combined. The Bear used to say he was "just a simple plowhand from Arkansas." But across many years of coaching he demonstrated a special gift for holding a team together, keeping them calm and, as he once put it, helping them play with "one heartbeat."

J.T., too, has developed a system for getting his kids to play as one, and to keep their composure. The truth is, he's deeply worried about this game. Except for the solid defensive line, anchored by Tank, and the linebackers, anchored by Mike Walker, the team was not synching in last week's practices, and some players, like newcomer P. J. Smith, have never run the veer offense.

There was much catching up to do in practice last week, but J.T. knew that three-hour practices would only fatigue his players' out-of-shape legs, so his assistants came up with a two-hour practice routine that was intense, but didn't push the players too hard. Now he's concerned about whether they're really ready for play. Reaching the fourth quarter, when muscles are burning and lungs are heaving, may be too much for them. The added emotion of going against Johnnie Thiel won't help them stay focused. J.T. hasn't been so unsure about the start of a season in years, maybe ever.

The Wildcats win the coin toss, and line up to receive the kick. Josh Medley, the Patriots' kicker, boots a high, hanging kick, and the silhouette of the ball back-flipping beautifully across the gray night sky is exhilarating.

Not until it lands in the receiver's arms do some of the Patriots finally allow themselves to believe that the 2005 football season has actually begun.

After a short kickoff return, Johnnie Thiel swaggers onto the field like he invented swaggering. And from the first play, he makes a statement, nailing a sweet, twenty-yard pass. On the next play, the Patriots make a strong rebuttal. Tank leads his defensive line on a five-man blitz and Tank drags his old friend down for a four-yard loss. Johnnie then comes right back with a ten-yard swing pass and, on the next play, sweeps left on an option, which he keeps, scampering for ten yards, and another first down. Then, he lofts a twenty-nine-yard pass to his wide-open running back, who takes the Wildcats down to the Curtis fifteen-yard line. Just minutes into the game, the Wildcats are poised to score.

J.T. can't stand still. He bends at the waist, hands on his knees, then stalks to his left, then his right, pulls at his hair, then bends over again. He takes his headset off, then puts it on again. He wants to yell at his players, but knows that won't do any good right now. In the press box, where he often watches over games, Leon tells J.T. through his headset, "Just relax, just relax . . ."

But Johnnie keeps attacking. He sweeps right and gains another seven yards. The Wildcats are now on the Patriots' eight-yard line. Then, on second and three from the eight-yard line, Johnnie drops to pass. His receivers are all covered, so he keeps the ball, spins out of the pocket, slides through a mass of defenders, and dives into the end zone. The extra point is good and the Wildcats are up 7–0 on a blistering first drive.

Johnnie has clobbered them. The drive went eighty yards, and Johnnie earned all but a few of them himself. He hit all three of his passes, for fifty-three yards, and ran for another twenty-nine.

After the kickoff, Kyle takes over at the sixteen-yard line for the Patriots' first drive of the season. But the drive is no drive at all. Kyle only manages five yards on two handoffs. On third and five, he drops back to pass. The coaches have long worried about a hitch in Kyle's windup, but have been unable to fix it. When he had finally recovered from his broken collarbone this summer, they even sent him to the renowned Manning Passing Academy, where Archie Manning and his sons, Peyton and Eli, train promising young quarterbacks. The Mannings couldn't fix the hiccup either.

Kyle has a receiver open down the left side, and the coaches are screaming, "Throw it! Throw it!" He pumps once, then finally releases the ball, but throws into traffic and is nearly intercepted. The pass drops for an incomplete and, on fourth and five, Kyle sulks off the field and over to where Jeff is waiting with arms folded.

After a short Patriots punt, Johnnie retakes the field. On the first play of the Wildcats' second drive, he stutter-steps backward, cocks his arm, and throws in one fast, fluid motion, drilling a bomb that flies fifty yards in the air. Johnnie's receiver is two steps ahead of the Patriots' safety, newcomer P. J. Smith, and the receiver makes a diving catch at the Patriots' five-yard line. Less than ten minutes in, the game is looking like a rout. The Patriots' fans are cringing and quiet in the stands.

P.J. comes off the field wide-eyed and scared, worried that he's just blown the game for his new team. Coach Tommy sends him right back onto the field, telling him, "Forget it. You're gonna learn right now that the most important play is the next one. . . ."

Johnnie has completed four passes in a row. The Patriots' defense is looking good on running plays, but keeps getting fooled by passes. In the next huddle, Tank pumps them up, exhorting them, "We've got to hurt this guy." On the snap, at first and goal, they do. The defensive line surges all over Johnnie, dragging him down for a ten-yard loss. The Patriot fans wildly shake their milk jugs and stomp the metal bleachers. Then on second down, the defensive line slams Johnnie at the line of scrimmage and pushes him back another yard. On third down on the sixteen-yard line, Johnnie finds a man open at the goal line, but under pressure from the defensive rush he throws too high.

The Wildcats settle for a field goal. Still, they go ahead 10–0, and Coach Doe is thinking: *If we can keep this up, set the tone and pace, we've got them . . .*

J.T.'s biggest concern before the game had been that his players haven't been acclimated to the intensity and pacing of a real game. Jeff has stressed that they don't have fresh legs. Johnnie and East St. John are clearly acclimated. Except for Joe, who played twice with Evangel, the Patriots aren't even close.

On their next drive, though, J.T. sees the first hopeful signs that his offense is settling down. After a solid Wildcats' kickoff, the Patriots take over at the twenty. Kyle looks less tentative, like he's settling down. He takes the snap, spins, and confidently stabs the ball into the gut of David Seeman, who gains six yards. On second down, Kyle hands off to Scotty Encalade, who gains four more yards and a first down, their first of the season. J.T. knows he could give the ball to Joe McKnight on every play and get right back into the game. That's how plenty of other high-school coaches would use Joe, but that's not how his team operates. He's selective about just when he gives Joe the ball. On first and ten, after their steady start, this is one of those times. Kyle takes the snap, half-steps to his left, and hands Joe his season's first possession as a Patriot.

Joe runs behind the left tackle and straight at two defenders converging on him, then does what he does best. He breaks through the two defenders and nearly plows over his own lineman's back, slides sideways between two more defenders, and bursts into the open field. Turning on the gas, within ten yards he has outrun every man on the defense, except one. That defender is running dead even with Joe, a few yards to his right. Joe edges closer and closer to the left sideline, past the fifty, then the forty.

He has a gliding, graceful stride that makes him look as if he's hardly pushing, and some teammates believe Joe only runs as fast as he needs to, just fast enough to stay a foot or two ahead. Now, Joe decides not to take any chances and accelerates. Instantly, he gains two yards on his opponent, then four, and as he crosses the twenty, and then the ten, the Patriots fans scream wildly. With the grace of a dancer, Joe streaks across the goal line eight yards ahead of his opponent. He casually drops the ball to the turf and loops back around to greet his teammates, who throw themselves all over him.

In the stands, ecstatic fans hug and kiss one another, and the Patriots' cheerleaders, who have lost some members and taken on new ones, stick to their most basic chant: "Let's go red! Let's go white! Let's go *red . . . and . . . white*!"

Knowing that every point will count in this game, J.T. calls for a two-point conversion. A lineman jumps the gun and they're called offside. The ball is moved back five yards and kicker Josh Medley comes on for the extra point. Josh had been reliable as the Patriots' placekicker last year, but of course he hasn't done much kicking in recent weeks. His kick goes wide, and the Patriots trail, 10–6.

J.T. realizes that Joe will be his team's saving grace tonight. He's not about to use Joe on every play, but decides to bend his own rules and let Joe play on both offense and defense. With East St. John's passing attack, he needs a special weapon in the defensive backfield, especially after P. J. Smith got beat so badly on Johnnie's bomb.

The decision immediately pays off. Stalking in the secondary, eyes wide, fingers fluttering, as Johnnie spirals another well-aimed pass at one of his receivers, Joe makes a perfectly timed leap and snatches the ball away for an interception. The Patriots offense takes over but, on second and long, while trying to wrestle his way to a first down, Kyle fumbles and the Wildcats recover.

Frustrations and emotions run high on both sides, and the scrumming on the line of scrimmage, the after-the-play forearms and shoulders start to get rough. Joe decides to make a statement to his old friend Johnnie. A few plays later, Johnnie can't find an open receiver and scrambles outside toward Joe's zone, chased by John Ruttley and Mike Walker. Just as Johnnie is about to step out of bounds, Joe dives after him and puts his shoulder into Johnnie's gut. Two penalty flags fly, and Joe is hit with a fifteen-yard personal foul for a late hit.

J.T. hates personal fouls. "Un-bee-*lee*-vable," he shouts, then points an urgent finger at Joe and yanks him off the field, keeping him on the bench for the next few plays.

Still, for Joe . . . the hit felt good.

With Tank, Mike, and Joe playing an aggressive game, the Patriots' defense is keeping the pressure on Johnnie. On a third-and-ten play late in the second quarter, he drops back to pass and Tank blasts past two blockers, faster than a 340-pound kid should move, and slams face to face with Johnnie, wrapping his arms around his old classmate and triumphantly spinning him down to the turf. He stands over Johnnie, like a prize fighter after a knockout, and again the Patriots' fans respond wildly.

The first half ends with the Wildcats up, 10–6.

During halftime, J.T. tells his team to settle down. "Just relax and play," he says.

The defense is making some impressive plays. Tank is on fire, and Mike Walker is stepping up. Joe is perplexing the Wildcats on both offense and defense, but the offense overall is a mess, with three possessions ending in punts and two more possessions resulting in fumbles. Kyle is throwing passes too short and, although his backs have made some nice runs, Kyle seems out of synch with them and making bad handoffs. On options and sweeps, which comprise a big chunk of the Patriots' offensive strategy, he keeps the ball when he should flip, flips it when he should keep it.

"You've got to give the ball up," J.T. reminds Kyle, then tells the others, "We're not dominating the ball the way we're capable of."

The Patriots have always been a better second-half team, thanks to the corrections they make at halftime. The coaches go from player to player, making numerous strategic adjustments. Leon, who's been watching from the press box, tells the linebackers to spread out more on pass plays. The other assistants urge the defensive line to close up the middle.

In the second half, the defense continues to play strong, physical football, putting even more pressure on Johnnie Thiel. They sack him twice and force a number of incomplete passes. On one play, Tank leads a herd of five Patriots who swarm over Johnnie and drop him for a ten-yard loss.

Kyle can't get the offense moving, though. When he does move the ball, the offense follows good plays with dumb mistakes: a fumble, an interception, a penalty. Unable to find their momentum, they're beginning to look like a band of sandlot novices. When a steady third-quarter drive across midfield is stopped two yards short of a first down, J.T. wants to show his team he believes in them, and decides to go for it on fourth down. Kyle is stuffed, just inches short, and the Wildcats take over. Fortunately, the Patriots' defense manages to keep the Wildcats out of the end zone, and after a scoreless third quarter the score remains 10–6.

As J.T. had feared, the game will come down to the fourth quarter. East St. John opens with a strong drive, taking the ball all the way to the Patriots' eleven-yard line. Penalties and the Curtis defense push them back ten yards. Then, on third and twenty, a Johnnie Thiel pass is picked off by Patriots' defensive back Kelby Wuertz. With ten minutes left in the game, the Patriots finally have a solid chance to pull ahead.

On third and long, Kyle makes a bold move. With the Wildcats defense playing in close to the line of scrimmage, expecting a patented Curtis running play, Kyle drops back and lofts a bomb to wide receiver Vincent Allen, but the pass is too high and too short, and it falls right into a defender's hands. It's the Patriots' third turnover of the game.

The Patriots defense once again steps up, stopping the Wildcats at the thirty-eight, and the Patriots bring in their punt-return team. Joe is poised to make one of his lightning-fast touchdown returns. He's dying to turn this game around.

But then the Wildcats suddenly line up for a field goal. The Patriot coaches argue, "It's a fake." "It's a punt." "It's a fake." "It's the punt, this is a punt." The Patriots mill around, confused, trying to figure out what's happening, when the place-kick holder takes the snap for a fifty-six-yard field-goal attempt, practically unheard of at the high school level, or *any* level. Improbably, the kicker boots a line drive and nails it clean. The Wildcats are up 13–6, with just a few minutes to go in the game.

"I can't believe that crap," J.T. says in disbelief, standing on the sideline and looking up at the goal posts as if there's got to be some kind of mistake. He then tries to calm his shaken team, reminding them that they're only down by seven points. "A touchdown and an extra point ties it," he tells them.

Joe figures now it's really time for some McKnight magic. He is back to return the kickoff, and the ball bobbles his way. He catches it and sees a big hole up the sideline. He can practically *feel* the route he'll take to the end zone. Planting his left foot, he tries to pivot to the inside of the approaching defenders. Incredibly, his foot slips and he tumbles to the turf at his own eight-yard line. Instead of a go-ahead touchdown, he's buried his team dangerously deep in their own territory. He trudges off the field, shaking his head, furious with himself.

Kyle trots onto the field and on first and ten turns to hand off to David Seeman, who runs into traffic at the line and is stripped of the ball. The Wildcats recover and go nuts, dancing and twirling onto the field, high fiving and chest-slamming each other, pointing number-one fingers over at the Patriots. It's first and goal from the seven.

The Patriots defense rallies, stifling a sweep on first and goal but, on second down, the Patriots are penalized for having twelve men on the field, and the ball is moved down to the two. Johnnie Thiel tries to run a quarterback sneak up the middle, but hits a rock-hard wall of Patriots and is stopped at the one-yard line. On third down, Johnnie again keeps the ball, but before he can take a step he is caught in Tank's beefy grasp, and Tank hurls him to the ground. On fourth down, East St. John's kicker easily boots a short field goal, and the Wildcats lead 16–6 with less than three minutes to play.

In any other season, the Patriots might still have a long-shot chance; the team has pulled off plenty of stunning, come-from-behind victories before. On the next drive, though, Kyle loses the ball on the snap. He recovers the ball himself this time, but he loses ten yards, then loses another ten when he's sacked on the next play. When a fourth-down attempt fails, East St. John takes over with less than a minute to go, and the game is over. Johnnie takes one last snap and runs down the clock. The Patriots have been clobbered, 16–6.

It's all they can do to force themselves to shake Johnnie's hand at midfield and mutter, "Good game." Johnnie completed fourteen of twenty-one passes for 231 yards. Kyle passed for just ten. Although the Patriots' offense rushed for a respectable 232 yards, they lost three fumbles and an interception.

Coach Doe tells J.T. that the Patriots were just discombobulated from the storm, adding, "I wouldn't want to play you in three weeks."

J.T. isn't so sure how they'll be looking, even then. This is only the fourth opening-day loss in thirty years, and the Patriots' first loss in nearly two years. The freshmen and sophomores have never lost a varsity game before, and the last Patriots' defeat was the 2003 championship game, with Johnnie Thiel at quarterback. Across the previous four hundred games, the Patriots have scored an average of thirty points, making tonight one of the poorest offensive performances in John Curtis history.

J.T. is worried about how the kids are going to take the loss. But after they gather at midfield for their postgame prayer, the field starts to fill up with Curtis parents and alumni, and it seems no one wants to leave.

At midfield, players mingle with cheerleaders and parents swap horror stories of their evacuation experiences. Everyone asks, "How's your house?" and "How's your family?" A few of the Patriots even make time for Johnnie Thiel, who asks about a few of his ex-teammates who are missing tonight.

It takes the Curtis coaches nearly an hour to break up the party and load the team on the buses.

Back at the school, the players shower, dress, and get ready to head home, or wherever they are holed up. J.T. decides to make a rare postgame visit to the locker room.

He doesn't want to be hard on them, but he doesn't think he should baby them either. They've just played one of the worst Patriot games in years, and he's not about to pretend he didn't notice.

"For all you new guys, at John Curtis school, we don't lose," he tells them. "This is *not* acceptable."

He tempers his remarks by pointing out some of the positive signs, like the highlights on defense. "It's just going to take time for us to jell," he says. Then, to emphasize that he has faith in them, he stresses, "We *will* . . . We'll get it together, I promise you."

He tells them to be back tomorrow morning for an eight o'clock practice, and then says to bring it in. They come together in a huddle in the middle of the locker room, heads bowed, for one last moment.

"Losing," J.T. says, "will never be accepted here at any level or for any reason. We can't use the storm as an excuse."

13

Big Green Indians

Enrollment at John Curtis continues to grow during the second week of school. However, if anyone has labored under the impression that life will snap quickly back to normal, the first post-Katrina weeks prove that New Orleans is in for a long journey of recovery.

Just as the psychologist had predicted, students aren't saying much about how they're feeling. J.T.'s sisters, Kathy and Alicia, have scheduled counseling sessions in the library, and have reminded students that school counselors are available for one-on-one sessions. So far, not a single student has scheduled a visit.

Kathy, who is both a school counselor and a speech teacher, one day takes special note of a kid in her ninth-grade speech class who seems exhausted and sad. His hair is greasy, he's got bags under his eyes, and his fingernails are dirty. She knows the signs of depression and stress, and asks him to wait after class.

"What's wrong, honey?" she asks.

The student, a Patriot player who lives in Kenner, explains how his house got flooded and needs to be gutted. He and his parents are living in a FEMA trailer. After a day of classes and football practice, he says, his mom picks him up and they try to find some fast food. Then, at night, they spend a few hours tearing moldy sheetrock out of their house, sometimes finishing at midnight, and he has to get up early again for school.

"I'm just so, so tired," he says.

Kathy realizes more deeply just how stretched to the max the kids are, both emotionally and physically. She also realizes that the teachers and counselors are going to have to start nudging kids to get them to talk.

While many boys and girls will keep their stories bottled up inside for many months, unable to fully explain to an adult what Katrina has done to them, a handful do begin to reach out.

Students know that J.T.'s door is always open. He often makes teachers and parents wait outside in the hall if a student stops by, knowing that when kids want to talk, you have to listen right away, before they change their minds or lose their courage.

During the second week of school, J.T. gets visits from a number of students and players, including Marcus Jones, a six-foot-three defensive lineman. Marcus says he wants to talk about a toothache, and J.T. invites him right in. Marcus sinks into J.T.'s couch and, in what has become a post-Katrina ritual, tells his storm story.

His mother, stepfather, and his one-year-old brother evacuated to Lake Charles, then had to flee because of Rita. They settled for a while in Baton Rouge, and Marcus attended Baker High School for a few days. Then they moved to Morgan City, forty-five minutes straight south of Baton Rouge, and Marcus enrolled in a school there. At neither school could he muster enough energy to join the football team. The roof of his home caved in during the storm, putting his bedroom out of commission, and forcing him to sleep on a living-room sofa. But he's hardly sleeping, sometimes going two nights in a row without sleep, and what really gets him is that, after a sleepless night or two, he'll break down crying, thinking about missing friends and starving babies, about looting and soldiers, killings and drownings. He feels like he's itching to start a fight, angry at everyone around him, and angry that no one seems able to stop the suffering.

"This is America," he's said to his mom countless times. *"Why?"*

Of course, she has no answer.

On top of that, now his tooth and jaw ache. Maybe it's his wisdom teeth, he wonders. J.T. takes him out of school and drives him to a local dentist, a Curtis graduate and former Patriot, Jimmy Burns. Burns can't find anything wrong with Marcus's teeth. He does notice an ulcer, and starts asking some questions. "Did you burn yourself?"

"No."

"Eat something hot?"

"No."

Finally, Marcus says, "I'm just so tired of sleeping in that front living room." Burns pulls J.T. aside and whispers his diagnosis, "Stress."

J.T. is keenly attentive to the transfer students. He's known many of his students since grammar school, and some since they were babies, having taught or coached their parents. It's odd now to see the unfamiliar faces of all the new kids the school has taken on. He keeps a special eye on them, knowing how hard it must be for kids to be coping with a switch to a new school.

They must now learn from scratch a whole new school culture; new social codes, who's in which clique. They have to struggle to find a niche for themselves within a well-established hierarchy of kids who have mostly been together since kindergarten. P. J. Smith has fit in well on the Patriots' squad, and seems to be making friends easily. Still, J.T. visits his homeroom teacher every morning to ask how he's doing. Lance Frazier, another new Patriot, is also struck by how attentive J.T. is to newcomers like him.

The senior from Chalmette spent a week holed up in the Domino Sugar plant where his father works. Their neighborhood was engulfed by twenty feet of water, and nothing was spared. His school, Archbishop Hannon, is nowhere near reopening. On his first day of class at Curtis, J.T. called him into his office and asked if he'd ever played football. "You should play for us," J.T. said. "We lost a lot of receivers." When Lance said he wasn't sure, J.T. told him to think about it at lunch and give him an answer. Lance arrived at practice that afternoon and found he had a new pair of cleats, pads, and a jersey waiting for him.

J.T. is also keeping his eye on Taylor Schwab, another transfer student from Chalmette. Taylor had been dying to start her freshman year at Andrew Jackson High, and was planning to try out for the cheerleading squad, the volleyball team, and the intramurals club. Her house was flooded up to the roof, and now she and her mom, sister, and brother are living in a River Ridge apartment while the house is gutted. She's already joined the Curtis spirit club and drama club, and is making new friends, but she can't stop thinking how she'd give anything to have her old life back. Another new girl, Brandi Armant, who lost her home in New Orleans East, has been feeling like an outcast since transferring to Curtis. Making the cheerleading squad has helped her feel less like the new kid, but she's struggling, and keeps looking for messages in all the upheaval. At one point she decides Katrina must have been a sign from God. But a sign of what?

For students and teachers alike, these are humbling days. Many kids who were at first too proud or embarrassed to accept handouts agree to take donated clothes or school supplies. Many parents are falling behind on tuition and have offered to work at the school. The Curtises decide to set up a program in which students do some manual labor around the school on weekends, earning one hundred dollars toward tuition for each day of work.

Keeping the kids focused on the daily routine is vital, but with the teachers' lives still in such chaos, it is hard for them to maintain a normal schedule. Many teachers are forced to take mornings and afternoons off to meet with insurance agents or contractors, breaking the rhythm of their classes. They're all trying to keep Katrina reminders out of the school, but the reminders are everywhere: in the unusually quiet lunchroom, where students are eating more and laughing less; in the classroom, where kids slouch and fidget, restless and unfocused.

Coach Rob, who also teaches honors history, is struck by the lack of enthusiasm his kids are showing. His classes are usually lively affairs, with kids encouraged to throw out impromptu questions, comments, arguments, or even jokes. He's been here thirty years and has taught many of these kids' parents. Sporting bushy, dark eyebrows and a bushy white mustache, he's a natural teacher, one of those who's dressed up his drab classroom with a crazy quilt of posters and maps. The concrete block walls are alive with history: a poster of all presidential elections, old roll-up maps of Asia and Europe, a replica of the Constitution, old newspaper pages.

This week, he throws himself into the story of World War II, the first "six-front war . . . it wasn't until World War I that any nation had fought a two-front war and this was a six-front war . . . ." He knows his stuff, and employs a casual teaching style, talking off the cuff about Lend-Lease and island hopping in the South Pacific, the battles of Midway and the Coral Sea. He often makes real-world comparisons between past and present, to excite his kids about historical events that can seem utterly irrelevant.

When he explains how, during the Depression, movie theaters were especially popular because people wanted a distraction from their difficult home lives, he mentions how that's just what New Orleanians need now—distractions from the aftermath of Katrina. Normally, that would prompt a lively discussion or, even better, an argument. Not this week. He gets no comments, no jokes, just down-turned eyes and shuffling feet.

The only glimmer of the old vibrancy is when he tries engaging them with a big question for discussion: How do we solve today's world problems? Mike Walker spits out one of his signature quips, "Drop a nuclear bomb," which earns a few chuckles. At least Mike is trying to be Mike.

When the bell rings, they tromp off toward the low-ceilinged lunch room, where mashed potatoes and gravy, creamed corn, and fried chicken patties await.

Principal Larry Manguno has begun meeting with students who've been referred by their teachers for failure to complete homework assignments. Usually, their excuse is the FEMA trailer—with less than 300 square feet for the whole family, there's no place for them to do homework. Manguno is also seeing more kids than usual lingering outside school at day's end, waiting for parents, friends, or relatives to pick them up. With the local McDonald's and other student spots like the Breakfast Club Diner, the Backyard Barbecue in Kenner, and the mall all closed, there's no place to just hang out.

Some of them have started making the school a second home. Science teacher Cathy Boucvalt, an enthusiastic redhead who has taught science at John Curtis for fourteen years and is popular with the kids, is finding that some students want to hang out in her classroom in the early morning and late afternoon, some of them even on Saturday.

They come to visit her at lunchtime, just to linger among the snake and reptile cages. Others come to use her computers, and she realizes how difficult a lack of Internet access has been for some kids. A few kids bring in pictures to show of their wrecked houses or their FEMA trailer, but they don't say much about how they're feeling. She cuts them slack any way she can, and she's glad that they're finding her classroom something of a sanctuary.

As the second week of classes winds to a close, it's become clear to all that they'll have to adjust to the new definition of *normal*. Post-Katrina, it's normal that gas stations are open one day, closed the next. It's normal for grocery store shelves to be half empty, and for stores to stay open only a few hours a day. It's normal for one neighborhood to have electricity and running water while, a few streets away, there is neither. It's normal for mountains of moldy carpeting and furniture to grow taller along street curbs, and for residents to simply duct tape their rot-filled refrigerators shut and haul them out. And it's normal for rescue workers to keep finding corpses in the attics of flooded homes, as they will continue to do for months.

Jefferson Parish is at least slowly emerging from the trauma; an advisory to boil drinking water has been lifted, and in a heartening sign of resilience, the Come Back Inn in Kenner has started serving its famed roast beef po'boys, and the Treasure Chest Casino has reopened to gamblers. In parts of New Orleans proper, and in Orleans, St. Bernard, and Plaquemines parishes, life still isn't functional at all. Vast sections of the city and its adjacent suburbs are still off limits, with no power, water, or sewer service. Streets are still covered in muck and debris, and military patrols still roam.

Hospitals are seeing waves of injured people who've fallen off roofs, stepped on rusty nails, become dehydrated, been bitten by snakes or dogs, cut themselves with chainsaws, and a slew who've developed strange infections from mosquito bites. Health officials are worried that the city's foul-smelling air is getting fouler, and might cause long-term respiratory problems. One culprit is the Alvar Street shipping terminal, where 52 million pounds of chicken parts are rotting in freezers lacking electricity.

Now that the local media is getting back on its feet, they're reporting more about just how badly public officials handled Katrina, and how badly they continue to handle the cleanup. The news stories seem to get worse by the day. More than 750 inmates have been freed from the Orleans Parish Prison. Dozens of New Orleans police officers have been fired, some for abandoning their posts during the storm, and others who were caught looting on videotape. Other officers have been suspended for beating a man in the French Quarter, an act that was also captured on tape. In Jefferson Parish, officials are under attack for evacuating the operators of the parish's pumping stations before the storm, a decision that residents believe allowed parts of the parish to flood.

As residents begin to learn these details, they are becoming increasingly enraged at the leaders and organizations who have so abjectly failed them, including President Bush, Governor Blanco, Mayor Nagin, the Red Cross, and FEMA. Many are also angry with God.

The official death toll has risen above one thousand, and continues to grow.

Times-Picayune columnist Chris Rose tries to temper all the bad news with his keen observations and wit, joking in print that the return of female strippers to the Déjà Vu club on Bourbon Street is "[O]ne small step towards normalcy—at least as that term is defined in the Big Uneasy." But he admits that nothing else is as it should be, no lines for lunch outside Galatoire's, no Saints games or movies or tourists.

"Inexplicable things seem to be the norm around here these days."

J.T.'s years of turning scared and skinny little boys into finely honed football warriors have taught him to believe in the steady progress of perseverance, and he feels that each day at the school is a baby step toward recovery. Tomorrow night's game will be another step. He's hoping this will be the game that gets his Patriots back in synch.

The only game he could line up for tomorrow was 250 miles away, in Fort Walton Beach, Florida, against the Big Green Indians of Choctawhatchee High. The drive there would normally take four hours, but will now take much longer because the twin spans of

Interstate 10 across Lake Pontchartrain lie in ruins. The Patriots' caravan will leave early tomorrow.

Although the Big Green Indians missed two games last year due to Hurricane Ivan, they've been unaffected by Katrina or Rita. They are a big 5A school and former Florida state champs. Though their record is 1–2, both losses were by just a field goal. J.T. and his assistants only received a scouting tape of the team yesterday, but from a quick review of the footage can tell they have a big front line and a fast-paced West Coast offense full of tricky pass plays, pitch-outs, and sweeps. Their quarterback takes snaps from the shotgun, a risky style for high school. He's jumpy and unpredictable, sliding left and right, twisting through defenders' outstretched arms like a dancer slathered in lard. The Curtis defense, with guys like Tank English and Oscar Ponce de Leon, may be big and stolid, but this guy's just plain magical. J.T. worries that his defenders will have a tough battle. Even on handoffs, the quarterback has this odd technique of bumping into his own running back. Sometimes it only *seems* like a handoff, and with the ball tucked sneakily in his gut, he jukes and spins by defenders for a first down.

The coaches spent many hours over the past week reviewing footage of the loss to East St. John, and one thing J.T. noticed was that Kyle seemed to be playing too gingerly. When Kyle assumed the starter's job, the coaches force-fed him an enormous amount of information about calling plays, reading a defense, and deciphering the hand signals coaches send from the sidelines. He seems to have absorbed those lessons well, and ran most of the offensive plays correctly against East St. John. His problem was a lack of confidence. He seems hesitant on the option, waiting too long to pass, and still protecting his recently healed collarbone.

He needs to be more aggressive and not afraid to run the ball. "Play to your athleticism," J.T. told him this week. If Kyle can't pick it up, there's a talented sophomore named Matt Saucier who's dying to step in.

Of course, Kyle was hardly the only problem. Offensive linemen were jumping offside and running backs were dropping balls. Josh Medley's kicking was off and the defensive secondary got beat on a few pass plays. J.T. is hoping that this past week of practice has

helped his players regain some ground. He knows how intent they all are on erasing the memory of last week's self-inflicted implosion against East St. John, and he thinks a solid victory against a big, strong team will do his Patriots a world of good.

It's a cool Florida Friday night, and stalking the sidelines, hundreds of miles from home, J.T. can't believe what he's seeing on the field. Play after play, his boys are dropping passes, missing tackles and blocks, fumbling the ball, and earning penalties. He's never seen so many fundamental screwups. The offense is disorganized and indecisive. The defense is unfocused and sloppy. His frustration grows with each lame play.

"Terrible by the center," he screams. "Just *terrible* by the center!"

"What is Mike *doing*?"

"Catch the ball!"

"Aw, keep your feet."

"C'mon, *get* his ass."

The Patriots look anything but fearsome tonight. They're playing like third-stringers, and J.T. thinks the somber six-hour bus ride may be to blame. Like some nightmare tourist excursion, the Patriots' caravan rolled through southern Mississippi and Alabama past swaths of devastation and ghost towns and leveled forests for mile after awful mile. On top of that, only a few parents have been able to make the trip. Most are back home working on their mold-infested homes or screaming at insurance agents or FEMA officials.

In a normal year, the Patriots would have played five games by now, and would likely be sitting atop a 5–0 record. In a normal year, no way would they be in Fort Walton, Florida, playing the Choctawhatchee Green Indians, a team they'd never ever heard of until a week ago, and still couldn't pronounce. Chocka-*what* . . . ?

Instead, the Patriots' offense spends most of the first quarter deep in its own territory and the defense keeps getting fooled by the Indians' elusive quarterback, who is steadily chewing up yards, making perfect throws, and converting crucial third-down plays. Early in the second quarter, Mike Walker gets fooled on a run to his

side and the Indians gain twenty. A few plays later, an Indians'
receiver fakes out defensive back Kelby Wuertz, dodging him to grab
a bullet of a spiral and breaking free of Kelby's outstretched arms to
sprint forty yards for the score. The Patriots are down 7–0.

The Curtis teachers realized this past week that things were going
to take much longer than they'd hoped to return to normal, and it's
looking like the Patriots are also going to need more time to regain
their rhythm.

Late in the second quarter, the Green Indians again drive steadily
toward their end zone, helped by a sneaky shovel pass that gains
twenty yards. On first and ten, an Indians' receiver finds a seam just
behind the linebackers and just in front of the safeties. The quarterback nails him, and though he's flattened by Joe McKnight, it's
good for a first down at the twenty. On the next two plays, the Patriots finally stop the kid, forcing two incomplete passes to set up a
third-and-ten with time running out in the first half.

The Green Indians then bring on their field-goal team. The kicker
lines up, the ball is snapped . . . but it's a fake. The Patriots defense
is stupefied as the place-kick holder flings a sloppy pass to a wide-
open receiver who makes the catch and falls into the end zone for a
touchdown.

The Patriots' coaches screech "Whose man was that?" and the
players argue, "That was your guy . . . Hell no, man, he was yours!"

The extra point is good, and the Green Indians go ahead 14–0.

In the stands sits J.T.'s closest friend, Pete Jenkins, a former coach
at LSU who's now with the Philadelphia Eagles. For twenty-five
years the two men have spoken by phone every Sunday morning,
and Jenkins probably knows J.T. better than anyone except Lydia.
J.T. had invited his friend to tonight's game and, knowing how
much this game means to J.T., Pete agreed. He has never seen J.T.'s
face so devoid of passion, so filled with doubt and fear. He's thinking, "This might be the poorest performance I've ever seen by a Curtis team."

With just seconds left in the half, Kyle leads the offense back onto
the field to try and squeeze in one or two more plays. The ball is
placed at the twenty, and in the huddle Kyle calls, "Thirty-base," a
handoff to David Seeman that will veer just right of the center.

Kyle takes the snap, steps to his right, and hands off cleanly. The center, Bryan Munch, and right guard, Andrew Nierman, open just enough of a hole for David to slide through. He then blasts past two linebackers and into the secondary.

The coaches have always known David has the potential to be a good runner, but worried that he was too laid-back for the job. As he gains twenty yards, then thirty, they're amazed at his burst of speed past midfield and into Indians' territory, screaming at him, "Hit it, David. *Hit* it."

He sees a clear shot at the end zone, but the Indians' safety has an angle on him, and is gaining ground fast. Then, seemingly out of nowhere, Joe McKnight intercepts the defender and with a shove sends him sprawling. David coasts the last twenty yards for the score, just as times expires.

The coaches are hugely relieved to be on the board before half-time, especially on an impressive eighty-yard run up the middle. In the locker room, they get right down to business. Coach Jerry gives a spluttering chew-out speech, pointing a finger at player after player, tearing into them about what they're doing wrong. Minutes later, when Jerry walks off, offensive lineman Chris Tusch speaks up, calling the other linemen around him. Tusch *never* talks, so when he opens his mouth, the others get totally quiet.

"They don't deserve to beat us," Tusch says softly, seemingly near tears.

J.T. has rarely seen a team so shaken, not even during last week's debacle against Johnnie Thiel. He decides to slow everything down, realizing his team just isn't ready for this. Despite two weeks of practices, they're still out of shape, and their minds are still elsewhere. They're too green, most of them playing anxiously and without confidence.

A few of his guys are making some great plays, especially Tank and Joe. David is an impressive surprise, and J.T. has actually been heartened by Kyle's performance. At least he hasn't fumbled yet. What's missing is the hard-to-teach X factor, the cohesion and synchronicity that develops in a tight team across a season. So, instead of screaming at them, J.T. goes easy. His team is hurting, nursing deep, hidden wounds.

After all, though he treats them like men, they're just *boys* . . . Just man-sized boys, some sleeping in 240-square-foot trailers or on relatives' floors or in temporary apartments. They lost the beds they'd slept in since childhood. They lost their favorite blankets and their bedroom slippers, their CD collections, and framed pictures of their girlfriends. Some of them had still kept a few stuffed animals from childhood hidden away on a shelf or in the closet, and those are gone, too. Also missing are the friends who evacuated and never came back. So, it's not a hard kick in the butt these boys need now, it's reassurance and comfort.

"Let's just go out and execute," J.T. tells them calmly at the end of halftime, before leading them in a short prayer. "Nothing fancy. And let's not do anything dumb."

The Patriots open the third quarter with their most impressive drive yet. David Seeman, on his first carry in the half, runs for a thirty-yard gain. Kyle follows with an eleven-yard run for a first down. Two plays later, Kyle again gives the ball to David. The offensive line opens a huge hole on the left, and he races twenty yards to score. Josh Medley boots the extra point and, suddenly, the game is tied at fourteen.

On the Indians' next drive, on third and long, Joe leaps to intercept a pass and runs it back twenty-five yards to the Indians' forty. Kyle then drives his team deep into Indians' territory, earning a hard-won first down on a spinning, dancing run of his own. Jeff, who coaches Kyle, sidles up to his dad and says, "He's starting to relax."

On third and goal, Kyle hands off cleanly to freshman running back Kenny Cain who carries two defenders into the end zone with him.

J.T. screams, "Atta *baby*," and the tiny contingent of Patriots fans shake as much noise as they can from their milk jugs.

With the extra point, the Patriots are up 21–14. It's their first lead of the year.

The Patriots' defense ruthlessly protects that lead through the rest of the third quarter and into the fourth. Jacob Dufrene stops one of those tricky shovel passes, and later sacks the quarterback. Mike Klein and Oscar Ponce de Leon each break through the offensive line to make key tackles in the Indians' backfield that drop them for a loss.

In the opening minutes of the fourth quarter, Kyle hits Joe for a ten-yard gain, then gives the ball to David who fights his way for a twenty-five-yard gain that takes the Patriots down to the Indians' thirty. Suddenly, the Patriots' offense is working.

On the same drive, having earned a first down on a keeper, Kyle drops back to pass and sees Joe sprinting to the right rear corner of the end zone. He winds up and throws, but the pass is high and a little short. The Indians' defender gains ground on Joe and they leap at the same time, but Joe leaps higher. He catches the ball with his fingertips and manages to plant both feet just inside the end zone before falling out.

The extra point misses, but the Patriots go ahead, 27–14.

Then, with five minutes to go, the Green Indians strike back, mounting an impressive seventy-yard drive that ends with a quarterback sneak into the end zone, cutting the Patriots' lead to 27–21, with three minutes remaining.

Over the years, J.T. has earned a reputation for greedily possessing the ball and running out the clock. The veer offense is built on the theory that if the offense can just gain three and a half yards per play, by hogging the ball they can win games.

Kyle trots back onto the field needing just a first down or two to secure a victory.

Everyone knew Kyle worked hard and had potential and grit, but he'd had so little real game experience that it was hard to tell just how he'd perform in pressure situations. It's not like he exudes confidence. He's the anti-Johnnie Thiel, a humble guy with an inward confidence and a calm belief in himself, who quietly grinds it out.

The coaches have been impressed with how he's come alive tonight. He's corrected many of last week's problems and, as Jeff said, seems more relaxed. But on first and ten at the twenty-yard line, he takes the snap and turns to his right, looking to give the ball to running back Scotty Encalade. Just as he's about to hand off, he's grabbed at the waist by a defensive lineman. As he stretches to get the handoff to Scotty, the ball squirts loose and bobbles to the turf, and a Green Indians player pounces to recover. They take over just fifteen yards from their end zone, with two minutes to go.

One of J.T.'s prime fears for his team in these early games is that they'll run out of gas deep into the fourth quarter. After fighting fiercely back from a two-touchdown deficit, now they might simply be too exhausted to hold the lead. The players aren't the only ones on the brink of exhaustion. His face is pale and drawn.

If the Green Indians manage to score on this drive, the game is tied. If they score and kick the extra point, the mighty Patriots of John Curtis Christian will be faced with their first 0–2 start since Richard Nixon was president.

On first down, the quarterback hands off to his running back, who slams into the wall of Tank, but still manages to twist ahead for two yards. On second down, a throw is incomplete. On the next snap, Tank inexplicably jumps offside, and the ball is moved ahead to the eight-yard line.

Then, on third and three, Tank redeems himself, all 340 pounds of him busting through the line to take down the Indians' running back for a two-yard loss. The Indians are now at fourth down and five, on the ten-yard line, with a minute to play.

Their shifty, jangly quarterback drops back to pass. He looks for his receiver who cuts across the middle and steps ahead of his defender, Joe McKnight. The quarterback rifles a beautiful spiral into the end zone, a perfect strike aimed right into the receiver's chest. At the last possible millisecond Joe dives, stretching like he's made of rubber, gets two extended fingers into the ball's path, and decisively flicks it out of reach. The Patriots coaches shout, "Our ball! Our ball!" and the meager Patriots crowd erupts.

The Patriots take over on their own ten-yard line, with barely a minute to play. All they need is one first down to run out the clock.

Kyle makes a clean handoff over the left tackle, and the Patriots earn two yards. The Indians call time out. On the next play, J.T. puts Joe in the backfield. He wants the ball in Joe's sure hands. Kyle's handoff is clean but Joe is slammed at the line. He keeps his balance and fights and pushes slowly ahead for four yards, and it takes four defenders to bring him down. Joe hits the ground hard and he's piled upon by the defenders who try stripping the football away.

When the officials break up the pile, Joe is lying face first on the turf, not moving. The Patriots have lost their team trainer, whose house was ruined by Katrina, so the Choctawhatchee doctor comes running out to look at Joe, who seems woozy and disoriented. The doctor, worried about a concussion, calls for a stretcher.

As Joe is carried off the field, Kyle pulls the offense back into the huddle and tries to settle them down, assuring them, "We can *do* this." They all know that if they can't get a first down right now, the Green Indians will get one more shot.

On third and four, Kyle runs an option to the right, and instead of pitching out to his running back decides to keep the ball himself. He plunges ahead, gaining two yards, then another, and seems headed for a first down. But he's dragged down a foot short.

The three-and-a-half-yards-per-play strategy has failed on this series. Three yards per play isn't enough, and it's now fourth and one. The Indians use their final timeout. If the Patriots punt, the Green Indians will still have thirty seconds to score. If the Patriots go for it and gain a yard, the game is over. If they go for it and get snuffed short, the Indians take over, ten yards from their end zone, with plenty of time.

The Choctawhatchee High School band starts playing pow-wow music, and it's like a taunt—you can't beat the Indians, just go home.

The Patriots all know they're lucky to be playing at all tonight. Dozens of New Orleans schools are still closed; some will stay shuttered all year. It's so much better to be playing football than at home pulling up carpets and tearing out walls. If they lose here tonight, though, it's like they won't know who they are anymore. They'll face that miserable six-hour drive back through Mississippi and Alabama, through coastal towns that look like ant hills stomped flat by evil feet, as losers. Some time past midnight tonight they'll drive through downtown New Orleans, past the alien shape of the Superdome, where their team won a rousing victory ten months ago before a crowd of 50,000. It will remind them of the team they *should* be, as well as of all the horrors that so recently occurred there, the rapes, the looting, the bloated bodies floating face down; the ruin of their city. Their pocked and putrid city. Their war zone of a sorrowful city.

They've been hit by two hurricanes over the past six weeks. They've lost teammates whose wounded families moved away. They've had to work in new players who transferred. They've had to travel all the way to Chocta-somewhere Florida. If they can pull it together here, right now, maybe they can prove that they're coming back, that they can spit out the vicious aftertaste of Katrina's ruin and push ahead. As J.T. has told them, they can't do anything about the past. But they can do something, right now, about the future. They can take their lives back.

In the stands, Pete Jenkins thinks he sees a mischievous sparkle spread across J.T.'s face. In fact, J.T. knows exactly what his players want, and decides to let them go for it on fourth down.

"There's always a point in the season where you're faced with a challenge and you see what you're capable of," J.T. will say later. "And you grow up."

This was that moment. In a show of confidence in Kyle, on fourth and a foot from victory, the play called is an off-center quarterback sneak. The Patriots' right guard, Andrew Nierman, loves the sneak. He's confident that he can pound open a hole in the line against any defender, and he's been pressing J.T. to run the ball to his side. "Just run it behind me," he pestered at halftime. Now, he'll get his chance, and the student most likely to become the school's valedictorian is thinking less-than-scholarly thoughts: *I'm gonna kill this guy, I'm gonna kill this guy.* Kyle takes the snap and steps backward a few inches as his offensive line slams with a *crr-ACK!* into the Indians' bulky defense. Later, when Curtis coaches review the game tape, they'll see Andrew's opponent fly five feet backward.

When Kyle sees the opening Andrew has blown open, he tucks his head, protects the ball, and dives with every ounce of strength he's got left into the breach. He's hoping for just one foot, just twelve lousy inches to ignite the Patriots' season.

Indians defenders pile onto him, scrumming to shove him backward, clawing at the ball, even as the officials wildly blow their whistles. When the scrumming stops, Kyle is at the bottom of a dogpile and no one can tell where the ball has landed. As the mound of players is finally pulled apart, it becomes clear the ball is lying right on the cusp. The officials bring the chains onto the field. The Patriots and their fans are frozen in the moment.

The chain is stretched out, and the ball's nose has just barely pushed past the first down.

With twenty seconds to go, in the last play of his first winning game, Kyle snaps the ball one last time and drops to a knee as the clock ticks to zero. It wasn't pretty, but they've scraped out a victory, and their record now stands at 1–1.

The players are pumped, but they're exhausted and emotionally drained. They celebrate a bit on the field, then amble off slowly toward the locker room to shower, and then to the bus for their dreaded six-hour ride home. Many hang their heads low, and Coach Jerry, who was tough on them at halftime, now has to remind them, "Cheer up, guys. We *won*."

Pete Jenkins comes down to the field to chat with J.T. He can see that his friend isn't relishing the victory.

"Not a very good team, is it coach?" Jenkins says.

"No, we aren't," J.T. says softly.

"And I don't know what to do, except go back home and work on getting a little better every day."

14

Homecoming

As the long, harrowing post-Katrina trauma tightens its grip on the city of New Orleans, in the town of River Ridge, a magical alliance begins to grow among the students and staff of the John Curtis Christian School.

Throughout the student body, and across the teaching staff, people are opening up their lives, sharing their homes, and coming together. One teacher and her two kids are living with Miss Merle, who has given them the front bedroom in which Mr. Curtis had recently passed away. The family gets a kick out of the exuberant displays of his art collection, the paintings covering the walls of every room, and the decoy ducks and Hungarian figurines littering the shelves of bookcases. They find themselves uplifted every time they walk across the front yard crammed with sculptures and wind chimes, flowering shrubs and perennials, a fanciful fountain, and a goldfish pond.

Kids have started hanging out at coaches' and teachers' homes after school, and are often invited to stay for a home-cooked meal. On Saturday nights, Leon and Sue are inviting students over to eat popcorn and watch college football.

Coaches and teachers give kids rides to and from school and practice because, with moms or dads off working in Dallas or Shreveport, a lot of two-car families are down to one. Transportation has long been a tricky issue at John Curtis, with kids coming from thirty to sixty minutes away, and the Curtises have always had to help with travel arrangements. Now, the kids are looking out for each other, devising their own car pools. Those with cars post notices on the school's bulletin boards or, at the end of the day, call out, "Who needs a ride to La Place?" Leon finds himself amazed at the kids' spirit.

At J.T.'s house, Joe and Tank have settled into a routine. They grew up together in Kenner and have been friends since fourth grade, but they've now grown much closer, often talking late into the night. J.T. overheard Joe tell a friend, "Tank is like my brother."

They rise early every morning and breakfast on Lydia's eggs, pancakes, or grits, sometimes with a mound of bacon, and they're pitching in with chores, washing dishes, and throwing in loads of laundry. They share a bathroom and drive to school with J.T. most mornings, usually returning home with him after practice. Among the comforts of life with the Curtises are Lydia's dinners. They devour big plates of meatloaf, chicken and dumplings, beef brisket, or red beans and rice.

A few years ago, when J.T. and Lydia added their big family room, they also remodeled the kitchen, and Lydia insisted on installing an oversized refrigerator. She's now glad she did. In the evenings during the week, and on Saturday afternoons after football practice, a procession of kids passes through the home. J.T. and Lydia rarely lock their front door and the kids will usually just knock once and walk right in, looking for Joe or Tank, and hoping to spend some time playing games on the PlayStation.

The house was already busy, with J.T. and Lydia's kids and grand-kids, their siblings, in-laws, nieces, and nephews stopping by at all hours. Now, it's downright bustling. P. J. Smith has become a regular, as has Robby Green. Mike Walker and Kyle Collura visit frequently, when they're not working on their houses with their dads. Being teen boys, they're always hungry and Lydia whips up sandwiches, soup, or macaroni and the kids crowd around her kitchen island, vacuuming up whatever she's prepared. Her grocery bill has soared, but that's fine; she's loving the chance to know the kids better.

She's especially happy to have been able to provide some stability for Joe, and thinks it's great for both Joe and Tank to be exposed to the day-to-day life of her big, wacky family. Sometimes she can't help herself from mothering them a little, and even finds herself correcting their grammar. When Tank says, "What time it is?" she'll look at him in that parental way and say, "What time *is* it." And when Joe asks, "Where Coach Johnny at?" she'll pester him, "You mean, 'Where *is* he'?"

Katrina's wreckage has drawn many of those in the extended Curtis family even closer together. For most, the communal time is therapeutic. But, for Joe, the rhythms of this new lifestyle are complicated and disconcerting.

Joe hasn't been accountable to anyone but himself for years and has come and gone freely from whatever house he calls home at that moment. Now, J.T. and Lydia are always asking, "Where are you going?" "Who will you be with?" and "When will you be back?" And he's still worried about how his mom will feel if he really settles down at J.T.'s.

Meanwhile, Tank's mom has finally managed to find a small house to rent in River Ridge. She'll be leaving Leon and Sue's place soon and Tank will be moving in with her. With Tank leaving, Joe will be at J.T. and Lydia's on his own, which makes him uneasy. He hasn't told anyone yet, but he's thinking about going back to Evangel.

Joe appreciates all J.T. has done for him, as both a coach and a surrogate father of sorts, and he respects J.T. completely. He's also close to Tommy, and will never forget the daily backbreaking weight-lifting sessions he's put him through. Inside the cocoon of the weight room, he opens up to Tommy more than the other coaches.

But, lately, he's looked on Mike Tucker as his primary role model. The similarities are just too hard to ignore. Mike grew up in a rough, African-American section of East St. Louis, the son of a struggling single mother. He was a good high-school football player, and briefly lived with his high-school coach. College was his escape route, after which he found a good job as a police officer, married a nurse, had three kids, and now owns a community mental-health center. He's helped Joe with money, or a bed, or a meal. This summer, he sent Joe to a two-week football camp in California, where Joe met Mike's niece and started dating her. Mike is a family man, a Christian man, and a good role model for Joe, a good *African-American* role model.

Joe doesn't want to abandon the Patriots the way he believes Johnnie Thiel did. But he's confused. Things have changed so much in these past few weeks, and he doesn't feel like he's really in charge of his life any more. He feels caged in.

He calls Tucker and tells him he just doesn't think he belongs at J.T.'s.

"I don't want to stay here no more," he says. "It just don't feel right."

Mike tells him that if Joe had come to live with him, he would have faced the same responsibilities and the same rules. "It's not a control issue," he says. "It's a *care* issue . . . You're in the best place you can be."

Joe says he'll stay a little longer, but once Tank leaves, he may just take off and head back to Evangel. The coaches would take him back in a minute.

When Joe accepted J.T.'s offer of room and board, he said he needed to go back to Evangel one more time for the fall dance, and J.T. told Joe he'd make sure he got there.

On the morning of the dance, Lydia tries to find a bus to take Joe the six hours up to Shreveport, but has no luck. Joanna is at the house and is worried about what will happen if Joe misses the dance. She calls Tommy and tells him, "If my dad lets him down here, he's gone." So, Tommy agrees to drive Joe, to spend the night, and bring him back again on Sunday. Joanna and Tank come along.

During the long ride, Joe opens up about his life, about being hungry as a kid, about his mom's struggles to raise three kids by herself. He also talks about how his father recently tried to rekindle a relationship with him, but that all he has are bad memories of a man who mistreated Joe's mother and neglected him and his siblings.

He says that his mother and brother recently returned from Innis. Before Katrina, they'd been living with Joe's grandmother, whose house flooded, and now they've found a small apartment. There's no room for Joe, though, and even if he wanted to go back to his old ways—sleeping a few nights here and there with relatives—he can't. The storm damaged many of their homes, eliminating that option.

Tommy and Joanna realize more deeply just how different life at J.T.'s house must be for Joe, and just how important it is for him to be there.

A few days later, Tank's mom picks Tank up from J.T.'s place to bring him over to the house she's rented, and she invites J.T. to come along, too. There's a small bedroom for Tank, and she's hung football posters on the wall. The bed is tiny, but she's bought new sheets and a nice spread. She's gathered bags of clothes from the Salvation Army and some local churches, and has laid some clothes on the bed and placed a pair of tennis shoes beside it. She has tried to recreate her son's old bedroom in Kenner.

When they get there, Tank sees that the room is really more of a closet. He's so big that he'll take up half the room himself. The three of them stand in the doorway of the room for a few moments, and Althea is waiting for Tank to say something, anything. Finally, he turns to his mother.

"Momma, I'm sorry," he says, "I love you, but, but . . ."

He finally builds up enough courage and starts wagging his finger like a firebrand preacher. "I *rebuke* this room. I *rebuke* this bed. I rebuke it, Momma, I *do*. This is *not* my bedroom." When he calms down, he tells her he's gotten used to the king-size bed in *his* room at J.T.'s. And besides, he says, as a grin breaks across his face, once his mom, his two aunts, and Miss Dee move in, "There's going to be too many women here."

They decide he can continue to stay with J.T. until she is able to repair their house in Kenner. While she hates being apart, she knows it's probably best that he stay with the Curtises, where he can watch a big-screen television and eat big meals and sleep on a big bed. She also knows it's good for her son to be in the presence of a strong father figure.

Joe is relieved to hear the news. If Tank is going to hang around the Curtises, he figures he will, too. He'll just have to adjust to the life, to all the questions and Lydia's grammar lessons. For a change, he's going to really stay put somewhere.

A few days later, Tank and Joe are sitting in the living room watching television after school, waiting for their coach to get home so they can all have dinner together. He's running late tonight. Joe asks Lydia if she knows where Coach is, and she tells him that J.T. is probably—*where else?*—still in the coaches' office.

"Well," Joe says, "call him up and tell him his two kids are *HON*-gry."

243

Joe and Tank bust out laughing, and Lydia realizes it's one of the first times she's seen Joe laugh.

The Patriots' third game of the season is at St. Charles Catholic, in La Place, west of New Orleans and not far from East St. John. St. Charles is the first of the 2A schools that were on the Patriots' original lineup for the fall. The school was not hurt by either Katrina or Rita and the Comets have played five games so far. They've won them all.

J.T. knows the coach, Frank Monica, because Monica coached Johnny and Jeff at Tulane. Louisiana football is like that, with complex relationships and backstories adding soap-opera intrigue to some games. This is the first time the Curtis boys have faced their ex-coach's team, though, due to Curtis's recent switch to playing 2A schools.

Even before Katrina, playing in the 2A district was going to be an adjustment, after twelve years of playing at the 4A level. This year, Curtis was originally scheduled to play in a New Orleans 2A district, but the LHSAA shifted Curtis to a 2A district far west of the city, requiring all Patriots' teams to travel long distances to games, and prompting Mr. Curtis's angry resignation as headmaster in protest. Now, however, J.T. is actually relieved to be in the district. The city schools he would have faced were ravaged by Katrina, including Peyton Manning's alma mater, Isidore Newman, whose season has been canceled and whose coach has been laid off. The Patriots might not have had a season at all, and J.T. figures Mr. Curtis is probably gloating about that, from up on high.

The Patriots' new district is no cakewalk, though. Four of their five opponents compiled winning records last season, with St. Charles going 8–2. "People who look at this district and don't think it is a true test are crazy," J.T. told sportswriters back in August. On top of having a good coach in Frank Monica, the St. Charles Comets have picked up a dozen good players who were displaced from their old schools by Katrina, including a speedy running back who had been P. J. Smith's teammate at Rummel High. In their first five games, the Comets have outscored their opponents 185–32.

So, J.T. has warned his players to expect a tough contest. And Johnny and Jeff have warned that their ex-coach is a scrappy, bull-dog of a competitor, who would like nothing more than to humiliate the vaunted Patriots of John Curtis.

The Comets' side of the field is packed with spectators and the visitors' stands, while much smaller, are filled beyond capacity. Hundreds of Patriots fans have come tonight, many of them more than an hour early, and the late arrivals are forced to stand alongside the fence beside the field. That's where Kyle's parents, Tank's mom, and David Seeman's mom are gathered, along with a crowd of students, teachers, and alumni.

Mike Walker's parents, Mike and Donna, arrived early, along with Donna's parents, who never miss a game and have driven two and a half hours from Mississippi. Mike's other grandmother, his dad's mom, is still in the hospital. Andrew Nierman's grandparents, Gram-mer and Gramper, never miss a game either, and have driven in from Texas. They always arrive early, to reserve good seats for Andrew's mom and for the Walkers. In the stands, the Niermans and Walkers, along with Jacob Dufrene's parents, decide on the cheer they'll chant for tonight's game: "Stomp the Comets!" Donna Walker's parents, Maw-maw and Paw-paw, have brought a huge garbage bag filled with homemade milk-jug noisemakers. And, as usual, Donna and her mom have brought her popcorn balls.

Along with J.T., the parents are all hoping their sons will finally find their rhythm tonight. J.T. is relieved that his players and the coaches finally had a full week to review footage of their opponent, and he feels good about the defense, which had a great week of practice. The linebackers and the secondary are still a little spotty, and the coaches have been moving players here and there, trying to find just the right lineup. Overall, the defensive line looks like it may become one of the best he's ever had.

The offense, though, still has quite a way to go. The front line is in synch, led by the threesome of Andrew Nierman and Chris Tusch at right and left guard, with Bryan Munch at center, but Kyle still hasn't found his groove. It certainly doesn't help that, except for Joe McKnight, Kyle's receivers and backs are as young and inexperienced as he is.

• • •

It's great therapy for the parents, teachers, and students to be in the stands, a brief reminder that life isn't all about dealing with walls tattooed by mold and roofs tarped in blue, and it's far better to be shouting "Go Patriots!" than arguing with insurance agents.

The Patriots win the toss, and David Seeman runs the opening kickoff back twelve yards to the thirty-three-yard line. Kyle takes the field, looking strong and confident. J.T. would love nothing more than for his team to jump out to an early lead.

On the opening drive, Kyle moves the offense steadily. On second and eight, at the Comets' thirty-five-yard line, he drops to pass. It's always a little unnerving watching Kyle pass. In addition to the hitch in his windup, he has a bad habit of facing the wrong way when he drops into the pocket. Instead of pedaling straight back or to his right on the snap, which would favor his throwing arm, he often backpedals to the left. When he passes, he has to first turn around, from left to right, then cock his arm, and throw. On this play, as Kyle backpedals, he sees Joe open deep down the left sideline but, by the time he turns around to throw, Joe is covered. Kyle takes two steps to his right and fires toward David Seeman instead. The throw is high and the pass is incomplete.

On third down, Joe again sprints toward the end zone and is wide open, but Kyle is looking for his tight end, Kevin Wild. Kyle backpedals, does his left-to-right spin, cocks, and throws a wobbly pass that soars over Kevin's outstretched hands and right into the arms of a Comets' defender, who runs the ball back fifteen yards.

"Jiminy CRICK-ets!" J.T. shouts, and rips off his headset, furious that the opening drive has ended with a turnover. He hates turnovers almost as much as personal fouls.

After the whistles have blown, Kyle is caught off guard by a Comets' linebacker, who flattens him and keeps him pinned to the turf for a few seconds. "Get *off* me," Kyle shouts, wrestling his way free and jumping up, looking for an official to call the penalty. When he sees that they're not going to throw a flag, he storms off the field, furious at both the interception and the late hit.

J.T. worries that Kyle will now lose his composure. As for the

Patriots' defense, though, the sucker punch just fires them up. On the first play of the Comets' drive, a sweep to the right, their running back has a clear path down the right sideline, but Mike Walker nimbly sheds a blocker, dives, and stops the runner with a one-armed tackle. He leaps to his feet and stalks defiantly back to the huddle, as his parents and grandparents wildly scream, "Yeah, Mike! Go, Mike!"

On the next play, a swing pass, Tank English makes a statement of his own. He gets a good read on the pass and overpowers his blocker, breaking up the play in the backfield. He's joined by Jacob Dufrene and Oscar Ponce de Leon, and they drop the receiver for an eight-yard loss. Two plays later, the Comets punt. The Patriots' third game of the year is ten minutes old, and the score is 0–0.

On the next drive, Kyle moves the offense down the field, helped by a long pass to Joe McKnight and two more nice runs by David Seeman. On first and goal, at the three-yard line, Kyle takes a quarterback sneak to within inches of the end zone. Then, on the next play, he plunges into the slot between Bryan Munch and Andrew Nierman. He's stopped at the line, but keeps his legs pumping as his blockers crack open a small hole and Kyle squeezes into the end zone.

The Patriots' fans roar, but Kyle's parents, Steve and Melody, miss the play entirely. With the bleachers filled, they are standing down at field level and can barely see over the heads of the players on the sidelines.

"What happened? I can't see," Melody keeps asking, and when she learns that Kyle scored she screams, "He *what*? He scored and I missed it?"

Kyle doesn't waste any time celebrating. He calls the offense right back into the huddle before the extra-point attempt. As the place-kick holder, Kyle takes the snap, tees up the ball, and Josh Medley nails a line drive for the extra point, to put the Patriots up by seven. As Kyle trots off the field, J.T. likes what he sees. Gone is the anger of the interception. Also gone is the tentativeness of recent weeks.

The drive seems to do the trick for the rest of the team as well. Play after play, the Patriots come into synch. J.T. senses that they're finding their groove, and he's encouraged by the subtleties of body language that only a coach can read: an extra confidence in their swagger, an eager, hungry look when they line up in their stance.

Washington Redskins coach George Allen used to say that football "isn't necessarily won by the best players. It's won by the team with the best attitude." Finally, J.T. feels his team is finding the right mix of trust in each other and confidence in their true talents.

On the Comets' next drive, the Patriots' defense shuts them down with authority. Mike is reading their plays as if he's a psychic, and then calling out last-second adjustments to the other linebackers and safeties, shouting out that the play is going to be a run or a pass, that it's coming left or right. He makes three unassisted tackles and Jacob Dufrene, Colby Arceneaux, and P. J. Smith each step up to make some great tackles of their own. The defense gives up just twenty yards and the Comets punt.

Kyle takes over on the thirty and drives the offense steadily, surely, a few yards at a time. The veer is back. The game is getting more and more physical, though, and Kyle is again flattened on what appears to be a late hit. The Comets have started cat-calling and trash-talking at the line, spitting out insults and expletives. At the end of a hard-fought ten-yard run by Joe, the two teams begin scuffling. Two flags fly, and the penalty goes against the Patriots, who are pushed back ten yards. In the huddle, Kyle tells the others to "settle down . . . Just ignore them and play the game."

Showing the trash-talking Comets just who they're dealing with, on first and ten at the fifty-yard line, J.T. calls for a left-of-center run known as a *trap*. The offensive line slams ahead like a battering ram and Kyle hands off to running back Blaine Roberts. The linemen blast open a hole big enough for a car to drive through and Blaine races down the field untouched for a fifty-yard touchdown. The Patriots are up 13–0.

The Comets are again shut down and on the Patriots' next drive Kyle flings a long, confident pass to newcomer P. J. Smith, who leaps over two defenders to haul it in, earning thirty-eight yards and moving deep into Comets' territory. Three plays and a short touchdown run by David Seeman puts the score at 19–0.

Before the game, Tank had told his teammates that after their loss to East St. John and the too-close-for-comfort win in Florida, he wanted a shutout tonight. A *real* Patriots' game. His fellow linemen— Mike Klein, Oscar Ponce de Leon, and Stephen Champagne—are committed. They're putting a wall of pressure on the Comets, but on the next drive, following a long kickoff return, the Comets' quarterback pulls off a few improbable third-down passes and brings his team down to the thirty. The shutout is in danger.

On third down and twelve, the quarterback drops to pass but Mike Walker blitzes like a wildman, arms flailing overhead and eyes ablaze. With Mike charging at him, the quarterback lets loose a hurried pass to his running back. In an impressive rebuke of gravity, Tank leaps over the receiver's head and picks off the ball. Then, in one of the most unlikely, spirited plays J.T. can remember, Tank rumbles ahead with an open field in front of him, cradling his first interception as if it's his first born. Tank is flying, but he's so intent on protecting the ball that after a dozen fast yards he trips over his own feet.

"Ho . . . lee . . . *MACK*-erel!" J.T. shouts on the sidelines, almost breaking into a laugh. The players swarm onto the field to throw themselves all over Tank.

In the press box, the announcers are impressed: "Tank's fast," one says. "Yeah," says the other, "for a fat dude."

Just before the end of the first half, Kyle caps another drive with another quarterback sneak for another touchdown. The half ends, 25–0, Patriots.

J.T. is all business at halftime, but commends his team for staying focused on the basics and for hogging the ball. Kyle hasn't been passing all that well, but his handoffs have been clean and the Patriots have been chewing up the field in five- and ten-yard increments. Of the twenty-four minutes in the first half, the Patriots were in possession for eighteen. Following Kyle's interception, they scored on their next four possessions, earning 283 yards and eleven first downs in the first half. The defense has allowed only one first down. This, at last, is a Patriots game.

They continue to play solid ball in the second half. Joe scores on a beautiful dancing, spinning forty-three-yard run, bringing the score to 31–0. For the first time in this ratty season, J.T. starts putting in his second- and third-team players, and they step up and manage to hold the Comets scoreless the rest of the game.

Mike Walker comes off the field, pumping his fist and shouting, "This is how it should be." On the bus home, they laugh and replay

Tank's comical interception over and over: "You would have *scored* if you hadn't tripped!," and congratulate Kyle, who scored twice. The bus is all abuzz with talk of how they're finally clicking.

J.T. lets his players enjoy the victory. After all, the Patriots had never played St. Charles before, and they scored thirty-one unanswered points against a previously unbeaten team. Best of all, they have improved to 2–1 on the season.

Back at the school, J.T. tells them "Nice game," and "Good defense," keeping it low key. They've got some tough opponents coming up, and he's not taking anything for granted. There's still work to be done, especially on offense, and he tells his players, "I'll see you back here, eight tomorrow morning."

On Friday, October 21, the Patriots are traveling west into sugar-cane country to play another district 2A opponent, the Rebels of Riverside Academy, on the banks of the Mississippi. New landmarks line the route, tent cities and trailer cities, makeshift villages of the disenfranchised. Scores of abandoned cars are orphaned beneath highway overpasses. Piles of garbage lie everywhere. Orange detour signs and traffic cones glow at every intersection. Downed poles and signs and trees and light posts and billboards are strewn everywhere.

Traveling east of downtown would be worse. The players would look out at mile after mile of ruined apartment complexes, flattened neighborhoods, ravaged shopping malls, fast food joints, churches, restaurants—all closed. Two months after Katrina, their city is still without electricity in many neighborhoods, many ATM machines are still without cash, and many gas stations are still without gas.

The Patriots have recently learned more details about some of their missing classmates. Linebacker Preston Numa, it seems, might be coming back in a week or two. It's been confirmed that Kenny Dorsey won't be returning, nor will running back Darryl Brister, or two of the team's wide receivers, Randell Legett and Brandon Scott.

Fortunately, a few of the new guys are playing well, especially receiver P. J. Smith. Unfortunately, another Katrina transplant, Lance Frazier, the kid from Chalmette, is out for the year. After playing at wide receiver in the first two games, he was visiting an ex-classmate from his old school, who's been displaced to Mississippi. The boys were driving ATVs and Lance fell off and shattered the bones in his forearm. "Rock bottom again," he told J.T., when he'd returned from three days in the hospital, following surgery to puts screws and plates into his ruined arm.

With his team so much in flux, and a tough opponent in the Riverside Rebels, J.T. is leery that last week's shutout may have been more a fluke than a sign of a definitive turnaround. That fear seems affirmed when his team finds itself off to a sluggish start against the Rebels, who have a huge defensive line and are shutting down the Patriots' running game. The Patriots manage to score on a field goal toward the end of the first quarter and, in the second quarter, J.T. decides to switch tactics and take a chance on Kyle's arm but, after mounting a strong drive into Rebels' territory, Kyle suddenly throws an interception. Five plays later, the Rebels score, and the Patriots are trailing 6-3 with less than a minute left in the half.

On the kickoff, the Rebels send a short dribbler of a kick down the field, apparently in an effort to keep the ball away from Joe McKnight, who earlier almost scored on a punt return. The Patriots refuse the bait, and wait patiently for the ball to dribble all the way back to Joe, then create a wall of blockers in front of him. Joe follows his blockers for twenty yards down the right side, then reverses field and sprints clear across to the other sideline, and is finally chased out of bounds at the thirty.

When Kyle comes onto the field, there's just thirty seconds left in the half. He takes the snap and drops for what looks like a pass, but then hands off to David Seeman, who breaks through the Rebels' big line, and powers his way all the way down to the ten-yard line. There's only time for one more play, and J.T. decides to play it safe. With five seconds left in the half, Josh Medley kicks his second field goal to tie the score. The Patriots are disgusted by the 6–6 score, frustrated they're not moving the ball better.

At halftime, J.T. speaks calmly to his shaken team, reminding them that they can't underestimate Riverside, whose record is now 5–1.

"We're a little flat," he tells them. "And that's okay. That's not unusual in the middle of the season. Sometimes you hit a little spell where you go a little flat. We won a big game last week, dominated it pretty easily, but you got to understand that the teams that play along the river, they have a little different, shall we say, *attitude*."

It's a bit of an inside joke, an effort to loosen them up. In the Patriots' new district, all of the teams are west of New Orleans, along the Mississippi. The players are beefy country kids from sugarcane country mixed with inner-city kids from La Place and Reserve. "They think they're a little better, they think they're a little tougher—I can't describe it exactly, other than to say it's just a little bit of an attitude," J.T. says. "So, if you remember what we've talked about in practice . . . and just execute."

J.T.'s calm pep talk does the trick and, in the second half, the Patriots come booming back, scoring fifteen unanswered points. Kyle throws two touchdown passes, one to tight end Jacob Dufrene and a beauty to P. J. Smith. The defense completely shuts down the Rebels' running game, and the Patriots escape from the sugarcane fields of Reserve with a 21–6 victory, and a 3–1 record.

After the game, J.T. calls the team together in the end zone.

"Except for that play we screwed up on and gave them the touchdown, we did a nice job of playing good solid defense," he says.

Then, sensing that his team is ready for the extra push, he says, "I knew that was a good team, but we can play better. Are we gonna do it better?"

"Yes sir," the Patriots respond enthusiastically.

"We'll begin that tomorrow," he says. "Eight-thirty. Clear?"

"Yes, sir."

"Come in for our prayer, please . . ."

On Monday, October 23, the school bulletin announces, "The Patriots will play their first home game of the season at Muss Bertolino Field on Thursday night. The game will be against the highly regarded St. James Wildcats. Thursday night will also be Homecoming for the Patriots. We hope to have a good crowd."

Unlike his boisterous father, J.T. does not readily display his emotions. He trusts the discipline of method over the adrenaline rush of pure feeling, and he doesn't ever ruminate. He's uncomfortable being left alone with his own thoughts and refuses to travel to coaching clinics alone, always insisting, as his dad did, that someone else drive with him. Instead of looking inward, *What am I feeling?*, he is always thinking outward, *What can I do next?* His philosophy of football has also been to strip out the emotion, which is why he doesn't pump his fists after touchdowns and, in victory, celebrates with little more than a satisfied grin.

But there's no denying the fervor of this bizarre season, and the emotions that he usually tries to keep off the field have now become his team's secret weapon. He knows, from the one-on-one sessions in his office, that players are still frustrated and angry about the excruciating, ongoing drama of the storm's aftermath. Yet, with every tackle, every triumphant quarterback sack, every reception, completion, and victory, they're throwing off a little bit more of the pain. And, as he watches a few players emerge as team leaders, he's beginning to realize that he's never had a team quite like this one.

Tank is playing like a kid with nothing to lose, manhandling opponents like they're dolls. Mike Walker's become just the leader he aspired to be, flooring J.T. with his fierceness. He's risen above anything the coaches expected eight weeks ago, overcoming his lack of speed with an intuitive ability to read plays and get his body to the right spot at the right time.

Andrew Nierman, the elder statesman of the offensive line, has rallied the younger linemen around him, building a strong wall of protection for Kyle. That protection has boosted Kyle's confidence, allowing him to start making big plays. What impresses J.T. most about Kyle is his ability to bounce back, to not get rattled.

Just two months ago, David Seeman was considered number three or four on J.T.'s list of running backs. The coaches have been stunned by his composure on the field and his ability to muscle his way for the extra yards. He's already racking up more yards than any Patriot running back has in years. And P. J. Smith is a delightful surprise, so much so that J.T. has decided to start playing him on offense and defense.

As for Joe, he's playing with every bit of natural ability and drive that J.T. expects. He's making up huge gains on kickoff and punt returns and, on defense, has had at least one interception per game. On offense, he's snaring passes at wide receiver and ripping off long gains at running back. He's never been one to take a stab at overtly leading the team, but his leadership by example has been outstanding. J.T. has also detected a new feeling of something else—inner peace? J.T. was well aware of how hard it was for Joe to adjust to the restrictions of living in his house and, while signs of unease remain—Joe still locks his bedroom door—he's felt Joe becoming more at home.

J.T.'s plan after Katrina was to get his players focused again on the one thing they could control: the game, the ball, and their opponent. With each game, that focus has increased, and the team has become a tighter machine.

The coaches are always amazed at how the culture of a team can change from year to year. Last year, with Johnnie Thiel as quarterback and a slew of senior starters, the team was sassy and bit mouthy. This year's young team, maybe because of all they've been through, is quieter, more serious, and its leaders all lead by example.

For the teachers, students, parents, and alumni of John Curtis Christian School, football games have become a lifeline to their former lives, and a deliciously exhilarating reminder of how good life can be, of how emotionally satisfying and inspiring it is to just watch a crushing competition on the football field of battle.

Screaming on Friday nights for the Patriots is like screaming *back* at Katrina, whose remnants lurk constantly.

Muss Bertolino, a few miles from the school, is the Patriots' traditional home arena. This may be the Patriots' homecoming game and the year's only home game, but there's a terrible irony about a homecoming at Muss Bertolino.

For a month, the field served as a staging ground for relief workers and a campsite for those left homeless by the storm, packed with hundreds of tents, campers, and trailers. During their weeks of re-shingling damaged roofs or covering them with tarps, the relief workers had set up lawn chairs, card tables, and charcoal grills, turning the stadium into one of the many such tent cities that mushroomed across the region after Katrina.

The relief workers and their tents are all gone now, and the field has been cleaned up, with the only major lingering sign of Katrina being the scoreboard, which was toppled and damaged by heavy winds. Officials will have to use a small, tabletop LED timer and scoreboard borrowed from a local basketball team.

J.T. considers the St. James Wildcats the toughest of his 2A opponents. The Wildcats played in 3A last year but lost a few students and were bumped down. Like St. Charles, they're a physical, smack-talking team with a highly touted running back and a great defense. Veteran head coach Rick Gaylie has been running a fast-paced Wing T offense as long as J.T. has been running the veer. An assistant St. James coach had told Johnny at a preseason game they were scouting, "My guys are animals, we're going to rip somebody's head off." In short, this should be just the kind of game Patriots' fans live for.

Many parents who had been unable to make it to previous games arrive early for tonight's seven o'clock homecoming contest. The Patriot team buses arrive an hour before kickoff, and the parking lot and stands are already packed.

A few homecoming traditions have been canceled. There's no official pregame tailgating party or Friday night Get Acquainted spaghetti dinner in the gym. Fortunately, the dance is still scheduled for Saturday night, and students have been buzzing all week about who's going with whom and who's wearing what, looking forward to erasing the memory of Katrina completely from their lives for one charmed night.

Lydia, as she always does at home games, sings the national anthem, and many parents in the stands feel their emotions rising in their chests, the pain and grief and anger and fear giving way to a deep sense of pride in being here on this perfect autumn night.

In what seems to have become a signature, the Patriots get off to a sloppy start. On the Wildcats' opening drive, P. J. Smith gets fooled by a receiver, and the kid hauls in a forty-yard pass. P.J. just barely prevents a touchdown by making a shoestring tackle, and the noise and energy seeps out of the Patriots' side of the stands. Soon, the Patriots defensive line rallies and, after three authoritative plays, they give up just six yards, forcing the Wildcats to punt.

J.T. figures that homecoming jitters are done now, and he expects the offense to find a groove, but as Kyle takes over for the opening drive, he looks tentative and a little shaky. He manages to earn a first down, but on first and ten he makes a bad handoff to Blaine Roberts, and the ball pops loose. As Kyle spins around looking for the ball, other Patriots and several Wildcats dive for it. The Patriots fans wince. When the players are pulled off the dog pile, it turns out that the Patriots have recovered. But on the next play, Kyle backpedals to pass and again drops the ball. He scoops it back up himself this time, but is quickly sacked for a fifteen-yard loss, and the Patriots have to punt. Kyle storms off the field, yelling at himself and at anyone who comes near him. The St. James defense has proven just as fast and smart as J.T. had warned. They swarm the ball and aren't easily fooled. Kyle is going to have to regain his composure fast, and he knows it.

On the next drive, after the defense again shuts down the Wild-cats' vaunted Wing T offense, actually pushing them back five yards over three plays, Kyle suddenly starts taking control in the huddle, speaking more loudly and urgently to his players, and barking orders at the line of scrimmage, pointing out shifts in the defensive lineup. His passes are still off; he's overthrowing and underthrowing. But he's taken charge.

After a steady drive to start the second quarter, helped by a huge David Seeman run on third-and-fifteen, the Patriots stall at the Wildcat's fifteen but Josh Medley nails a field goal, and they go up 3–0.

Then, just when the team seems to be getting in synch, the defense falls off its game. The Patriots' secondary is badly fooled by another long pass on the Wildcats' next drive, and the receiver sprints eighty yards for a touchdown. Mike Walker chases the receiver all the way into the back of the end zone, and is stunned that his team has let the Wildcats go ahead. An uneasy quiet spreads across the John Curtis grandstands.

On the field, the Wildcats begin taunting the Patriots. "John Curtis ain't *nothin'*! *Y'all are going* down!" Mike finds himself struggling to keep his anger in check. Even from their spot in the stands, his parents can tell he's barely controlling his temper.

J.T. warns his players not to get lured into fights and to avoid on-the-field conflicts that might draw a penalty flag. His advice is that they just point up at the scoreboard and walk away.

But there's no scoreboard tonight and, even if there were, it would show the Patriots losing 7–3.

For many weeks now, Mike has been living in the FEMA trailer his parents ordered, which turned out to be the right choice. His dad parked it right in the driveway, and he and Mike have been tearing out carpeting and sheetrock almost every night. At first, they were at least able to take showers in their house, since the water there was still working. Then the water line was crushed. Apparently, after sitting in a lake for two weeks, the foundation of the house sank, cracking the water pipe. Mike and his folks now have to cram into the two-foot-square box of the trailer's shower stall.

Their first trailer meal was roast chicken with macaroni and cheese, which Mike's mom served so proudly that it was as if she had dug deep into her hunter-gatherer genes and accomplished something heroic. She is still commuting ninety minutes to Baton Rouge and his dad is commuting ninety minutes to Hammond. Mike's sister comes home from college on weekends to help around the house. With four of them in the trailer, there's no privacy at all.

Mike's dad wakes up at five to get an early start on the commute, and the family learned right away that when one person wakes up in a FEMA trailer, everyone wakes up. At night, after Mike's football practice and his parents' hour-and-a-half drives home, they eat a quick dinner, then trudge into their former living room, kitchen, and bedrooms. They're making steady progress in gutting the house and are already talking about a Thanksgiving Day return, but there are plenty of ups and downs.

Before Katrina, the Walkers loved entertaining, whether it was neighbors or Mike's teammates. Some nights, six of Mike's friends might sleep over, and they'd get up at three in the morning to gorge on peanut-butter sandwiches. Now, Mike is visiting other friends' houses or J.T.'s house, and the trailer is ghostly quiet. Only once did Tank and Andrew Nierman visit Mike, and Donna yelled at the three boys, "Don't all stand on one side! It'll flip over!"

The players all know Mike's situation and how hard it's been on him. The trailer was embarrassing at first, but by now it's become a badge of honor. For the thousands of New Orleanians who are coping with trailer life it says: I'm a Katrina survivor.

Mike isn't just a survivor, he's come alive in a whole new way. And, in what's fast become an infuriating game against the trash-talking Wildcats, he makes a proud survivor's statement. Feeling more energized than he has all season, the taunting from the Wild-cats only spurs him on, and he begins stuffing guys at the line, breaking up pass plays, making bruising solo tackles, and repeatedly sacking the quarterback.

The offense comes alive, too. Late in the second quarter, the Patriots are looking at fourth down and four at the ten-yard line. Instead of trying for the field goal, J.T. decides to go for the first down, and calls a 30 Base, the most basic play in his offense.

Kyle takes the snap, and turns to hand off to Joe. The teammates actually collide at the line of scrimmage, and the Wildcats, unable to tell which player has the ball, swarm all over Joe. By the time they realize he doesn't have the ball, it's too late. Kyle has slithered around them and into the end zone, completely untouched.

The extra point is good and the Patriots take a 10–7 lead into halftime.

After Kailen Fenerty is crowned the Patriots' Homecoming Queen in the halftime pageant, the second half is all Patriots' defense. A St. James drive is dashed by a Kelby Wuertz interception. On the Wild-cats' next drive, their quarterback lobs a high downfield pass, and Joe stops, pivots, and leaps above the receiver's head to snag the ball. He sprints fifty-five yards down the sideline and, by the time he crosses the goal line, there isn't an opponent within twenty yards. The Patriots go up 17–7.

On second and fifteen, on their own five-yard line, the Wildcats' quarterback can't find an open receiver, and is grabbed by line-backer John Ruttley. When the quarterback tries to throw, Oscar Ponce de Leon slaps his arm and the ball drops to the turf.

Mike Walker dives flat out, arms stretched like he's Superman. At first, Mike thinks he's merely recovered a fumble, but Colby Arce-neaux is bouncing wildly up and down beside him, screaming, "It's a touchdown! Dude, it's a touchdown!" It's the first time Mike has scored since his playground years. In the stands, his parents are on their feet, shrieking and hooting. They're bombarded by jubilant hugs and kisses from other parents. Mike's teammates crowd around him, punching and shoving him, pounding him on the shoulders, and head-butting his helmet. It takes a full thirty seconds for the players to break apart and line up for the extra point. Tears streak down Mike's mother's face.

The Patriots hold the Wildcats scoreless in the fourth quarter, for a 24–7 victory and their third consecutive win. They are now 4–1 and, with the short six-game schedule, if they can win their last district game next week, the district championship will be theirs, and they'll be headed for the playoffs.

Later that week, Mike's mom gives him a framed collage she's made that includes a blown-up photo of Mike's touchdown, and a newspaper headline that reads, DEFENSE LIFTS CURTIS TO WIN OVER DISTRICT FOE ST. JAMES.

Mike hangs it in the small cubby of the trailer that has become his bedroom.

15

State

Thanksgiving 2005 is a poignant, difficult time for the city of New Orleans, for those who are back in their homes, for those who have lost their homes, and for those spread far and wide in cities, towns, and trailer parks they never wanted to call home.

Officials are encouraging residents to return, with promises that the city's tap water has finally been deemed drinkable and that electricity is being steadily restored. In the French Quarter, there are some meek signs of recovery. Although Café du Monde remains shuttered, as do most of the quarter's world-famous restaurants, a few of the buggy drivers have returned, offering mule-drawn carriage rides to the scant few tourists who have braved the trip out of support for the beleaguered icon of good times.

An open-air carriage ride is a hard sell, though, with the air still filled with the stench of rot from the piles of beef, chicken, pork, and other groceries emptied from the freezers of Zara's Supermarket onto Prytania Street in the days after Katrina. The street is now a swarming breeding ground for flies, and the sidewalk is slick with maggots. Who can blame residents for their reluctance to return?

Just as Mayor Nagin had warned only days after the storm, it's looking like New Orleans will become a city half its former size. Officials say more than one hundred thousand residents have become permanent citizens of Baton Rouge, and tens of thousands of others are staying put in Houston, Atlanta, and other cities, not expected to return any time soon. School officials say just ten thousand students will return to city schools this year, and only twenty thousand next year, down from nearly sixty thousand before the storm. Even in Jefferson Parish, the student population is at thirty thousand, down from a prestorm enrollment of fifty-one thousand.

Nagin has fired three thousand workers, half the city's workforce, and the only available jobs seem to be at fast-food joints, some of which are so desperate to reopen they're offering six-thousand-dollar signing bonuses and eight-dollar-per-hour salaries, up from five dollars and fifteen cents before Katrina. Officials are worried about a post-Katrina brain drain as middle- and upper-class residents with the means to relocate are replaced by low-income workers.

Meanwhile, morticians and coroners continue the sorrowful task of counting and identifying the dead. So far, Louisiana has put the death toll at 1,057, and hundreds more have died in Mississippi and Alabama. Even now, two full months after the storm, bodies are still being discovered and will continue to be found in ruined Lower Ninth Ward and New Orleans East homes for months. The death toll will rise to nearly fifteen hundred.

Similar to the essays the *New York Times* published on the victims of the 9/11 attacks on the World Trade Center, the *Times-Picayune* has begun running a poignant series of articles, "Katrina's Lives Lost." The newspaper's Thanksgiving Day installment includes a profile of Roy "Lucky" Tidwell, a World War II Purple Heart recipient who raised parakeets and rabbits. He and his wife drowned in their Gentilly home.

As the weeks have passed, everyone has realized that it's not the clothes or appliances or cars or even the houses themselves, but the irreplaceables that are missed the most: wedding and baby albums; classic LP records; love letters; a handmade rifle handed down from a grandfather. Emotions are still hair-trigger. Like many others, Lydia can't help it, she still cries at some point every day, at the slightest provocation.

And Thanksgiving, it turns out, will not be the turning-point holiday many had hoped. Instead of hosting a big meal, many New Orleanians go out to eat, though it's a battle to find an open restaurant. Others leave the city to spend the day with relatives in unsullied homes, well away from all the ruin, filth, and stink.

• • •

For the Patriots of John Curtis Christian School, this year's Thanksgiving, as every year, means early morning football practice.

The traditional Thanksgiving practice is more about taking time in a formal way to engage in some team fellowship, rather than an intense workout. J.T. puts players through just a few drills on goal line situations and special teams, and reminds them what to expect of their next opponent. The real point of the practice is the devotional that follows.

Like many John Curtis traditions, the Thanksgiving practice and devotional started in 1975, when the Patriots won their first championship. That year was the first time J.T.'s team had made it so deep into the playoffs, and, not wanting to take any chances, he called for an early Thanksgiving morning workout so players would still have time to spend the holiday with family. In the locker room afterwards, he hosted an impromptu prayer session and asked players to mention something they were thankful for. The tradition grew from there, and the session is now open to all parents and alumni; it's a chance to stand up, state their name, and tell others what they've been up to since they left Curtis.

This year, as J.T. looks out at multiple generations of Curtis grads, he realizes that the crowd is bigger than normal.

Men and women who are now among a dying breed—those who graduated while Mr. Curtis was still the school's leader—take turns saying a few words about what the school has meant to them. Ex-Patriot David Gilmore, who was part of two championship teams, in 1975 and 1977, turns to the young men now proudly carrying the Patriots' mantle and tells them, "Guys, this is the best part of your life right now. Treasure. Every. Moment." As he says these words, the younger Patriots nod their heads, not one of them doubting that he'll ever forget a minute of this ridiculous season.

J.T. then steps forward to address the large crowd. Normally, the Thanksgiving devotionals come easily to him. This year feels different, and he can't help thinking, *What would my dad say?* It's been hard not having his father's spiritual guidance just a quick phone call away, and the responsibility of serving as the school's spiritual leader suddenly feels like a heavy load. J.T. reminds the crowd that they've all faced uncertainty before, and they will again. J.T. tells them, in words his dad so often used, "We must walk by faith, not by sight." He urges his players and alumni, "Have faith that God is in control. Trust that he has a plan for the school and for each of our lives."

Following a brief prayer, J.T. concludes with his traditional plea for restraint, addressing the players' mothers: "Mommas, make a big plate of food, cover it in Saran Wrap, and put it in the fridge. Your boys can eat as much as they want, eat 'til they're sick, but not until Saturday."

J.T. has been worried about this holiday, knowing that so many of his kids—Mike Walker, Kyle Collura, Joe, and Tank—won't be back in their own homes. To at least make sure that the two Patriots who've become part of his own home enjoy a well-deserved holiday, he's invited Joe and Tank to spend Thanksgiving with his family.

The Curtises, as they do every Thanksgiving, meet at the home of J.T.'s sister Kathy and her husband, Darryl. Kathy cooks a turkey and, as always, everyone brings a dish: J.T. and Lydia bring a barrel of mashed potatoes; J.T.'s daughter, Joanna, brings her asparagus and egg dish; his sister Alicia brings a bounty of pumpkin, pecan, and apple pies; and sister Debbie brings a turducken—a rolled-together concoction of turkey, duck, and chicken that is a New Orleans tradition. Dozens of siblings and cousins and in-laws fill the house with noise, and everything feels as it should be.

Except for one thing, which hits them all hard as the forty-plus family members, along with Joe and Tank, begin to take their places around the dinner tables. Mr. Curtis isn't with them, and this is the family's first Thanksgiving without him.

When they were growing up, J.T. and his siblings would ask their dad on weekends, "What are we going to do?" And he'd always respond, "The three Fs!" which meant family, food, and fellowship. Then he'd take them into New Orleans for a big meal at Arnaud's or Antoine's. As one who so loved food, Thanksgiving was Mr. Curtis's favorite holiday. He'd preside like a king at court, ogling the mounds of savory food.

His absence is suddenly, strikingly conspicuous. One by one, the Curtises say a few words of thanks, then a few heartfelt words for Mr. Curtis. "It's because of your strength that we're all here," Kathy says. "And we miss you."

Finally, Miss Merle stands up to say a simple, perfect, final blessing. "Your daddy would be so happy to see all of you together like this."

Over the past three weeks, the Patriots have played with inspired fervor.

A week after their homecoming victory, in the last of their four district games, the Patriots faced the Donaldsonville Tigers. The defense was again suffocating, giving up just one first down in the first half. Kyle kept his composure, playing with authority and poise, giving up no fumbles or interceptions. By the third quarter, the Patriots were up 34–0, thanks to David Seeman, who made three touchdown runs, and to a nicely executed touchdown pass from Kyle to Joe McKnight. Even with the second- and third-team guys playing in the final quarter, the Patriots emerged with a 34–15 victory, improving their record to 5–1 and securing a playoff berth.

A highlight of the Donaldsonville game was the return of linebacker Preston Numa. After two months in Baton Rouge, and playing a few games at Woodlawn High, he and his mother finally made their way back to the city. She choked up as she watched him march onto the field, as if she were watching her child walk for the first time. He couldn't stop grinning on the sidelines, and she was so happy to see how comfortable he was to be back with his friends. As she watched him wait for the kickoff, she kept thinking, *My child is smiling again. He's at peace again.* She and Preston have found a stark, cramped two-room apartment that Preston calls the "psych ward."

In their first playoff game, against Loyola Prep, the Patriots walked away after a 53–13 ransacking. Joe scored twice, including an eighty-two-yard run, and David scored once, racking up 100 rushing yards. David's scrappy tenacity has become a powerful complement to Joe's speed and finesse. He's been a testament to J.T.'s coaching style, and the assistants are thrilled to have someone other than Joe to carry the ball.

On November 18, the Patriots faced the Yellow Jackets of Kinder High, a team that had upstaged them in a 1978 semifinal game. A headline in the local paper blared, WILL HISTORY REPEAT? and J.T. held it up in the locker room before the game and admonished his players, "Don't . . . let . . . it . . . happen . . . again. Not this team."

The game ended as a 50–18 rout. On their first offensive drive, the Patriots scored easily, capping an eight-play march down the field with a quarterback sneak into the end zone. The Yellow Jackets fumbled on their first possession and Kyle marched right back downfield, throwing a beautiful sixty-four-yard touchdown pass to Joe, the first of three McKnight TDs in the game. J.T.'s system may not showcase stars—he put in plenty of second- and third-team players throughout the game—but Joe is getting deserved attention for his extraordinary gifts from scouts around the region, and further afield.

The sportswriters have acknowledged the Patriots' impressive season with some fawning ink, paying particular attention to Joe's contributions. On Thanksgiving morning, Joe is the focus of a *Times-Picayune* article: "MCKNIGHT MOVES: Curtis' do-it-all performer will play, 'wherever they need me,'" that gushes about Joe's all-purpose abilities. "Call it speed," wrote Billy Turner. "Call it a burst. A wiggle. On punts, he has the ability to make the first guy miss. Then he accelerates in a step. Call it a balance most people do not possess. Or call it an indescribable something. But whatever it is, Joe McKnight has it. When the John Curtis football team needs it, it's there." Turner also quotes East St. John's Coach Larry Dauterive, who declared, "He's ready for the NFL now."

J.T. is pleased to see Joe get his due, and knows such stories will impress the college recruiters. But he's even more pleased with Joe's response to one of Turner's questions. Turner mentions how Joe had started the season with Evangel, and asks why he decided to come back to Curtis.

"Coach J.T. teaches you how to be a man," Joe said. "That's the difference. The difference is Coach J.T. works with you on the things you're going to need in the future."

•   •   •

Each week, before and after games, parents have met on the field or in the stands to check in with each other about the latest word from their insurance company or the progress they've made rebuilding their home. Patriots games have become the highlight of their week, like group therapy sessions, but more fun and with better food.

As Tank's mom, Althea, puts it, "It's what gets me through."

This season had started so badly that it's hard to believe how far they've now come. None of the parents necessarily expected a normal year, nor a great one. They just wanted a season. *Any* season. But now, with the Yellow Jackets blowout, the Patriots find themselves two playoff victories away from a trip to the state championship.

Amidst the celebrating after the Yellow Jackets game, in one of many moments J.T. knows he'll cherish forever about this crazy season, Robby Green found J.T. and asked if he could skip the next morning's practice. With his mom still living in Dallas with his younger brother, and his dad still in Baton Rouge, Robby has been bouncing all over the place all season long, one night with his dad, one night with his mom, and many nights in River Ridge with friends or, occasionally, in Joe's room or Tank's room at J.T.'s house. The Yellow Jackets game was the first time they'd all been together for weeks, and Robby wanted to head to Dallas with his family for the weekend. J.T. has always been so unwavering about requiring players to be at every practice, making a total commitment to his team. This season, though, he's had to bend his rules and the result has surprised him. Instead of slacking off, his kids have worked even harder for him.

"Sure, son," J.T. told Robby. "Go see your family."

As Robby ran off to join his mom and brother, his dad pulled J.T. aside to thank him. "He's grown up so much this season," he said. "I've watched my little boy become a man."

On the afternoon of Friday, November 25, the coaches and players pile their Thanksgiving-stuffed selves onto the team buses for the drive to Joe Yenni Stadium in Metairie for the semifinals of the 2A playoffs and a rematch against Riverside Academy.

In homage to Mr. Curtis's penchant for boosterish T-shirts, the school has been selling green and black, camouflage-style shirts with orange bull's-eyes on the chest that read SHOOT FOR STATE. As parents gather in the parking lot and the stands, they laugh when they realize they're all wearing the same shirts. The cheerleaders have painted signs, HOME OF A PATRIOT, and put them in players' front yards. J.T. and Lydia's small front yard has sprouted a garden of colorful signs with 4 and 99, Joe's and Tank's numbers.

When the Patriots had surged back in the second half against the Rebels of Riverside five weeks ago, pulling off a 20–6 victory after trailing 6–3 at the half, the Rebels threw down a challenge as the Patriots left the field: "We'll see you again."

Again is tonight.

The Patriots' offense gets off to a typically slow start, and have to punt on their first two possessions. The defense, however, is brutally unyielding. They give up just one first down in the first quarter. They're swarming over the Rebels' ball carriers and slamming their quarterback for five- and ten-yard losses.

In the second quarter, in an effort to roust his offense, J.T. orders Kyle to go to a no-huddle offense, a fast-paced drill they practice regularly but rarely use. The shakeup does the trick, and the offense begins to find its rhythm, racking up sixty-five yards in five quick plays. Joe caps the drive with a six-yard touchdown run, the kick is good, and the Patriots are up 7–0.

On Kyle's next drive, he lofts a high spiral to P. J. Smith, who makes a leaping catch over his defender's head, spins out of his grasp, and then slaps away one last would-be tackler to dive into the end zone for a forty-one-yard touchdown. On the next series, one play after recovering a Rebels' fumble, Joe scores his second touchdown of the night on a seventeen-yard run, and the Patriots take a 21–0 lead.

The Rebels aren't giving up yet, though. On their next possession, they seem to come alive, spreading out their offense and putting the ball in the air. They take over at their sixteen-yard line and start moving steadily, gaining five yards on one pass, and then another nine, to earn their second first down of the game. On first and ten from the thirty, the Rebels' quarterback again drops to pass, but is suddenly confronted by Jacob Dufrene and Stephen Champagne blitzing.

In another play that the Patriots will remember fondly from this whole insane season, as the Rebel quarterback backpedals away from the blitz, he flips an ill-advised screen pass. Tank gets the read, nimbly cuts in front of the receiver, and picks it off.

Though Tank has shed some of the weight he had gained during his displacement, he's still well above three hundred pounds. No matter. He starts chug-a-chugging down the sideline and, when his teammates realize what's happened, they rush frantically into the fray, rallying around him, making precision block after precision block to clear his path. Tank crosses the twenty and, at the fifteen-yard line, puts an impressive stutter-step juke move on one defender, who flops to the ground. Tank then leaps like a hurdler over the fallen body of one of his own teammates.

As Tank closes in on the end zone, a Rebels' running back manages to catch him from behind, and jumps on his back. Never slowing for a step, Tanks carries the guy for the last four yards right into the end zone. The amazing thirty-yard run is his first ever touchdown and it kicks off a rapturous celebration of laughing Patriots, who swarm euphorically all over Tank in the end zone. They're going so wild that Tank is actually worried they're going to get penalized for celebrating too much, and he starts urging the others to clear the field.

In the stands, the roars are deafening. Tank's mom is surrounded by a dozen family members, aunts and uncles and cousins, as well as Tank's older brother. They go absolutely berserk, screaming and laughing until their throats ache.

The final score is 42–0, a deeply satisfying shutout. The Patriots' defense held the Rebels offense to *negative* twenty yards in the first half and sixteen yards for the entire game.

When the Patriots roll through their semifinal playoff game a week later, with a 39–7 victory over the Eagles of Ouachita Christian, they finish the season 9–1 and are headed to the 2A championship game. Their opponent will be the foul-mouthed, trash-talking team they'd beaten 31–0 in their third game of the season, the St. Charles Comets.

When the Louisiana Superdome opened in 1975 in downtown New Orleans, on a site that was once a cemetery, it was the largest domed structure in the world. In addition to hosting the annual college Sugar Bowl game and more Super Bowls—six—than any other stadium, Louisiana's high-school championships have been played at the Superdome since 1981. Reaching that stadium, home of the Saints, with its bright-green AstroTurf and awesome klieg lights, has become the Patriots' annual goal.

But the Superdome is now a bulbous symbol of human suffering and chaotic failure, remembered as the Terrordome, and nowhere near ready to host football.

The five high-school championship games, one for each of the five districts, will be played three hundred miles away at Independence Stadium in Shreveport, on Friday and Saturday, December 9 and 10. The Patriots' game is set for Friday at one o'clock.

On Thursday, the entire student body, from both the upper and lower schools, descends on the high-school parking lot for the traditional prechampionship cookout, where parents serve up burgers and jambalaya and coaches run around telling players not to eat too much. "You'll cramp up tomorrow!" Tommy keeps shouting.

Next, J.T. ushers everyone into the gym for a pep rally, an afternoon-long celebration with balloons, noisemakers, and GO BIG BLUE banners on the walls and in the stands. Acting as master of ceremonies, J.T. introduces the team's seniors, calling their numbers as they jog through rows of cheerleaders throwing confetti in their faces. Assistant coaches and teachers stand in the corners, some with their children atop their shoulders. The cheerleaders host a shouting contest between the high school and grammar school, and the little ones win. The gym is filled with the shrieks of young voices.

J.T. finally quiets everyone down and hands the microphone to Gary Greaves, the scrawny player and 1975 alumnus whose dad had begged J.T. to let his son play, and who then helped J.T. win his first championship.

"It's amazing," Greaves says. "Thirty years ago this weekend, we won our first state championship." He mentions the "troubled" 1974 team and how he and his teammates used to work out with plastic weights in a corner of the gym, never dreaming they'd be one of Louisiana's best teams a year later.

"We were champions, but we weren't born champions," he says. "It didn't happen without a lot of hard work and dedication." This year's Patriots, nodding, know exactly what he's talking about. Then David Gilmore, the ex-Patriot who spoke so eloquently at the Thanksgiving devotional, tells them an old saying, "What you give, you keep. What you don't give, is lost forever. What that means is, tomorrow, at the end of the game, when the whistle blows, make sure you have nothing left to give."

J.T. then heads them all out of the gym for one last prechampionship ritual.

Back in 1975, Mr. Curtis had been so nervous the afternoon before his school's first championship game that he found himself pacing the halls. Finally, he grabbed a few members of the marching band and told them to get their instruments and "Follow me!"

He led the small band through the halls, stopping to bellow into each classroom, "Follow the band, everybody. Follow the band!" The whole school proceeded right out the doors and into the street and paraded through the neighborhood, Mr. Curtis high-stepping Mardi Gras style the whole way.

This afternoon is overcast and spitting rain, but that doesn't stop hundreds of students, parents, and teachers from taking over the streets of River Ridge for a big loop.

The Patriots then load the buses and the caravan heads to Shreveport, arriving well after dark on Thursday night. J.T. tells the bus drivers to go straight to the stadium. He wants to practice for an hour before checking into the hotel and eating dinner.

The players gather in the end zone, slowly walk the length of the field, and then back to the end zone. J.T. always insists that players get a feel for the playing field before a game, inspecting the turf beneath their feet for any aberrations, divots, or bumps. It's a chilly night, and the players are bundled in sweatshirts and sweatpants as they perform passing, blocking, and kicking drills.

The stadium is empty and, when the practice is over, J.T. calls them together at midfield, and the players begin clapping and shouting, "Let's do this, baby!"

Coach Johnny prompts the final chant of the night: "Let me hear *state* on three," and the mighty Patriots of John Curtis Christian School holler out in perfect unison, "One, two, three, *state*!"

The final word echoes into the night.

• • •

On Friday morning, December 9, the team meets for breakfast at the hotel, then gathers in a banquet hall a few hours before their one o'clock kickoff. J.T. goes over some last minute instructions, reminding them to "Play hard, and play smart."

Thoughts of his father are much on his mind; he knows how much his dad would have loved to have been here. In the locker room at the Superdome before last year's championship game, Mr. Curtis had stopped in to visit with his son.

"Are you nervous?" he asked, and J.T. chuckled.

"No, sir. I'm not nervous," he said, though it wasn't entirely true. Memories of the heartbreaking loss in the previous year's championship game were still fresh.

As if reading his son's mind, Mr. Curtis said, "If you're prepared, you're not nervous." He then walked out to take his seat at the fifty-yard line.

In that game, the Patriots broke a 14–14 fourth-quarter tie with a long punt return by Joe McKnight, then a fifteen-yard quarterback sneak for a touchdown by Johnnie Thiel, who played brilliantly and was named the Most Outstanding Player.

"This is not about the prize, this is not about the trophy," J.T. told his team after that game. "It's what you do that separates you in later life. You have to find a way to get things done, to handle adversity like you did tonight. You must do things with a *purpose*."

J.T. has delivered hundreds of speeches to his team over the decades, becoming so skillful at motivating others that New Orleans area companies sometimes hire him to give inspirational talks to their employees. His style has always been businesslike, focusing on his work-hard message, accepting hardship and setback as the price of victory. He's tried not to reach for loftier messages, which was his father's domain.

Now, many miles from home and with his father seven months gone, he decides to give a different kind of speech. He takes a moment, searching for just the right words.

"It's very meaningful that we are here today," he says. "I hope it will be as meaningful to you as it is to us." Opening a tattered bible, he says, "One of my dad's favorite bible verses was Psalm 127," and then reads the passage slowly to his team:

Sons are a heritage from the Lord. Children are his reward.
Like arrows in the hands of a warrior, sons are born to one's
   youth.
Blessed is the man whose quiver is full of children. They will
   not be put to shame.
For when they contend with their enemies at the gate, they
   shall be blessed.

Then he reads the verse a second time ". . . *Like arrows in the hands of a warrior* . . ."

J.T. closes the bible and takes off his reading glasses.

"That kind of sums up where we are," he says softly.

His players lean in.

"You are our *children*, and you are loved."

As he looks around him, into the sleepy eyes of Kyle Collura, the joyful eyes of Tank English, the wide eyes of Mike Walker, and the fiery eyes of Joe McKnight, he tells them they've done amazing things this year. Then he says, "This is more than a football game, guys." He reminds them that they could win a hundred thousand football games, and they'd all be in vain if they didn't strive to be good people above all else.

"Is it important to win? Yes. But is it who you are?" The players shake their heads, and J.T. continues, "No. Our prayer for you is that your character always be sterling, so that all that you do, from this day forward, won't be in vain."

The players then join hands, bow their heads, and pray.

On the last day of the season, as it has been from the first, old man Curtis's presence is everywhere. As the players arrive at the stadium and walk into the locker room just hours before kickoff, they find a surprise.

The assistant coaches met secretly two weeks earlier and decided to order new uniforms for the game: red pants with white stripes and blue stars running down the side, the uniforms Mr. Curtis had wanted his players to wear decades earlier. They are hanging neatly in each player's locker. The coaches haven't even told J.T.

As the team suits up, J.T. comes into the locker room for a pep talk. His pregame face, typically stone-cold serious, breaks into a wide, reluctant grin when he sees the uniforms. At first, he sticks to business, telling them that their victory over St. Charles earlier means nothing. That game is in the past, he says, and a team can change a lot in two months, and the Comets are "capable of big plays on offense and defense."

After a short prayer, "Lord, we ask that we might play as Christian gentlemen . . ." J.T. looks around the room.

Normally so bold and booming, his voice once again becomes soft.

"Listen to me," he begins.

The room grows quiet as his players and coaches lean in toward him, the only sound a dull echo from the three thousand fans outside in the stands.

"Thirty-four years ago, my daddy . . ."

He can't finish the sentence and tears well in his eyes.

"My daddy wanted those pants thirty-four years ago . . ."

He's crying now, and his team remains silent, transfixed.

"I never got them for him, but I was *wrong*," he says. "They look pretty good."

He clears his throat, wipes his face, and then finds the voice that has helped inspire so many Patriot teams to reach this game. His daddy might be gone, but his Patriots are right here where they belong. "I want you to wear those pants with pride, because I know he's smiling from ear to ear today as he watches down on you. Make him proud . . .

"Make him *proud*. Now let's *go!*"

Then, like the fearless warriors they've become, young men who've seen terrible things and grown stronger for all the hardship, they charge out the double doors, up the tunnel, into the chilly afternoon, and onto their green-grass battlefield.

• • •

In the stands, John Curtis parents, students, teachers, and alumni spring to their feet as their team charges across the field in their flashy new uniforms.

Joe McKnight's mom is in the stands with Joe's little brother, an eighth-grader who hopes to be a Patriot next year. She loves her son, and it hurts being separated from him, but she's always comforted herself by thinking that he's doing what he loves most, playing football.

Tank's mom is there, too, having driven up last night with Tank's older brother and a gaggle of family members. They've brought along T-shirts that they had made, with a photograph of Mr. Curtis on the front and a caption that reads, WE'RE #1 BECAUSE OF YOU. Tank's brother gives T-shirts to Miss Merle and Lydia and one of the coaches, who drapes the shirt across the back of Mr. Curtis's empty chair, sitting as is now custom, at the fifty-yard line.

Robby Green's mom and younger brother have driven in from Dallas, and are sitting with Robby's dad. Preston Numa's mom is here with Preston's older half-brother, whom he hasn't seen for a few years. Mike Walker's folks have arrived with his sister and his grandparents, along with their milk jugs and their popcorn balls. Kyle's parents have also brought along T-shirts, with a photo of Kyle, Tank, and Joe on the front, and the whole team on the back, and they give shirts to Joe's and Tank's moms.

Parents and alumni have converged from all across the Katrina-ravaged South for one last, sweet taste of Patriot football, hundreds piled in the stands on this sunny, wintry afternoon, ringing cowbells and waving flags and signs, with bellies full of tailgate food. The *chucka-chucka-chucka-chucka* of the coin-filled Curtis noisemaker milk jugs will rattle in the background throughout the entire game.

As the players head over to the sideline, the empty chair reminds Joe of what Mr. Curtis said to him before each game: "I want you to score me two touchdowns tonight, Joe." Whenever Joe scored, Mr. Curtis always found him, shook his hand, wiped his face with a towel, and gave him a water bottle. Joe touches the chair in memory of the old man, as do many others.

J.T. yells for Lance Frazier, the kid who lost his home in Chalmette, then broke his arm in the middle of the season and hasn't been able to play since. He's now suited up for his first game since the cast and sutures were removed, but the doctors said he's not ready to play yet, and he knows he'll spend the game on the bench

"Frazier, where's Frazier?" J.T. shouts.

When Lance trots up, puzzled, J.T. asks him, "You think a kid from Chalmette can handle the coin toss?"

In the biggest game of the year, in the toughest season of the kid's life, J.T. decides to give him a chance to contribute. Frazier is a senior, and J.T. knows this is the last football game of his high-school career.

"You think you can handle that?" J.T. asks again.

Frazier scampers happily out to midfield with the two co-captains. When the ref flips the silver dollar in the air, Lance calls out "heads," and the Patriots win the toss. Coming off the field he's greeted with the high-fives and hugs of his teammates.

In the stands, his mother is suddenly so overcome that she covers her face.

When the Patriots faced St. Charles earlier in the season, the game was defined by emotional, aggressive play, filled with late hits, penalty flags, and tempers. Last night, in a pregame interview, the St. Charles coaches appeared on television wearing John Curtis sweatshirts. Johnny and Jeff, who had played under Coach Monica at Tulane, knew Monica well enough to assume he was just messing with them. Many of the Curtis coaches and players were offended by the gesture, and they're stoked to play.

"Let's get ready to RUM-buuuuuuulllllllllll," the stadium announcer bellows, and rumbling is exactly what's in store.

Though the Patriots' opening drive is a herky-jerky progression, with good plays followed by mistakes or penalties, they quickly find their rhythm. The defense keeps a tight clamp on the Comets' offense, while Joe makes a beautiful fifty-yard touchdown run on a punt return. Kelby Wuertz then picks off an interception that sets Kyle up for a three-yard score. The Patriots miss the extra point on both scores, but well into the second quarter they're up 12–0.

On the Comets' next drive, Jacob Dufrene causes a fumble, then scoops it up, taking it into the end zone, and giving the Patriots an 18–0 lead. As the Comets grow frustrated, on the next play, the Patriots' prospects take a turn for the worse.

Following Jacob's touchdown, J.T. decides to try to make up for the two missed extra points, and calls for a two-point conversion. Kyle drops back to pass and, just as he releases the ball, he's hammered by two Comets' defenders. He flies backward and his head bounces off the hard December turf as his pass soars beyond Joe's reach.

As players withdraw toward their sidelines, Kyle remains flat on his back. He finally stands slowly, but is wobbly and starts looking around like he's just lost his car keys. A couple Patriots turn to help him, and Kyle is muttering like he's drunk, "Hey, why are we wearing red pants? These are *awesome*."

"What's wrong with him?" Coach Johnny screams from the sideline.

The team doctor and a few coaches rush to the field and, as Kyle is helped to the locker room, he keeps asking where he is and why he's wearing red pants.

J.T. always tells his players, whether they're starters or second or third team, that every single Patriot is just one play away from being called up. That's why he makes sure all players get repetitions and valuable playing time at practices.

After Kyle is escorted off the field, the doctor assures Kyle's mom that "He just got his bell rung." J.T. crooks a finger at sophomore Matt Saucier, a lean, baby-faced kid from the town of Marrero. They can only hope he can hold onto the eighteen-point lead.

Matt's first play, a handoff to Blaine Roberts, earns five yards. On second and five, Matt scrambles to the right on an option, and is within a yard of the first down, but he decides to pitch the ball backwards to his running back, Scotty Encalade, making a terrible pitch that Scotty almost fumbles. The Patriots actually lose a yard.

On third and long, Matt scrambles for a nice ten-yard gain and a first down. After two short gains, he throws a pass well short and behind the intended receiver, P. J. Smith, and the pass is intercepted. The defender takes off and gains fifty yards before he's tackled. The Comets then grind their way down to the ten-yard line. Several plays later, the Comets have pushed tenaciously to the two-yard line. On third and goal the quarterback has a man open in the end zone and throws. Joe deftly steps in front of the receiver, steals the ball, and sprints the entire length of the field. The Patriot fans roar, but there's a penalty and the play is called back. The half ends with the Patriots holding their 18–0 lead.

In the second half, the Comets get even more physical. When Joe takes another long touchdown run down the sideline, a Comet defender lunges at his feet after the whistle, apparently trying to trip him. Joe just skips out of reach and the kid falls on his face. Joe then does a U-turn, stands above the kid, drops the ball by his face, and walks away.

On the Comets' next possession, while Joe is standing near their sideline, he's slammed to the turf by a Comet defender, who stands there, apparently waiting for Joe to retaliate. Joe gets up and trots away.

Replacement quarterback Matt Saucier continues to struggle. He again makes a terrible pitch to running back Scotty Encalade, which a Comets defender scoops up and runs twenty-eight yards for a touchdown, which cuts the Patriots' lead to 24–6.

When Matt next takes the field, he fumbles again, and the Patriots fans let out a collective groan. The Patriots recover the ball, but then Matt throws an incomplete pass and, after the play is whistled dead, he's slammed to the ground by yet another late hit from a Comets defender. At this point, Joe's had enough of the dirty plays. He's not going to let another of his quarterbacks get hurt. He shoves the guy back, *hard*, words are exchanged, and the teams come to the verge of blows.

A few plays later, Joe completes yet another stunning run for his third touchdown of the game. He is followed deep into the end zone by a Comets defender, who jabs him with an elbow, but Joe just drops the ball and trots off. On the same play, Blaine Roberts, standing at the one yard line, is blindsided by a crashing late hit. It's a blatant foul that's not called by the officials, but he's not taking the bait. He stands up, points to the scoreboard—PATRIOTS 30, COMETS 6—and jogs away.

Josh Medley kicks the extra point and, for the first time all night, it's good.

• • •

In the fourth quarter, Officer Craig comes onto the sideline with a surprise.

He's brought championship T-shirts, just like the ones Mr. Curtis would have unveiled about now. Craig walks up to J.T. and unfolds a shirt. On the back is a photo of Mr. Curtis and his favorite quote: KNOW THE TRUTH AND THE TRUTH WILL SET YOU FREE.

J.T. smiles and turns back to the game, but then swings around and grabs the officer in a huge bear hug.

Across the final quarter, the score remains unchanged. J.T. puts in the second- and third-team guys, including his third-team quarterback, and even puts Lance Frazier in for one play, choosing a play in which he knows there's no chance he'll take a hit. The game ends Patriots 31–6.

Joe is named the game's Most Outstanding Player, and he runs into the stands to show his mother the trophy. He asks J.T. if he can skip the bus ride home and stay behind. "You do that, kid," J.T. says. "You stay with your mom."

The game was a bruiser, but the Patriots have clinched their twentieth state championship to cap the most improbable season in the team's remarkable history.

In the locker room, J.T. tells his players how proud he is. "It was not an easy journey," he says. "And I want you to be proud of that journey. I also want you to know, I miss the guys who aren't here." He lists a few names of players who've been permanently displaced, including Kenny Dorsey. "I miss those guys and wish they were part of this," he says. "And they *are* a part of this."

On the noisy ride home, the players snap photographs of each other with their cell phone cameras, striking tough-guy gangsta poses. They pound on the seats and the ceiling, singing rap songs and gospel songs, chanting and clapping and laughing. Every now and then someone lets loose a gorilla scream, "STATE CHAMPS, BABY!" and the others howl back. Eventually, inevitably, the rowdiness dwindles and, as dusk turns to night they watch movies on

their portable DVD players or listen to their iPods. As New Orleans draws closer, a somber silence creeps over them.

Tomorrow, they'll gorge themselves on jambalaya at the championship party, an almost annual Curtis ritual, and soak up the congratulations of their classmates. They'll clip the newspaper articles and tuck them safely away. Then, their season will be over.

Sitting up in the front of the bus, Johnny Curtis is already worrying about the letdown.

"Monday's gonna be interesting," he says quietly. "Like a new day in a new book.

"What are they gonna do when they don't have to go to football practice? When they gotta go home to the trailer at three-thirty? Go tear out sheetrock at three-thirty? I think there's gonna be another healing time, trying to figure out what we're going to do with our lives."

Down the dark highway toward their ruined city, an uncertain future awaits.

Epilogue

In August 2006, the spotlight was back on New Orleans, shone by a media that loves anniversaries. However, a year after Katrina, there was still much work to be done.

There had been some signs of recovery in recent months. Restaurants were reopening in the French Quarter, which was busy again with tourists. And noted Big Easy chronicler Andrei Codrescu bleakly observed that the displacement of massive numbers of New Orleanians was actually good news for the rest of America, which would now enjoy a bounty of music, coffeehouses, festivals, and parades—and guns. "You will no longer experience any faith in your government," he added. "If you have any."

Indeed, outside of the hopeful downtown hotspots, the sorrowful reality of modern New Orleans was that it had, as feared, become a city half its original size. Streets in the Lower Ninth, in New Orleans East, in Gentilly, and the Faubourg Marigny, and further east into Arabi and Chalmette, were still littered with mounds of debris, abandoned cars, piles of wrecked lumber, mattresses, and appliances. Electricity was still out in many sections, and traffic lights remained dark at four-way intersections.

Despite all the large, positive billboards—LOWES NOW HIRING and WE WILL REBUILD, and the occasional other hopeful signs, like rows of newly planted trees at an exit off I-10—a pervasive feeling of sadness and loss lingered well into 2007, a feeling that no positive slogans or optimistic platitudes could easily fix.

The final death toll along the entire Gulf Coast was estimated at just above 1,800, with New Orleanians accounting for more than 1,400 of those fatalities.

Harder to measure were the long-term effects of the scores of thousands of New Orleanians who had moved away and might never return: the musicians, artists, chefs, and everyday folks whose character gave shape and vitality to the city's unique culture. While displaced residents continued slowly to return throughout 2006 and into 2007, the city's population remained in the mid-two-hundred-thousands, down from nearly a half-million before Katrina. St. Bernard Parish's population was down to a third of its pre-Katrina level of 64,000. Even those numbers might represent a plateau rather than a trend. Many residents returned to find that New Orleans had become a less hospitable place, and a survey by the University of New Orleans in early 2007 found that a third of New Orleans residents, especially those with graduate degrees, were thinking of leaving within two years. On every level, the region continued to struggle to gain back what was lost.

Public-school enrollment was down by half; there were fewer hotels, restaurants, hospitals, day care centers, libraries, and jobs; more than fifty thousand FEMA trailers were still being occupied. Only one statistic rose dramatically: crime, which surpassed pre-Katrina levels and gave New Orleans the highest per capita murder rate in the nation.

The barge that destroyed Kenny Dorsey's home was cut apart and removed in early 2006, as was the ruined John Curtis school bus. But, by early 2007, the Lower Ninth was still more of a morbid tourist destination than a neighborhood. It *still* looked like Baghdad, and tourists aimed their video cameras at houses that had landed atop cars, asking, *Why? Why aren't armies of garbage collectors roaming these streets, cleaning up the mountains of wreckage? Why isn't the military here, helping this city rebuild?*

Elsewhere across Greater New Orleans, everyday life was still far from normal. Roofs remained covered in blue tarps, and trailers squatted in front yards beside fat storage boxes called PODS (portable on demand storage). After months of emptying trailer toilets by hand, many residents had learned to connect the pipes right to the city's sewage system. Most trailers sat up on blocks, and many folks had built small decks off the side, decorated with hanging plants and optimistic landscaping around the fringes.

One unexpected side effect of the devastation of a once-great American city was the patient kindness that emerged in Katrina's aftermath. People made eye contact and nodded hello in the months after Katrina. At four-way intersections without traffic lights, drivers were solicitous and patient. Despite the rising murder rate in certain neighborhoods, many of the city's survivors seemed to be looking out for each other, sharing subtle we're-in-this-together gestures like those that occurred in New York after 9/11. And yet, New Orleanians justifiably remained baffled by the lack of progress, feeling abandoned and hurt, as if America had moved on.

With their city's lingering troubles no longer televised, few Americans had a clue or interest in what a bipartisan Congressional report in 2006 called a national failure.

"It remains difficult to understand how government could respond so ineffectively to a disaster that was anticipated for years," the report had said. "If 9/11 was a failure of imagination, then Katrina was a failure of initiative. It was a failure of leadership."

Though the Patriots of John Curtis Christian School and their families faced their own ongoing struggles, the lessons of their triumphant season continued to guide them.

Despite months of repair efforts, and an almost desperate desire to get back home by Christmas, many John Curtis families continued living in temporary apartments or with relatives or in their miniscule FEMA trailers, well into 2006, and beyond.

Mike Walker's home had been mostly gutted by Thanksgiving 2005, and he even moved a futon and television into the living room of his empty house soon after the championship game. It took months longer to find contractors to finish installing new sheetrock, to paint the walls, and refinish the floors. The family started moving back home in March, but didn't complete the final repairs until May, when they celebrated with their first home-cooked meal in twenty months: roast chicken, broccoli, macaroni and cheese.

Kyle Collura and his dad had also finished gutting their house by late 2005, and Kyle's dad continued working at night and on weekends to rebuild the walls and repair the damage. The family celebrated Christmas in their cramped, two-bedroom rental at the Mark Twain Apartments in River Ridge, and Kyle's mom kept reminding him, "Hey, it's better than a trailer." They moved back into their home in Kenner on March first.

As of early 2007, Tank English's mom was still fighting with her insurance company and FEMA, waiting for contractors to repair her home. As she'd feared, too few of her clients returned to New Orleans and she was unable to reopen her day-care center. Tank continued living with J.T. and Lydia, and was still there in early 2007.

Joe McKnight began spending more and more weekends with his mom and younger brother in late 2006, but was also still living with J.T. and Lydia in early '07.

Enrollment at John Curtis Christian School dwindled some through the 2005–06 school year, as displaced transfer students switched back to their old schools, many of which slowly continued to reopen throughout the year. At the start of the 2006–07 school year, enrollment at John Curtis was just above 600. While some parents continued to struggle to pay tuition, the Curtises decided not to kick anyone out for failure to pay, and kept working out creative payment plans with families.

Curtis students who had been displaced by Katrina continued trickling back to the school. Among them was Patriots running back Darryl Brister, who at the start of the 2006 season had moved in with J.T. and Lydia, sharing a bedroom with Tank.

Kenny Dorsey's family never returned to New Orleans. They relocated to a suburb of Birmingham, where Kenny played for the Homewood High football team—the Patriots—who went undefeated in 2005 and became Alabama's 5A state champs.

His teammates and coaches gave him a nickname: Hurricane Dorsey.

• • •

284

Because most of the 2005 Patriots were juniors and sophomores, nearly all the starters returned in 2006, and the team began the season ranked twelfth in the nation by *Sports Illustrated*. They got off to a fast start, winning their first three games.

The team had been so disappointed in 2005, when they were unable to play Cottonwood High, that J.T. sought out an even bigger game for 2006.

On September 29, the Patriots traveled to Birmingham to face Hoover High, the school featured in MTV's reality show, *Two-A-Days*. At the time, Hoover's Buccaneers were ranked number one in the nation by both *USA Today* and *Sports Illustrated*, having won their fourth consecutive 6A championship in 2005.

The Patriots found themselves quickly down by two touchdowns in the first half but, in the second half, mounted the most dramatic comeback in team history, scoring twenty-eight unanswered points to stun Hoover with a 28–14 victory. Joe scored half those points, but after the game he told a reporter, "None of this means anything if we don't win state."

In December, the Patriots again made it to the 2A state championship game, a rematch against the St. Charles Comets, this one played at the Superdome. (The team was joined at the Dome by the newest Curtis, Jeff and Toni's son, who was three days old.)

By the fourth quarter, Kyle and the offense had racked up more than 400 yards—a third of them by David Seeman—as the Patriots' defense allowed only eleven yards. The game ended in a 41–7 rout, and David was named MVP. The victory gave the Patriots their twenty-first championship, capping their eleventh undefeated season.

At the end of the '06 season, *USA Today* ranked the Patriots number two in the nation, and named J.T. Coach of the Year. In a subsequent interview with *Sports Illustrated*, J.T. said the experience with Katrina had given his players "a deeper appreciation of football . . . and changed their perspective on life in general."

J.T. now keeps two photographs of the 2005 team hanging in his office: a before team picture and an after picture. He wants to always remember the kids who never came back, and the kids who led his Patriots to their most emphatic championship.

• • •

In early 2007, a number of Patriots earned college football scholarships: Tank English signed with Arizona State; Andrew Nierman with LSU; Preston Numa with Purdue; Jacob Dufrene with Kentucky; Colby Arceneaux with Ole Miss.

But, as is usually the case, many of the senior Patriots said good-bye to their football careers after the state championship game. As of early 2007, two players who helped lead John Curtis to its 2005 and 2006 championships, Mike Walker and Kyle Collura, had not yet been recruited to play Division I college football.

Joe McKnight signed with the USC Trojans, where he hopes to follow in the footsteps of Reggie Bush, who, in 2006, in his first year with the New Orleans Saints, contributed to one of the team's best seasons, bringing them to within one victory of the Super Bowl.

Joe was chosen by ESPN as the nation's best high-school football player of 2006. In December of that year, he traveled to Arizona to play in the U.S. Army All-American Bowl, which gathers together the country's top players. Before the game, Joe was interviewed by the high school athletics and recruiting magazine, *Rise*, which asked him what he wanted people to be saying about Joe McKnight in ten years.

"That he's a great person," Joe said. "Not a great football player, but a great person."

Acknowledgments

Without "A Testament To Faith," Wright Thompson's incredible story for ESPN.com in December 2005, this book might never have happened. I'm grateful to Wright (no relation) for inadvertently introducing me to the Curtis family, whose dedication and commitment to their school and to each other has humbled me.

Across the months I spent getting to know J.T. and the rest of the family, I realized I had never met a family quite like them. I love you all and I thank you for entrusting me with your story. Likewise to the Patriots and their parents, I'm thankful for the time you patiently spent with me. There were far too many stories to fit into this book, and I hope that the many families who were still struggling to recreate a home for themselves have done so by now. This book is homage to your resilience.

Many thanks to Jody Hotchkiss for kicking off this project, and to Michael Carlisle for insisting that day that I immediately get in my car and drive to New Orleans.

Thanks to Blaise and his New Orleans mix tape (Alan Toussaint and Elvis Costello, Professor Longhair, The Meters), and to the other New Orleans musicians, living and dead, who provided the soundtrack for the writing of this book: Louis Armstrong, Bonerama, The JBs, the Morning 40 Federation, and others.

As always, to my wife and sons, for their wonderful and inspirational support.

And, finally, to the city I've come to love, I pray for your recovery.

Notes

The majority of this book is based on scores of interviews conducted with J.T. and other Curtis family members, as well as the coaches, teachers, and students of John Curtis, and with many of the 2005 Patriots and their parents, especially Melody Collura, Donna Walker, Shirelle Wiltz, Althea English, Ken Dorsey.

Many of the students wrote essays about their Katrina experiences, and I'm grateful for the time they spent opening their hearts so movingly on the page. Other interviews include the following: Mike Tucker, Pete Jenkins, Larry Dauterive, Johnnie Thiel, Ronnie Alexander, Bill Kurd, Craig Gardner, and Bob Whitman.

It bears repeating: Wright Thompson's amazing "A Testament to Faith" was the first to put into print the story of the 2005 Patriots. As of early 2007, the ESPN.com story was still accessible at http://sports.espn.go.com/espn/news/story?id=2259022. Unfortunately, the video footage that went with the story was no longer free.

Depictions of Katrina and its aftermath relied heavily on the following: Douglas Brinkley's impressive *The Great Deluge* and Jed Horne's damning *Breach of Faith,* as well as *Time* magazine's *Time: Hurricane Katrina: The Storm That Changed America* and CNN's *Hurricane Katrina: CNN Reports: State of Emergency*, as well as CNN's online archived coverage of the storm, and Spike Lee's film, *When the Levees Broke.*

Indispensable to this book was the amazing blog that the *Times-Picayune*'s reporters and editors posted when they were unable to publish a print edition.

CHAPTER 1

9   an LSU coach suggested they consider J.T. Interview with Pete Jenkins.

14 *The percentage . . . highest in the nation* Brian Thevenot and Matthew Brown, "From Resistance to Acceptance," *Times-Picayune*, May 19, 2004.

20 *"If he can't play, he'll run away from home"* Dave Krider, "Legends of High School Football," nflhs.com, Nov. 21, 2005.

20 *"That's what makes high school football so special"* ibid.

25 *"fiercely proud and independent"* Chris Rose, "Louisiana Ambassadors Say Hello to Ya'll," *Times-Picayune*, Sept. 6, 2005.

25 *"Sometimes we bury our dead in LSU sweatshirts"* ibid.

25 *America's third-most football-crazed state* Christopher Lawlor, "Mississippi in state of football bliss," *USA Today*, Aug. 25, 2006.

25 *"This is Louisiana. When it's crawfish season . . ."* Jill Lieber, "Prep Football brings Hope in Katrina's Wake," *USA Today*, Sept. 15, 2005.

26 *"That's the nature of the business. We're a private school"* J. T. Curtis interview with Bill Elder, WWL-TV, 1990.

26 *"We're the Rolls Royce of athletic factories"* Josh Peter, "Patriot Games," *Times-Picayune*, Dec. 3, 2000.

27 *"People don't know what's inside my heart"* ibid.

28 *"The defense doesn't know what . . ."* David Purdum, "Gold Rush," *American Football Monthly*, Vol. 9, June 2004, p. 14.

28 *"Love him or hate him, you've got to respect him"* Josh Peter, "Patriot Games," *Times-Picayune*, Dec. 3, 2000.

29 *"J.T. has committed the ultimate sin in America"* ibid.

CHAPTER 2

39 *Elmo Lee . . . daily workout* Bill Bumgarner, "Not the Average Joe," *Times-Picayune*, Aug. 24, 2006.

41 *"God blessed me with ability"* ibid.

49 *"Boy, be careful"* Dave Krider, "Legends of High School Football," nflhs.com, Nov. 21, 2005.

CHAPTER 3

58 *"Watching his practice is like watching a college practice"* Purdum, *American Football Monthly*, p. 13.

63 *Katrina began her raucous life a week ago* Hurricane Katrina: *CNN Reports: State of Emergency* (Kansas City: Andrews McNeel Publishing, 2005), p. 9.

64 *"I want everybody out of Plaquemines Parish"* Douglas Brinkley, *The Great Deluge: Hurricane Katrina, New Orleans, and the Mississippi Gulf Coast* (New York: William Morrow, 2006), p. 5.

64 *Animals are being evacuated . . . piranhas* Brinkley, *Great Deluge*, p. 40.

CHAPTER 4

70 *"Monday is going to be too late"* CNN, Aug. 27, 2005.

70 *"We have been very blessed so far"* Cooperative Research: History commons, "Hurricane Katrina," www.cooperativeresearch.org/timeline.jsp?timeline=hurricane_katrina.

71 *Camille . . . killing seventy-five overall* Jed Horne, *Breach of Faith: Hurricane Katrina and the Near Death of a Great American City*, (New York: Random House, 2006), p. 20.

71 *Katrina is as strong as Camille . . .* Horne, *Breach of Faith*, p. 21.

73 *"This is not a test . . . This is the real deal"* Cooperative Research, "Hurricane Katrina," www.cooperativeresearch.org.

74 *the storm is "really scary"* Brinkley, *Great Deluge*, p. 57.

74 *"I've never seen a storm like this"* Brinkley, *Great Deluge*, p. 58; *CNN Reports*, p. 10.

75 *Mayfield "scared the crap out of me"* Horne, *Breach of Faith*, p. 32.

76 *"this is an economically depressed city"* Cooperative Research, "Hurricane Katrina," www.cooperativeresearch.org.

77 *President Bush calls Governor Blanco . . .* ibid.

77 *"I do not want to create panic. But . . ."* Brinkley, *Great Deluge*, p. 87.

77 *"I want to emphasize . . ."* Cooperative Research, "Hurricane Katrina," www.cooperativeresearch.org.

78 *spending frivolously on gambling boats . . .* Brinkley, *Great Deluge*, p. 194.

86 *more than one hundred thousand don't own a car or have access to one* Brinkley, *Great Deluge*, p. 626.

86 *pump operators . . . ordered by Broussard* Brinkley, *Great Deluge*, p. 131.

86 *"The birds are gone"* Brinkley, *Great Deluge*, p. 122.

87 *"The potential for destruction is enormous"* *CNN Reports*, p. 15.

88 *CNN correspondent . . . an "eerie feeling"* *CNN Reports*, p. 17.

88 *"Go Home Miss Thing"* Brinkley, *Great Deluge*, p. 95.

CHAPTER 5

91 *a football field every thirty-eight minutes* Elizabeth Kolbert, "Watermark: Can Southern Louisiana be saved?" *The New Yorker*, Feb. 27, 2006, pp. 47–50.

Notes

91   *"living on borrowed time"* ibid.

93   *"a thirty-foot wall of water. Take this seriously"* CNN Reports, p. 20.

93   *police officers are washed out* Brinkley, *Great Deluge*, p. 152.

102   *a floating table with two elderly women* Brinkley, *Great Deluge*, p. 317.

CHAPTER 6

109   *"I'm not going to make it"* Brian Thevenot, "City a woeful scene," nola.com, Aug. 30, 2005.

112   *"They're just pushing them to the side"* Melinda Deslatte, "Nagin details latest storm damage," nola.com, Aug. 30, 2005.

112   *"Free samples over here!"* Mike Perlstein and Brian Thevenot, "Even a cop joins in the looting," nola.com, Aug. 30, 2005.

112   *"The police got all the best stuff"* ibid.

112   *"like Sodom and Gomorrah"* Ed Anderson and Jan Moller, "Looting difficult to control," nola.com, Aug. 30, 2005.

112   *"It's just heartbreaking . . . This is catastrophic"* Jan Moller, "Notes from a Plane Flight," nola.com, Aug. 30, 2005.

118   *"Please roll up the sleeves of your shirt"* Horne, *Breach of Faith*, p. 65.

118   *a thousand rubber rafts* Horne, *Breach of Faith*, p. 89.

CHAPTER 7

131   *"hundreds, perhaps thousands" are dead* CNN Reports, p. 46.

131   *Mark Twain . . . Mardi Gras Time: Hurricane Katrina: The Storm That Changed America*, (New York: Time Books, 2005), p. 33.

CHAPTER 8

141   *corpses in Jefferson Parish must wait* Michelle Hunter, nola.com, Sept. 2005.

142   *radio host . . . the "scumbags"* CNN Reports, p. 29.

142   *Dennis Hastert . . . be bulldozed* "Hastert: New Orleans 'Could Be Bulldozed,'" *The Associated Press*, Sept. 2, 2005.

142   *Richard Baker . . . "finally cleaned up public housing"* Gwen Filosa and Gordon Russell, "Public Housing Takes a Blow to the Gut," nola.com, Oct. 9, 2005.

142   *ghost towns for as many as nine months* Geoffrey Lean and Andrew Gumbel, *The Independent*, Sept. 4, 2005.

144   *Seven officers will later be charged with murder* Shaila Dewan, "Police Officers Charged in Deaths in Hurricane's Aftermath," *New York Times*, Dec. 29, 2006.

CHAPTER 9

152 *"When you hit, hit hard"* Eric Zweig, *Gentlemen, This Is a Football: Football's Best Quotes and Quips* (Ontario: Firefly Books, 2006), p. 71.

153 *The school spends $450,000 a year* Lars Anderson, "Aiming for Perfection," *Sports Illustrated*, August 28, 2006.

164 *Tommy Henry . . . heard about coaches* Mike Strom, "SLIDE RULE: Local Coaches Are Questioning Whether Some Schools Have Taken Advantage of the LHSAA's Decision to Grant Displaced Athletes Immediate Eligibility," *Times-Picayune*, Oct. 1, 2005.

CHAPTER 10

172 *"The tasks before us are enormous"* Robert D. McFadden, "Storm and Crisis: The Overview: Bush Pledges More Troops as the Evacuation Grows," *New York Times*, Sept. 4, 2005.

172 *"Bobby's world"* http://bobbys0411.blogspot.com/2005_09_01_bobbys0411 _archive.html, "Bobby's World."

CHAPTER 12

203 *unprecedented mental-health disaster* Adam Nossiter, "Storm and Crisis: Hurricane Takes a Further Toll, Suicides Up in New Orleans," *New York Times*, Dec. 27, 2005.

203 *"people walking around with an endemic"* ibid.

208 *"At Curtis, we only threw the ball"* Lori Lyons, "Thiel Eager to Show Patriots Why He Left," *Times-Picayune*, Sept. 30, 2005.

208 *"I hope he has a nice career"* ibid.

209 *"Tighten your belt up"* Jill Lieber, "Prep Football Brings Hope in Katrina's Wake," *USA Today*, Sept. 15, 2005.

209 *"Everyone is trying to get back there"* Lori Lyons, "Storm Produces Rare Matchup of Cats," *Times-Picayune*, Sept. 30, 2005.

214 *Coach Doe . . . we've got them . . .* Bill Bumgarner, "East St. John Holds Off Curtis," *Times-Picayune*, Oct. 1, 2005.

CHAPTER 13

227 *"one small step towards normalcy"* Chris Rose, *Times-Picayune*, Sept. 27, 2005.

CHAPTER 15

266 *"McKNIGHT MOVES* Billy Turner, "McKnight Moves: Curtis' do-it-all performer will play," *Times-Picayune*, Nov. 24, 2005.

266 *"He's ready for the NFL now"* ibid.

266 *"Coach J.T. teaches you how to be a man"* ibid.

267 *"I've watched my little boy become a man"* SRC: espn.com.

272 *"If you're prepared, you're not nervous"* Bill Bumgarner, *Times-Picayune*, Dec. 12, 2004.

272 *"This is not about the prize"* ibid.

EPILOGUE

281 *"You will no longer experience any faith"* Andrei Codrescu, *New Orleans, Mon Amour: Twenty Years of Writings from the City* (Chapel Hill, N.C.: Algonquin Books, 2006), p. 272.

281 *city half its original size* Coleman Warner, "Area's Rebound Slow but Steady," *Times-Picayune*, August 26, 2006.

282 *survey by the University of New Orleans* Shaila Dewan, "New Orleans' New Setback: Fed-up residents giving up," *New York Times*, Feb. 16, 2007.

283 *a national failure* U.S. House of Representatives, *A Failure of Initiative*, (U.S. Government Printing Office, 2006), p. 13.

283 *"It remains difficult to understand"* ibid., p. 14.

286 *"That he's a great person"* risemag.com, December 19, 2006.

Further Reading

___. *Hurricane Katrina: CNN Reports: State of Emergency.* Kansas City: Andrews McNeel Publishing, 2005.

___. *Time: Hurricane Katrina: The Storm that Changed America.* NY: Time Books, 2005.

___. National Oceanic and Atmospheric Association, and National Weather Service, *Hurricane Katrina: Service Assessment*, Department of Commerce, June 2006.

___. U.S. House of Representatives, "A Failure of Initiative," Washington, DC: U.S. Government Printing Office, 2006.

Barry, John M. *Rising Tide: The Great Mississippi Flood of 1927 and How It Changed America*, New York: Touchstone, 1998.

Bissinger, H. G. *Friday Night Lights.* Cambridge, MA: Da Capo Press (movie tie-in edition), 2004.

Bissinger, Buzz. *Three Nights in August: Strategy, Heartbreak, and Joy: Inside the Mind of a Manager.* Boston: Mariner Books, 2006.

Brinkley, Douglas. *The Great Deluge: Hurricane Katrina, New Orleans, and the Mississippi Gulf Coast.* New York: William Morrow, 2006.

Codrescu, Andrei. *New Orleans, Mon Amour: Twenty Years of Writings from the City.* Chapel Hill, NC: Algonquin Books, 2006.

Dent, Jim. *The Junction Boys: How Ten Days in Hell with Bear Bryant Forged a Championship Team.* New York: Thomas Dunne Books, 1999.

Gay, Timothy. *The Physics of Football.* New York: Harper, 2005.

Halberstam, David. *The Education of a Coach.* New York: Hyperion, 2005.

Horne, Jed. *Breach of Faith: Hurricane Katrina and the Near Death of a Great American City.* New York: Random House, 2006.

Lewis, Michael. *Coach: Lessons on the Game of Life.* New York: W.W. Norton & Co., 2005.

Lewis, Michael. *The Blind Side: Evolution of a Game.* New York: W.W. Norton & Company, 2006.

Further Reading

Marx, Jeffrey. *Season of Life: A Football Star, a Boy, a Journey to Manhood*. New York: Simon & Schuster, 2003.

Piazza, Tom. *Why New Orleans Matters*. New York: Regan Books, 2005.

Rose, Chris. *1 Dead in Attic*. New Orleans: Chris Rose Books, 2005.

Thompson, Wright. "A Testament to Faith," espn.com, December, 2005.

Zweig, Eric. *Gentlemen, This Is a Football: Football's Best Quotes and Quips*. Richmond Hill, ON: Firefly Books, 2006.

Index

297

Index

About the Author

Neal Thompson (www.nealthompson.com) is a veteran journalist who has worked for the *Baltimore Sun, Philadelphia Inquirer,* and *St. Petersburg Times,* and whose magazine stories have appeared in *Outside, Esquire, Backpacker, Men's Health,* and the *Washington Post Magazine.* He is the author of *Light This Candle: The Life & Times of Alan Shepard, America's First Spaceman* and *Driving with the Devil: Southern Moonshine, Detroit Wheels, and the Birth of NASCAR.* Thompson and his family live in the mountains outside Asheville, North Carolina.

If you would like to learn more about the John Curtis Christian School or about making donations to the school or scholarship funds, you can visit johncurtis.com or write to Mark Naccari, Business Manager, 10125 Jefferson Highway, River Ridge, LA 70123.